Revelation and Faith

Revelation and Faith

Theological Reflections
on the Knowing and Doing of Truth

The Samuel Robinson Lectures for 1984
Wake Forest University

BY
THERON D. PRICE

 MERCER
UNIVERSITY PRESS

ISBN 0-86554-260-0 (casebound)
ISBN 0-86554-261-9 (perfectbound)

BT 127.2 .P74 1987

Price, Theron D.

Revelation and faith

The paper used in this publication meets
the minimum requirements of American National Standard
for Information Sciences—Permanence of Paper
for Printed Library Materials, ANSI Z39.48-1984.

Library of Congress Cataloging-in-Publication Data
Price, Theron D., 1916–
    Revelation and faith.
    "The Samuel Robinson lectures for 1984,
Wake Forest University."
    Includes indexes.
    1. Revelation. 2. Faith. 3. Theology, Doctrinal.
4. Theology, Practical. I. Title. II. Title: Samuel
Robinson lectures.
BT127.2.P74   1987   231.7′4   86-33224
ISBN 0-86554-260-0 (alk. paper)
ISBN 0-86554-261-9 (pbk. : alk. paper)

CONTENTS

To
Leslie
and
Our Children
and
Their Children

PREFACE

This book is about God as self-revealing, and about the kind of human response to that revealing by which persons come into knowledge of God. The *central concern* of theology is to give clarity to this knowledge and to the divine-human relationship that is both its condition and its content. As an *intellective discipline,* theology seeks to render faith as understanding. It does this by interpreting the reality of God, and our knowledge of him, in relation to our lives in this world.

A glance at the table of contents will show that no more than this is undertaken, but surely that is enough. There is no intention to treat the whole of Christian doctrine. I simply point toward the meaning of revelation and the nature of faith, and try to practice theology as the interpretation of the relationship of revelation and faith to each other and to our life in this world.

In the doing of this kind of theology, I have sought to establish a *perspective* not only on the meaning of Christian faith-and-life, but also on Christian faith-and-life as *meaning*. Christian faith has to do with knowledge and acts, with experiences and relationships; that is, with the meaning of our life in this world. The book is, therefore, a reconsideration of our life in this world from the perspective of Christian faith: that is, it has to do with the knowing and doing of truth. As such, it is an invitation to review and reflection. One must decide the meaning for oneself. This is urged as important, for it has to do with the knowledge of truth, the meaning of the gospel, the service of God, the understanding of neighbor, the fulfillment of our human pilgrimage. I have not sought to be "right" or "current" or "clever." The only intended aim is to see and state the truth (never reducible to speech, much less to dogma), and to avow our perfect freedom in God (truth's only source). If some reader should see, in my understanding of truth and freedom, a willing if cautious betrothal of the rational to the romantic, I can acknowledge the general accuracy of that vision and expect that the wedding should be happy.

Where would a catalogue librarian put the book? If certain aspects, both of content and style, were eliminated it could be thought of as a study of some of the crucial problems facing constructive theology. It also contains (what is not very happily called) "practical" theology, introducing certain issues basic to any serious religious concern—the reality of human distress, the plurality of religions, the meaning of mission. Perhaps, especially, it could be used by university and seminary students as an orientation to the formal study of theology.

The book is not, in any sense, an examination of current theological discussion. It is an attempt to verbalize the religious and moral "vision" that has shaped my faith and that my faith has shaped. I have sought, also, more to illumine the questions than to provide solutions. This explains, in part, the appearance (sometimes side by side) of theological materials that are not easily compatible with each other.

In a way important to myself, this work is a witness (somewhat in retrospect) of what has been seen and heard and known along the way. Now from retirement, it is also a sort of account of my stewardship as a teacher. As such it has revived memories of work and fun, as well as of some pain. More especially, the work of writing has paraded before me forty years' worth of dear friends and faces. To these, and to all readers, here is the faith that has held me more faithfully than I have held it.

There are those who will like what I have tried to do (or at least parts of it) and others who will not. I am happy to believe that the two sides will not divide up neatly into Protestants and Catholics, conservatives and liberals, Americans and non-Americans. The book is written for the Church, and finally for the Church as that host of women and men who confess faith in God through Jesus Christ, but who have never made a sustained study of Bible and history, theology and mission. Some ideas that appear in the book may distress certain of these readers. This will be due in part to various kinds of failure on my part—of knowledge, or understanding, or sympathy, or vision. It may also be traceable to some readers' assumption that their own understanding of the gospel must be identical with the gospel itself. In such case, the writer invites the reader to think this over and make such adjustments as seem needed for the sake of truth. Perhaps the reader should not carry too much guilt over having made this identification. If guilt is to be assigned, most of it must point to teachers and pastors who have found it easier to adjust to the misunderstanding than to lead faith beyond it. Beyond this problem, such persons as are accustomed to reading theological works will find no great strain in doing this one. Those who are not so accustomed will, here and there, find difficulties. In what follows, I hope that all these readers, as well as fellow-students, pastors and colleagues, will find light rather than darkness, help rather than confusion.

Regarding one present-day problem with language, I still call God "Father" rather than "Mother," and will probably continue to do so. Ordinarily, I also use "he" as a generic pronoun for a human person. This is simply the way I learned, and still speak, English. So far as I can tell, it is not resistance to more recent ways of speaking. Pardon is begged in advance.

Good theology springs from the soil of worship: the saving story, the great hymns, the liturgical words and gestures, the treasury of prayers, the familiar "I believe," the reading and preaching of biblical texts. All is done in relation to meaning, to life in this world and the next, and to the glory of God. It is theology's business to sort this out and to make its significance as plain as possible. One job theology needs to do is to recognize and display the inseparable connections of understanding, conviction and action. Dogmatics, ethics, worship, spirituality, and activity belong together. The power and appeal of the current "liberation theology" appear to lie in its implementation of this fact. The same connections, in a quite different way, appear in Geoffrey Wainwright's *Doxology: The Praise of God in Worship, Doctrine, and Life* (New York: Oxford University Press, 1980).

Mention was made above of "witness." More than incidentally, this book is a witness (a testimony) to the love and support of my wife, two sons, and daughter. In ways more rowdy and personal and loving (than theological) they have contributed to who I am and what I have done more than they can ever know. The book is dedicated to her, to them, and to their children.

My wife, Leslie, has read and commented on the work as it progressed. Sometime, when our children desire and feel ready for doing so, I should like for them to read and reckon with what their father has thought (and thinks) is of ultimate consequence. This book, in part my "witness," is written for all who will read it, but especially for them.

For all, but especially for them, I offer the collect in which we pray to God,

> Who alone can order the wills and affections of sinful men, to grant unto His people that they may love the thing which he commands, and desire that which he promises; that so, amid the sundry and manifold changes of the world, our hearts may surely there be fixed where true joys are to be found.

Greenville, South Carolina   —Theron D. Price
Easter 1986

ACKNOWLEDGMENTS

In the long term, this book is a belated response to the urging of two friends, Samuel S. Hill and the late Carlyle Marney. Neither is guilty of anything in it that may be found wrong-headed or unacceptable. In the short term, the book is an expansion and development of "The Samuel Robinson Lectures in Theology" given at Wake Forest University, Winston-Salem, North Carolina, in October 1984. Thanks are gladly expressed for the honor of the invitation to speak on that important foundation, and for the kind hearing, the courtesies and friendly acts, that accompanied our visit there. This pertains especially to the inviting committee of Wake Forest University and to colleagues of its department of religion. I mention also that the substance of several pages of chapter 3, in a slightly different form, was first used as a part of "The Lectures on Christian Theology" at Stetson University, given in the winter term of 1979. Pleasant memories of both visits survive and still warm the heart.

This should be a good place, as well, to express my appreciation for and to Furman University, which has provided my professional and (in some real sense) spiritual home for more than twenty years. The Furman department of religion forms around me the first circle of this warmth and stimulation. My debt is extended by the generous provision of typing and printout by university secretaries. My thanks to John H. Crabtree, Jr., vice-president of the University for Academic Affairs, for authorizing this much-needed service. I also remember gratefully the kind ladies at Southeastern Seminary, Wake Forest, North Carolina, who cheerfully and accurately rendered most of a first-draft manuscript into near-perfect type. Southeastern's Dean, Morris Ashcraft, made available this service to me during a pleasant fall term as a guest professor at that institution in 1984.

A word is necessary about the relation of this work to H. R. Niebuhr's *The Meaning of Revelation* (New York: Macmillan, 1941; paperback reprint, 1960). Over the years, Niebuhr's book provided for me a structure of ideas (a sort of critical framework) in and through which I reckoned with such issues as the knowledge of God, the relation of nature to faith, the limits of historical reason, the relations of internal and external history. This is the work most often quoted in my own book, and I am congenial with the whole of what it is concerned to affirm. Along with literal quotes, and nonliteral allusions, I should guess that many sentences of my own have unconsciously paraphrased lines of Professor Niebuhr. I have sought to reassert the values of his book, now a generation old. I have done this principally in two ways: one, by bringing certain points of Niebuhr's thought into conversation with Karl Barth, and, to a lesser degree, with Paul Tillich; two, by developing their thought, and my own, in relation to a selected number of biblical texts and current issues in the life of the Church. I am aware of much good theological work since their time, but those mentioned here provide ways of reckoning with truth that are now all but "native" to myself.

There is one further matter. I have understood and approved Niebuhr's recognition that "Jesusism" is not a synonym for "Christianity." I have felt, however, the need to discuss the theological questions, common to his interests and mine, in the light of Jesus' own concrete example and teaching, and in relation to New Testament texts generally. It seems needful, for what I am attempting, to reckon (though not *in extenso*) with the Kingdom of God as the primary focus of Jesus' work and teaching, and also with *agapē* (both as defining the Kingdom's character and power, and as the summing up of all the Law and the Prophets). This *agapē* is viewed as the inner reality of God's being, the way in which he does justice with mercy. It is how he *rules*. This love in Jesus Christ, coming to our kind as grace, defines what we mean by God's rule, both its judgment and its promise. This grace makes repentance and gratitude essential ingredients of ethical faith. It is the substance of what we respond to as revelation.

A word should be said also of James Denney of Glasgow (d. 1917). Denney was a part of a study of mine, done in earlier years, of nineteenth- and early twentieth-century British theology. The study included B. F. Westcott, Charles Gore, R. W. Dale, A. M. Fairbairn, P. T. Forsyth, and some others, along with Denney. Denney became favorite reading for me, and when I turn to him still, I vibrate to the quality and sharp clarity of his language and thought. In chapter 3 of this book, I have bodily taken over and used for my own purposes a sermon of his, "The Rich Man's Need of the Poor," from *The Way Everlasting* (London: Hodder and Stoughton, 1911). My own use of it in chapter 3 is in connection with social ethics and with Christology. Also, in chapter 2, where I have praised the understanding of traditional theology as a helpful interpretation of grace and faith, I have composed six paragraphs that repeat or paraphrase materials of Denney's found in *Jesus and the Gospel* (London: Hodder and Stoughton, 1909) and in *The Christian Doctrine of Reconciliation,* (London: Hodder and Stoughton, 1917).

A final and more personal word is about William Owen Carver (d. 1954), the greatest teacher to date in those seminaries supported (generously, if with growing suspicion) by Southern Baptists. Carver was a great expounder of Scripture, a good historian of missions, an insightful student of the world's religions, and a statesman of the Church. My years as his student and as his graduate fellow remain important beyond the telling. In Carver, I first began to find the Church, began to see what the Bible as a whole is about, and began to see something of God's relation to creation and history as well as to devotion and doctrine. It would be impossible to trace all of the ideas that inform this book, but I do not doubt that many of them first germinated in his classrooms.

The hands of these people (and of many others, perhaps especially Calvin and Barth) are upon me yet, and I am grateful. I hope I have honored them, not by copying them but by wrestling (with their help) with the great and recurring verities that were central to their faith and are to mine.

Chapter One

Introduction: A Somewhat Personal Perspective on Theological Work

For a world to take shape, it too must become a metaphor, and therefore any or all of its parts will, to those who are in on the secret, bear metaphorical relations to other parts. Only in pure chaos would "types, shadows, and metaphors" be unthinkable—or else in the Godhead Himself. Hence existing human beings confront, in the universe of experience, a terrible and never-ending paradox.

—Perry Miller

An introductory chapter should, presumably, introduce something. This one sketches a *perspective* upon theological work itself. It aims at helping readers turn already-held notions of the nature and function of theology into fairly clear ideas. It seeks to focus some of the forces, divine and human, that enter into theology's formation. It rather clearly reveals the author's own ideas and tendencies. Hopefully, it suggests something of the importance of theology for the life of faith.

If the theology that follows were thought of as a stream, two sources (more than others) affect the direction and force of its flow. One is the historical Christian tradition—the confession of God in Christ, reconciling the world to himself and revealing himself as present in his work. This one living tradition is accessible to us in both Bible and Church (that is, originally, in the Sacred Scriptures of Israel and of the primitive Christian community), and (in postbiblical times) in the Church's interpreted experience of God in Christ through worship, preaching, and good works. While these two forms of the one tradition are inseparable, like a good Protestant I see the former exercising a normative pressure on the latter that I do not ascribe to the latter in relation to the former. This confession of God in Christ, despite all the variables, Christological and other, that have attended it, has been and is at the heart of the Great Tradition. The Bible and the life of the Church are redolent of it. It is this tradition that serves to focus and define what Christians affirm about grace and calling, about the human condition and possibility, about the meaning and goal of history. This great tradition is an objective fact traceable, surely, in any theology recognizably Christian.

The second source, affecting the force and direction of the stream of theology, is the subjective apprehension, here and now, of the Christian confession through worship and fellowship, experience and study, life and work, as well as through decisions made about the nature of truth and about critical method. What I have to say, and have said in what follows, results from my own attempts at faithful and critical interaction with the historic tradition. It also reflects, and in some sense results from, the way I have absorbed (and sometimes re-formed) the learning and insights of my great teachers.

Having attempted to describe the two principal sources that affect the stream of theology, we need to have a look at the nature of the stream itself. (This is developed in such ways as, it is hoped, to enhance the discussion of theology found in the first part of chapter 4.)

While theology is never simply defined, I find myself congenial with the understanding both of theology and of theological education to be found in a brochure circulated, around 1982-1983, by the Vanderbilt Divinity School. "Theology," the brochure states, "names neither a set of doctrines nor a scholarly discipline, but the understanding, knowledge, and thinking distinctive to the Christian faith. Theology occurs when faithful people self-consciously and reflectively begin to understand the statements and symbols of faith and how they bear upon the world." This theological understanding will most fruitfully crystallize, as I see it, when it results from the encounter (in the mind of faith) of the historic revelation with the social realities of the present world, that is, in the encounter of the unchanging with the emergent elements that are always the two poles of religious knowledge.

One reason the Vanderbilt statement is such a welcome emphasis is that it is also a needed corrective to three deficient motives for theological study recognizable from the recent past: one, to train technicians for ecclesiastical jobs; two, to provide support for the preferences and programs of a denomination, school, or party; and three, to afford theological teachers an opportunity to talk with each other. The proper work of theology is the service of revelation and faith. It renders this service to God in the name of the whole Church for the sake of the whole world. Good theology gets beyond "denominations," "schools," and "fads"—even beyond "academic disciplines" and "ecclesiastical schedules." Because theology is a servant of faith and a participant in faith, it must engage those transcendent powers and historical actualities apart from the conjunction of which theology would never have arisen.

If such things be true, theology is the most vulnerable of intellectual endeavors. It must, by its very nature, concern itself for more and other than cultural, ecclesiastical, or academic approval. It must accept no sovereignties alien to itself, because it is finally answerable to God alone, its only sovereign. It must be true to itself, but it is true to itself by being true to more and other than itself. It may surrender to neither prudence nor pride. It must be true to the great tradition. It may reflect the author's mind and heart; it may not simply reflect the author's milieu. Theology must seek to be creative, not merely imitative. Perhaps, as in classical tragedy, it should carry some value as catharsis. From time to time, surely, it should entrance and delight as well as instruct or move. This must be done without too much looking over the shoulder. The true light is always *before* us; and to follow that light requires as much freedom as faith. Theology is at least as free as it is vulnerable. It is the "kept mistress" of no interest on earth, whether cultural, philosophical or ecclesiastical.

Always theology is concerned with *meaning,* indeed—to borrow the title of a published lecture by Huston Smith—we human beings are "condemned to meaning." It is theology's business to reckon faithfully and critically, in terms of Jesus Christ, with the meaning to which we are "condemned." This meaning must be sought out, identified, and interpreted. It is this concern for meaning that alerts the moral awareness to the tameness or triviality of much religious thought. Brave theology is done imperfectly and at hazard.

Theology aims to give guidance, in the light of its meaning, to the "doing of faith." It seeks to form and nurture the believer's life in the world. This is something other than providing justification or support for what one was going to do anyway. It aims at more than positive thinking or inward assurance. It challenges the mind. It distinguishes the issues. It addresses the conscience. It strengthens the arm. It guides the feet.

Theology's essential involvement with meaning defines another aspect of its task. Its task, as a rationale of faith, is fully as much to clarify questions as to provide answers. It offers no quick solutions to unexamined questions. Even its real answers—including, as they do, both truth and our historically limited perceptions of truth—must, from time to time, be reviewed and revised. Humility and hard work are required. Theology, as involvement with truth-larger-than-ourselves, leaves no more room for moral smugness and intellectual sloth than for insincerity and self-serving.

Theology's involvement in meaning forbids an identification of itself with any specific culture. For example, the historical roots of the biblical story are deep in the life of Israel and the ancient Near East. Biblical faith knew its most spectacular historical expansion in the Eastern Mediterranean and, later, in the whole Western world. But Christian faith does not allow any confinement of revelation and faith to the Mediterranean world, whether Israel or the West. The early Christians confessed God's truth-and-grace-in-Christ as truth-and-grace-for-them only because they were convinced that it was truth-and-grace-for-the-whole-world. Christian faith speaks to each time and each place and each culture because its truth and grace are for all times and all places and all human groups. This is to be affirmed of Christian *faith;* it is not to be claimed for any one organizational, theological, or liturical expression of Christian faith.

Difficulties for theology emerge from this fact. One perennially difficult task of theology is how to be universal and *at the same time* historical. Another is how to balance conviction of truth with honest appreciation of pluralism. These words only barely conceal the Gnosticism and the authoritarianism (or Fundamentalism) that provide illustration of the two difficulties just mentioned. There is at least some help for these difficulties to be found in parts of what follows.

Good theology requires *knowledge*. This is true in both senses; knowledge as insight (which is, by honest faith and experience, accessible to all) and knowledge as information (which not all have). This distinction underscores the reason why faith as such must be present in theological work, and also why faith alone does not qualify a believing person to formulate that faith as understanding. That requires knowledge as information, and such knowledge (as the building blocks of theology) must rest upon a responsible grasp of such things as Bible, Church history, ethics, and so forth. Such knowledge requires long, hard work. In order to enrich its own intellectual functions and to establish points of contact with other areas of intellectual concern, such specialized knowledge even needs to be supplemented with knowledge of philosophy, sociology, psychology, art and literature, the natural and life sciences, and the history and phenomenology of religion. Clearly, no one can do all this as it deserves to be done, but one can do what one can do. In our present world situation, it also should be emphasized that good theology, more and more, needs a knowledge of world religions both as a means of self-understanding and as a point of contact for dialogue and mission.

Even more than insight and information are needed for the theological task. *Inspiration,* perhaps, is the right word—that is, being breathed upon and quickened by the divine Spirit in such way that the movement of our life and the functions of our understanding are made harmonious with God's. This spiritual inspiration illuminates and enkindles rational knowledge. It produces what we may call "reasoned faith." The reasoned faith necessary to theology is a dialectical movement between loyalty to the tradition and freedom in the Spirit.

Putting religious truth in these terms could be illustrated from either Bible or art. To illustrate it from art might quicken our sense of the Bible's meaning and use, as well as disclose an understanding of faith as knowledge. China provides the illustration.

In the late fifth century A.D., the Chinese critic, Hsieh Ho, wrote a book entitled *Ancient Chronicle of the Classification of Painters.* Persons more knowledgeable than I have referred to this work as both celebrated and overwhelmingly influential. Hsieh Ho's famous Six Principles (or Canons) were to serve, in China, as the basis for all subsequent works on the theory of art. Art was a reproduction of the movement of life itself and the artist was to give resonance or rhyme to this movement.[1]

---

[1]The *Ancient Chronicle of the Classification of Painters* (a work I have never seen) is discussed in some measure by most studies of Chinese painting. My use of this work is secondhand from Mario Bussagli, *Chinese Painting* (London: Paul Hamlyn, 1969) 45ff.; also from François Foucade, ed., *Art Treasures of the Peking Museum* (New York: Henry N. Abrams, Inc., Publishers, n.d.) 13, 18.

In the *Ancient Chronicle,* Hsieh Ho bases the quality of all painting on the observance of "six principles." The sixth of these expresses the artist's *loyalty to the tradition.* The first, however, and the most important, contains the whole essence of art. In Chinese it reads *Ch' i yün sheng tung: Ch' i,* spirit or vital breath; *yün,* agreement or resonance; *sheng,* life; *tung,* movement. Chinese friends have told me that these four characters are all but impossible to translate, though an acceptable idiomatic rendering could be *bringing life into resonance with the spirit of things.* Hsieh Ho held that where the artist failed to achieve this harmony, his work would be bizarre or lifeless. Failure at this point was a fault that technical skill alone could not repair; but where the harmony was present no failure of technical ability could completely spoil the work of art. The depth of this aesthetic insight may be highlighted by the recognition of Hsieh Ho, and of other critics, of the great difference between "reproducing the movement of life" and "conforming to the appearance of objects." True "likeness" never lies on the surface. It is captured only by a spirit at once captivated and free—a spirit which probes for realities lying beneath the surface.

The five other principles of art could be learned, says Hsieh Ho. This first one, the resonance of the spirit with the rhythm of things, must "grow in the silence of the soul." It is acquired by neither skill nor effort. It is the mysterious movement of the universe by which the soul is awakened to its potential and commissioned for its work.

The Bible, as the primary sourcebook of faith and theology, offers itself to us on similar grounds. It is not a catalogue of right answers to all questions: indeed, it raises more questions than it answers. It is more a guide to the art of living. In the mysterious manner of grace, it draws faithful souls into harmony with the deep and universal rhythm that summons them. But just as no amount or quality of words (*ch' i* or *yün*) is art, so no number or quality of biblical words (*grace* or *revelation*) is faith. Art and meaning emerge when the artist paints and the viewer sees. Faith and truth appear when God summons and trusting persons respond. It is theology's business to interpret that summons, and rightly to depict the meaning and implications of that response.

Some part of an epistemology lurks in any view of knowledge as entailing both information and inspiration. In this instance, it is a view of knowledge as *realization.* "Realization" is from the same root as "realism," and is used here, philosophically, to affirm two ideas. One, truth, in its own right, is a transcendent and original reality. (It exists in and from

God as its only source, is conveyed to us by his own Word and Spirit, and does not depend for its reality upon our acknowledgment of it). Two, knowledge of the real were better described as insight than as information. (Such knowledge reveals the difference between holding a rational opinion that a fact is credible, and being persuaded of its reality or truth or beauty in one's inner being.)

The Christian doctrine of knowledge (as well as that of numerous others) affirms that we can, from history and from experience, "realize" transcendent truth, and experience it as grace. This realization is the work of faith. Faith draws life into resonance with the divine rhythm. It is not produced as the conclusion of a syllogism. This is the basis, in my own understanding, for calling faith a corollary or interface of revelation. It is a corollary in the sense of being a consequence of revelation and flowing "naturally" from it; an interface, in the sense that the two magnitudes (or "sacred spaces") perfectly correspond up to so far as faith reaches. Revelation and faith correspond; they are not coterminous. Part of theology's work is to understand the nature and significance of this correspondence and of this distinction.

At any rate, concrete acts of "knowledge as realization of truth"— in literature, in art, in theology—require that the real be *really realized*. For example, a theology or an art that fails to transcend the merely subjective cannot long persuade us of its hold on reality. The sense of reality emerges from the readiness, the courage and joy, to see truth as it is and to interact with it with both information and feeling. In short, whether in art or theology, something is calling us, and not much happens until we answer. Christian faith-as-realization affirms that we know who is calling us, and also that—in essence—we know what he is saying.

This grasp of reality implies *a harmony of intellect and feeling* which T. S. Eliot called the "unified sensibility." It also appears to be kin, in some degree, to William James's belief that philosophic systems, at bottom, are "visions" chosen more for aesthetic than for merely logical reasons.

This "unified sensibility" responding faithfully to the Reality that summons us is our best available track leading to judgments of truth and value. These judgments will be and will remain fallible, since no "vision" of Truth is commensurate with its Object. Still, such judgments are inescapable, for the nature of theology prevents its being merely descriptive. By definition, theology must reckon with truth and value. To say otherwise were itself a judgment about the nature of knowledge whose norm is not acknowledged. Two truths affect this fact: one, God is living God—he not only is to be confessed, but met and engaged, again and again; two, "souls" are always in process of formation, and are never the same on any two days. We unfinished souls daily face God not as Idea but as a Presence of the Word and Spirit. (One lasting element in Emil Brunner's work is the understanding of truth as "encounter," rather than as abstract idea.) There appears to be no way of avoiding responsibility for this *meeting* and for the repeated decision making that the meeting entails. These decisions are made between true and false, beautiful and ugly, good and bad—even *good and bad theology*. Refusal to acknowledge normative conclusions about its meaning and task brings theology under a foreign yoke. To accept conclusions about its meaning or task as established by norms alien to itself is a forfeiture of responsibility and, possibly, of faith.

So, we *must make judgments* of truth and value. This attends all theological work, and to recognize that no one in the world (or no institution in the world) can do this as it needs to be done is no excuse. Whose knowledge is complete? Whose heart is pure?

These limitations of character and of knowledge do not, however, prevent the doing of theology in ways that are wonderfully bright and stirring and helpful. The limitations do remind us—it is obvious if we pause to consider—that the doing of theology is clearly more appropriate for some than for others. More than feeling, sincerity, or the desire to be useful is necessary. Everyone, for example, may give personal testimony of faith, or share moral and religious insight with others. Not everyone, on the other hand, has the *relatively adequate* knowledge to illumine theological truth. This is important to realize; for every failure to illumine the truth tends to obscure it. Everyone is called to faith and understanding. Not everyone is given a theological vocation in the stricter sense.

Two related conclusions may underwrite the importance of this point of view and give it formal shape. On the one hand, theology, as a formulated understanding of the divine self-communication, addresses itself to persons—persons who must make life-shaping judgments of truth and of personal relationships. It must do more, and better, than offer surface answers to questions of depth. On the other side, theology, as the reasoned interpretation of faith, ascribes *quality* to religious experience and offers normative guidance for judgments of value and duty. In other words, theology is as morally committed as it is intellectually serious.

It has always appeared to me—and this part of my understanding was a gift of my religious heritage before it became a deliberate theological choice—that any description of experience-as-qualitative of necessity implies norms of judgment. Experience is relative to something that is not relative. Except on such a presupposition, experience cannot be said to have quality. In the long run, neither could it be described as having meaning.

This conviction makes me quickly congenial with what, in literary circles of a generation ago, came to be called the "New Criticism." Qualitative judgments of truth and value, of meaning and relationships, are involved in any *understanding,* whether of faith or poetry.

Theology, like the New Criticism, has high respect for tradition. It aims neither at the novel nor the esoteric. Its Pantheon houses no god named Fad. Its proper sign is not a weathervane, but the Cross. Theology seeks the meaning of the past in light of the present, and of the present in light of the past. One form of theology's respect for the past is its courage and humility toward the continuing presence of the past. Theology stands on the shoulders of its predecessors. It celebrates and also seeks to illumine its heritage. It shows respect for the great tradition through a utilization of it that is both faithful and critical.

The preceding argument reminds us that good theology may regard itself as neither final nor detached. The overriding reason why theology is never final is that our sense of relatedness to the external world (mundane or transcendent) discloses sublimities that can be depicted only in symbolic language. Any terms used to describe that relation must, therefore, be imprecise. The whole world is a metaphor of the Transcendent: it cannot be compassed by the finite understanding, even a faithful understanding. Furthermore, as H. R. Niebuhr convincingly reminded us, we have no *detached* knowledge whether of God or of ourselves. Knowledge of God, of history, of persons, is knowledge in which we *participate* as active and even as generative factors. No language exists uncolored by our partial perceptions of its meaning. No point of view, established outside ourselves, is accessible to us. Every gift of the Spirit flows through the filter of our own capacities and limits as persons. *God* speaks to us, but we *humanly* hear what he says.

The linguistic imprecision, just mentioned, reflects not simply the sublimity of faith's "object" in comparison with the finite character of all speech. It is also a difficulty arising from the intellectual and moral limits of the writer/speaker himself. The problem is not simply the agony of images and metaphors that haunt the mind, but only stubbornly take shape as words. It is that a rare singleness of heart is demanded—the concentration of the mind and heart on the truth and importance of the subject, the humility to see and hear. Purity of heart alone is surely not the same as theology, but no good theology is possible without it. Good information and purity of heart, these—not cleverness or the smugness of being right—are necessary conditions of a theology that matters. And such a theology is as distant from the exotic and faddish as from ecclesiastical expediency and sloganeering.

All of the above is compatible with a further observation. Theology, while being a *personal* enterprise, is never a *private* one. Theology is one form of attention to the tradition. As such it is found in the public sphere. But it is also personal witness to others on a reflective level. To say seriously that God has spoken *to all* requires each of us to add, with consternation and humility, "Then God has spoken also *to me.*" The public tradition takes precedence over the individual perception. I can believe God has called to me only because I am convinced he has called to all, and I must be concerned for that sovereign and redemptive Word. But if God has disclosed himself *also to me,* then I must report not only what I have read but, as well, what I have heard and seen and known. Theology, in such a context, could be described as the combination of the public tradition and the personal reckoning.

This combination of the public tradition and the personal reckoning can be illustrated with the following. Anyone who reads Eliot's somewhat difficult essay on Dante learns indirectly of Eliot almost as much as directly of Dante. This is not all loss: in measure, it is even as it ought to be. Perhaps, to a smaller degree, the same is, and needs to be, true of theology. At any rate it can be seen that something similar is visible in the theology that follows.

So the theologian is involved personally in his work. Nonetheless, he must remember that God—not himself—is theology's subject. Partial vision and moral limits put the theologian at a distance from the Subject, even as his faith draws him near. He is a witness, not an expert. He prophesies in part, and will continue to do so until faith is sight. Yet, he can still work in good heart. Authenticity is possible within such limits as these, even if infallibility is not.

Encouragement could come by calling to mind also for theology something Flannery O'Connor remembered about fiction. "Every novelist," she writes, "has his preoccupations, and none can see and write everything. Partial vision has to be expected." At the same time we need to add, as did she, "that partial vision is not dishonest vision unless it has been dictated."[2]

If, through literary art, Flannery O'Connor can help us to see the human limits of theological effort, she also can show us some of its amazing reach. For the greater difficulties in theological work relate even more to the limitless character of theology's Subject than to the limitations of its practitioners. The fiction writer, she says, is "concerned with ultimate mystery as we find it embodied in the concrete world of sense experience."[3] So is the theologian.

Taking Flannery seriously might help us to avoid two traps that theology, for its very life, must escape. One is the desire to reduce the mystery in the interest of exactness and verifiability. This desire feeds, too often, on the assumption that knowledge transcends faith. While no apologetic should be proffered on behalf of intellectual fuzziness, good theology must insist that true clarity is not achieved through reduction of the mystery. The mystery inheres in the subject itself. This fact of mystery remains a theological problem for some because, for at least two centuries, what has regarded itself as rational thought has tended to equate mystery with either ignorance or superstition. Good theology disappears quickly in the sands of that desert.

The second trap is perhaps more dangerous than the first. For, if we have been living in a world increasingly convinced that the farthest reaches of reality are accessible to reason alone, we have also seen in reaction (always in *reaction*) a fundamentalist assertion that the mystery will and does yield to convictions of a biblical and theological literalism. Reason alone cannot explain the Transcendent, but surely (they say) the Transcendent can be comprehended and, for some, demonstrated, by belief in the inerrancy of biblical texts, and in the interpreter's capacity—"by faith"—to escape the limits of historical reason.

This latter claim is intellectually less impressive than Rationalism. Perhaps, more accurately, it is itself a *religious form of unconfessed ra-*

---

[2]Flannery O'Connor, *Mystery and Manners,* ed. Sally and Robert Fitzgerald (New York: Farrar, Straus and Giroux, 1979) 133.

[3]Ibid., 125.

tionalism. God is no longer hidden, only revealed. Doctrine is now the systematically ordered body of revealed truths. It has been forgotten that all theology, even if sincere, is a partial witness to the truth. This sort of literalism, however devout, effectually denies that the Transcendent is trancendent. Perhaps its current popularity in American Christianity, in Islam, and, among some Israelis, even in Judaism, is a cause for some alarm. It is much more a call to free and fearless faith.

In the chapters that follow, I have tried to write with responsible freedom and meek fearlessness of what I have learned, and also of what I have seen and heard and known. The overall *shape* of my (not very original) thought is determined by what I have learned; its characteristic *flavor* by what I have seen and heard and known.

Obviously, what follows does not aim at an exposition of the whole of Christian doctrine. I have tried to focus, to clarify, from the perspectives of my own faith and understanding, what should serve as basic to an understanding of the whole. This is why I have talked of divine revelation, and of faith as its only human corollary. Theology has been understood as the work of explicating the meaning of revelation, the meaning of faith, and of both in relation. Were a full-scale system of theology indicated (or presently possible) the doctrine of God would be, essentially, a doctrine of him who, because of what he is, acts as he does; and who, through what he does, is shown to be who he is. This is the story of redemption as revelation. Looking closely between the lines, this reminds us that the doctrine of God is a doctrine of trinity-in-unity and unity-in-trinity. The doctrine of Christ would reckon him as the one who, being the mediator of saving grace, is the medium and norm of the revelation. In other words, his identity as Son of God appears precisely in his fully human obedience even unto death. To confess his deity is to acknowledge his Lordship by taking on his obedience. All roads to Christology begin at the Cross. The Church, as the product of the revelation and as the steward of faith, would be understood in terms of its function as mission in and to the world. The nature of the Church is an inference from the life and work of the Church. Other subjects of theological reflection would similarly be dealt with.

It is hoped that the sketch of the following understanding of the relation of the old and the new in theological exposition is neither indefensible nor offensive. Were I to characterize my own theology, I should tend to see it as both primitive and of current usefulness, and to hope that it is both simple and profound. The language, certainly, is not so current as some, and no one is a good judge of profundity in his own case. My close attention to all the language of this book does attest to the belief that the biblical categories, understood, still speak with clarity and power. Far from being exhausted, the language of this tradition more often witnesses to heights and depths that we have not explored than to fatigue from having carried so much heavy freight for so long a time. It would seem that the need is less for new language with which to kindle faith, and more for faith with which to appreciate the heights and depths that the language descries but cannot compass. One necessary function of faith is to break open into life the realities of revelation that, otherwise, were only words: to discover the glory in their familiarity; to probe for their true import and engage them at close quarters with mind and heart; to find in them their final simplicity and its cosmic scope—that is, to know for oneself the truth of God in Christ in that little child's simplicity that is both the despair and hope of every aging saint.

A further reflection in a personal vein: theological work is carried on through times both of vivid self-awareness and of obliviousness to self.

Numerous times in the preparation of what follows, I have, in self-awareness, stopped at some of the most serious parts of what I was doing—and laughed! How remarkable (or, perhaps, how ridiculous) that this kind of creature would undertake to speak of God, of truth, of knowledge, of the meaning of neighbor. It seemed like measuring the weight of a black hole in milligrams. Yet, one speaks of God, finally, because one must. Theology is not an explanation of God. God is known, but God is not comprehended even in faith's response to revelation. Theology is faith's finite effort to project reasoned reflection in the direction of its infinite Source. Theology is more than this, but it is also this.

Numerous times also, working on the back porch in the warm days of summer, I have been much closer to crying. From the back of our yard, in plain view from a little bower formed by a forsythia bush around a small statue of my chosen saint, Brother Francis has watched me with quizzical eyes. He perhaps understands; he surely rebukes. In a world full of need and empty of peace, would a real disciple sit there at that glass-top table and *write* about faith? If theology is reasoned reflection on faith's Source, it is also a summons to morally responsible *involvement* in the world.

At still other times, obliviousness to myself would sometimes occur and absorption in the subject become all but palpable. Then the effort to reduce the theological vision to literary form would lead back across the threshold of self-awareness. This swing, from absorption to self-consciousness and return, invariably turned out to be fruitful.

On the one hand, it was at this threshold that essential connections between language and knowledge became most apparent—and theology can no more endure a breach between language and knowledge than can poetry or science. At the same time, across this threshold would come the most electric impressions one receives of himself in relation to his work. This increased awareness is usually not too much fun: it finds one uncomfortably caught between what Rilke called "a threatening insecurity and the numinous attraction of the inexpressible."[4] In that kind of tension, one becomes concerned for more than the connections between language and knowledge. There, also, one finds out more of what it means to be a feeling and deciding, as well as thinking, person—and one is inclined either to exult or weep, or both.

One would surely flee this situation did not two convictions arrive with the self-awareness: one, that both joy and equanimity lie always *beyond* such discovery of the self; the other, to avoid meaning deliberately is to reduce one's personhood. There are no easy escapes.

It is all-important, for theology and for life, that we approach this tension with courage and freedom, a freedom that religious persons are too prone to fear. It being God's world, such fear is not only unworthy, it is unrealistic. The "soul" is made to search and find, it needs no defense against discoveries of the mind. Such a defense would be ruinous to both. Where such defense becomes habitual the relations between our sanity and our vitality are broken. There is a reason for this.

The revelation in which God is disclosed to us is the same revelation in which we are uncovered to ourselves. Faith, in one angle of vision, is the courageous freedom—the power—to accept ourselves, and to manage our lives, in such light. This power is one form of our freedom to establish effective unity between doctrine and existence without the sacrifice of mind to "soul." Christian faith does *not* call for—by its very nature, it forbids—such a *sacrificium intellecti,* and a too enthusiastic haste to offer it up may suggest that a smaller altar is needed in some cases than in others.

Sacrifice of the intellect is a denial that faith seeks and establishes the integrity of the *whole* person. Healthy faith in the whole person (a far

---

[4]Rainer Maria Rilke, *Letters to a Young Poet,* trans. M. D. Herter Norton, rev. ed. (New York: W. W. Norton and Co., Inc., 1962) 66-67.

better term than "correct belief") is the power to bring harmony between what we consciously confess as truth and what goes on in the mental depths. Thus the secret of dealing with the unconscious is not how to suppress it so that others and ourselves not recognize it: it is so to infuse it with healthy deep-running faith that it can assert itself without destructiveness. This integrity, as Ann Belford Ulanov has suggested, allows faith to flourish which otherwise would flag in the face of experiences it could not account for.

There is also a communal, as well as individual, dimension of this truth. The mind of faith, cleansed of its destructiveness and suspicions, is enabled to turn from itself to focus with generous love on the neighbor-brother-sister. This not only enables us to see them in their true light as God's beloved children, it reaches out to include them in the circle of faith, the community of *agapē*. They come to find, with us, both strength and help in time of need; that is, they do not have to leave religious ground to find nurture needed for their living.[5]

This power of faith derives, as the historic Church has always known, from faith's participation in God's actual life. My own understanding of this conviction of faith is largely affected by those from whom I have learned: chiefly, from William Owen Carver, Karl Barth, and H. R. Niebuhr. I believe God is objective to ourselves (not merely "being itself"), and when speaking of God in objective terms, I intend to confess God as both existent and sovereign. Of course, one does not say "objective" meaning God is an object. God is objective, as I intend the word, in the sense that he is actually met and known and not merely imagined. Through our faith, God makes himself known to us as an existent self rather than as a "principle of being." Subjective knowledge of God means actual knowledge of the objectively real God by a knowing subject. I still find no problem in saying "God is there," provided we also mean, "God is here." Anthropomorphisms are not the major theological problem.

In America, this point of view has been given two of its clearest and most compelling expositions by H. R. Niebuhr and Abraham J. Heschel. Niebuhr sees knowledge of God as historically and socially determined *relation*. The relation is *given,* but it never excludes the subject's active par-

---

[5]*Vogue* magazine is not usually regarded as a prime theological source, but two main points found in the preceding two paragraphs appear in some interview-answers on spiritual hunger, by Ann Belford Ulanov (with Deborah Mason) in *Vogue* (December 1985): 377-78.

ticipation in it. Heschel has helpfully reminded us that in historical event, which seems to reveal a divine side to human affairs, we are actually involved with the human side of divine affairs. A section in each of the following chapters wrestles with some of the complex questions that leave the truth of such good affirmations less than patent.

In what follows I have sought to make clear what I have meant and also to make it difficult for others to misunderstand. Attention has been paid to a maxim of Aristotle's *Poetics*. He states that the action of a play should be coherent and as concentrated as possible. Where the action does not match these requirements, the audience becomes confused or indifferent. I hope that the following chapters may show that same coherence and focus that the philosopher thought to be required of plays. Failures here and there to accomplish this could possibly be traced to my allowance of a "flow of consciousness" in some places, and to recognizable Victorian patterns in my English. The forms of my expression are, perhaps, more coherent than concentrated. In defense of the style, I believe that the careful choice of words, the use of qualifying phrases and clauses, of near-synonyms, parallelisms, and rephrased repetitions, do make it hard for readers to misunderstand what is being said. It might be germane also to add that the argument is more often spiral than linear.

In theology, as in art, one should be ready to acknowledge personal involvement in the subject. In the present time, when the physical sciences, as well as social anthropology, have shown we are inevitably parts of our experiments (and even interfere in them) I would not disguise the fact that there are autobiographical projections hidden in the shadows of my theology. This is a disvalue only where the theology is nothing but autobiography, or where one's ground is chosen for a reason other than interest in the truth.

Theology's primary concern is for God, and for self only in God's light. But this primary concern for God excludes no issue or interest arising from faith's interactions with life in this world. In this sense, nothing lies outside the proper concern of theology. In the last chapter of the book I have dealt with faith's relation to only two of these concerns: religion(s) and mission.

So, now the getting ready is over and we are prepared to take on what is ahead. Chapter 2 deals with revelation as God's self-disclosure in and through which he addresses us. Chapter 3 treats of faith as loyal and obedient response to that disclosure and address. Chapter 4, in part, presents theology as the ordered exposition of the revelation as given to faith. It seeks to understand what God has made known, to reckon with faith as the interface of revelation, and to comprehend history, experience (and all things else) in relation to God as the object of faith. It does not alter the primary character of theology as a doctrine of God to add that it attempts to think Christianly upon the whole human pageant and pilgrimage.

We shall move forward, then, already knowing that difficult questions must be met along the way and that there are no prepackaged answers to them. No gifts of grace will remove us from the common human toils through which we struggle. God is for us, but we must quit ourselves like brave men and women. We are elect in Jesus Christ, but we never "have it made." The gifts and the calling are sure, but the way is before us. We pilgrims move forward, remembering with Luther, that

> This life, therefore, is not righteousness but growth in righteousness; not health but healing; not being but becoming; not rest but exercise.
>
> We are not yet what we shall be, but we are growing towards it; the process is not yet finished, but it is going on; this is not the end, but it is the road.

Chapter Two

The Meaning
of Revelation

We saw that the mode of revelation . . . consisted in a coincidence of divinely guided events with minds divinely illuminated to apprehend those events, so that there would be no "revealed truths," but there would be "truths of revelation." The essential revelation is an act of God apprehended in a complete living experience, in which subjective and objective factors are both active; it is not capable of isolation from that experience, and is only renewed so far as the experience itself is recovered or renewed.

—William Temple

In what follows, revelation is taken to mean the divine self-disclosure. God discloses himself, not in the sense that we are enabled to comprehend him but in the sense that we are brought to know him. This disclosure is a communication. The communication is received, and is therefore receivable. The first Christians, for example, were Christian at all only because, in Jesus Christ, they had received this communication through responding to it. This experience of God became the form of their knowledge of God. They believed that God had made himself known in Jesus Christ and began to see this knowledge of God in Jesus as the lens through which to view themselves and the world. The report of this "making known" on God's part became the Christian story. It was narrated as the story of Jesus Christ. The story through which this knowledge came, and comes, was told as a cause for rejoicing. It was called "good news." This story gave rise to a rich tradition of interpretation, and the interpretation flowered into a variety of Christological endorsements. This rich

tradition is visible and this Christological variety traceable in that early
Christian literature that became the canonical New Testament, and in some
other that did not. Church history, on its bright side, is a continuation of
this tradition, and an ongoing commentary upon it. This chapter takes up
some aspects of this story as revelation and addresses certain questions
bearing on our understanding of it.

The first Christian people were convinced that God had really disclosed himself, had given knowledge of himself in Christ. This was the
substance of their Christian existence. Being in Christ was, for them, both
the fulfillment and the transformation of their knowledge of God. To put
this in terms more familiar to Athens than to Jerusalem: If faith in God was
the *form* of their existence, Jesus Christ was its *matter*—Jesus Christ, trusted
as Savior, believed on as Lord, and followed as Exemplar. Early Christians could no doubt distinguish the form and the matter of their faith; they
would have found it inconceivable ever to divide them. The connection between their experience of Jesus Christ and their knowledge of God was essential to the character of both.

The Old Testament, taken as a whole, had presupposed that creation, history, and human experience are media through which such revelation of God is given. God gives knowledge of God, and in Scripture is
regarded as the only source of that knowledge. Nature, history, and experience are *media of awareness* through which human perception of the
revelation had been most recognizable and compelling, but they do not seem
to have been regarded as *sources* of it.

This Old Testament understanding finds both continuity and transformation in the New. Old Testament and New are at one that God's self-
disclosure as person involves no reduction of his presence in creation, history, and experience. This is the continuity. The transformation comes by
the arrival of a decisive fact, interpreted as revelatory by those first believers. Through that fact, as 'lens,' the whole of creation, history, and
human experience is reread and newly understood. I mean, of course, the
whole event of Jesus Christ, whose life, death, and resurrection mark him
out—for those who are held by this faith—as the human and historical revelation of God. He who thus lived, died, and was raised, is viewed as the
embodiment of the divine presence, the unique exposition of the Father's
will (Jn. 1:14-18), to tell whose story is to delineate the divine purpose and
activity. In him, as risen Lord, faith found the God of 'then' and 'now'

coming to us with truth old and new. Jesus Christ (of the place, Nazareth; of the time, first century), is the revelation of God beyond time and place.

Jesus Christ, then, was taken by Christian faith as the fruition of the revelation known of old in Israel. He emerges out of that tradition and is its end point, its *telos*—the goal at which the whole process of creation and history had aimed.[1] Also, in the New Testament view, Christ carries beyond the earlier revelation as its completeness and fulfillment: its *teleiōsis* as well as its *telos*—the quality of reality beyond which another *telos* is unimaginable.

As being both of history and beyond it, Jesus Christ is seen also as the transformation of the whole series of revelatory events. This is why the New Testament treats him as the clue to the understanding of that whole history, the touchstone of its truth. This is theological conceptualizing on a massive scale, and we must not let its significance be lost in familiarity. Of whom can it be said—of whom should it be said, "This one discloses the divine meaning asserted in the creation, in history, and in the human experience"? Or, "This one impels us towards a redefinition of our world, our history, and the human condition"? The Christian faith has affirmed that it is Jesus Christ of whom this can and should be said. It is the conviction of the truth of such an answer that produced Karl Barth's remarkable treatment of the inseparable relation between the creation of the world and God's covenant in Christ.[2]

In the New Testament all the ongoing activity of God's self-revelation is interpreted by this determinative, personal event—Jesus Christ. He embodies and interprets the meaning and purpose of creation, the nature and end of humanity, the being and character of God. Creation and humanity, with Christ as the reality of both, are the forms in which, in the

---

[1]Father Teilhard de Chardin spoke of Christ as both the bearer and the goal of the upward movement of the universe toward the divine. Cf. R. P. McBrien, *Catholicism,* study ed. (Minneapolis, 1981) 487. In Christ, as the Omega-point of humanity, there is an actual, and for us a potential, breakthrough into the divine. I know how unhappy Karl Barth was with such an idea, and reckon that I understand why. It is, all the same, a brilliant metaphor.

[2]Barth's radical Christological reading of creation and humanity causes him to view Jesus Christ as the essential key to understanding the creation. Creation for Barth is the external basis of this covenant in Jesus Christ, as the covenant in Jesus Christ is the internal basis of creation. See Barth, *Church Dogmatics,* III.i,228-32, passim.

New Testament, the Eternal Love objectifies himself. The cross of Christ as the embodiment of this love is thereby the climax of creation and of the divine revelation in our humankind. His life and death open the door also into eschatological time. In relation to the reality and purpose of this Love alone, these forms have their own meaning and place—their reason. As the New Testament sees the matter, the *substance* of all God has to say, he says, in a nutshell, here: Jesus Christ is the Word God speaks; or, in Jesus Christ the divine love is given concrete existence as human person.

The decisive meaning and mystery of the eternal Word, which human speech cannot contain, are revealed in this personal event, this human life, Jesus. This Word, the Word that was in Jesus Christ, was made neither speech nor book but flesh and dwelt among us (Jn. 1:14). No written words, including this New Testament verse, are univocal with this Word.

This way of putting the matter seems pregnant indeed: it is equally problematical. Questions both of linguistic and historical character begin to surface between the lines. Let us look first at some of the linguistic matters.

1. THE VOCABULARY OF REVELATION

No words are equal to the Word; yet words are required if the reality of the revelatory events is to enter our understanding as meaning. Words are inadequate; they are also necessary. This is why one must either presuppose or examine the *vocabulary* of revelation. It would be useful, surely, to examine it.

The Hebrew verb regularly associated with the act and idea of revelation is גלה. Used transitively, and this is our principal interest here, it usually means to uncover, disclose, or reveal. This usage was long established in Near Eastern tradition, as indicated by parallel meanings appearing in the cognate languages.

To uncover one's ear (as in 1 Sam. 9:15; 20:2) means to reveal to that person, to make something known to him. To uncover the eyes (Num. 24:4) means to enable one to see, that is, to bring one into understanding. Secrets are also revealed (Am. 3:7; Pv. 20:19) so that what were otherwise not known is brought to light; or hidden, published.

When God is its subject, the *niph'al* state of this verb (נגלה), usually passive in Hebrew usage, is reflexive in meaning. Thus נִגְלָה means not, "he has been revealed, or is revealed"; but, "he reveals himself, or he himself is revealing." So, in a sense both interesting as language and important as theology, God reveals himself. This he does—as to Jacob at Bethel (נִגְלוּ, Gen. 35:7); as by his own word to Samuel at Shiloh (נִגְלָה, 1 Sam. 3:21); or to the ear of the prophet Isaiah regarding Israel's moral folly (נִגְלָה, Isa. 22:14). In Aramaic Daniel, the same verb is used of the communication of mysteries that are known only to God (גְּלִי, Dan. 2:19); or God reveals deep things to those who have wisdom and understanding (גְּלָא, Dan. 2:21-22).

To summarize: In varying contexts the verb can be rendered to disclose, lay bare, make known, show, uncover. God is the acting subject of this verb, and (in its religious and theological usage) is not its object except where he is also its subject. Through the action implied in this verb persons are caused to know what would remain unknown except disclosed; to see what would remain hidden unless uncovered.

It is probably worth noting, since it illustrates a recognizable element in the Hebraic understanding of things, that, in Biblical usage, the verb גָּלָה has no corresponding noun (no מִגְלָה, m., or תִּגְלָה, f.). The significance of this, I believe, is that, for the Hebrew religious perception, revelation is knowledge or power that God gives, or acts that he does in establishing or illuminating his relations with human beings. It is not simply a religious *idea* arising in people from a native power of perception or abstraction.[3]

The New Testament language is more similar to the Old Testament here than it looks, even though the Greek verb does carry a corresponding noun. The New Testament verb most commonly used of "revealing" is

---

[3]I owe to my friend and colleague, B. Elmo Scoggin, the following information regarding the use of גלה in medieval and modern Hebrew. There is in use, since the Middle Ages, a feminine noun, תִּגְלָה which means 'discovery'. E.g., the discovery of America was a תִּגְלָה גְּדוֹלָה, a great discovery. Also using the same root is הִתְגַּלוּת, likewise a feminine noun, meaning 'revelation' in the abstract sense, E.g., "that you attended Harvard is a התגלות, a revelation to me." If one uses the term "revelation" in the biblical sense of a "divine revelation," the Hebrew uses גִּלּוּי שְׁכִינָה. Thus, "the will of God came to him as a גלני שכינה," the disclosure of the *Shekinah*, i.e., as a revelation. In modern Hebrew, it is becoming common practice to use several words for revelation interchangeably: גִּלּוּי, 'discovery, revelation'; גִּלּוּי שְׁכִינָה if divine revelation is specifically intended; הִתְגַּלוּת, 'revelation'; מַעֲמָד, 'a stand, position'; as well as תִּגְלָה, 'discovery'.

ἀποκαλύπτω, to uncover, unveil, lay bare, disclose, bring to light, reveal.[4]

The corresponding noun, in the New Testament, is ἀποκάλυψις, a revelation or disclosure. What seems to keep even this Greek noun from being a merely abstract idea is the Old Testament impact upon the New Testament usage. For a revelation is that which God has done or is doing, has made or is making, has given or is giving. So that if one asks, "What does the New Testament mean by revelation?" the answer might be "It is an act of God by which his purposes are brought to pass, for example, an act by which the light of salvation is given to the Gentiles" (Lu. 2:32); or "the way in which God makes known the open secret of his purposes of grace" (Eph. 3:3); or the disclosure of those ultimate realities associated with what the New Testament calls the "last days," such as the unveiling of Christ's glory through our sharing of his sufferings (1 Pet. 4:13), or "the disclosing of the sons of God when the whole creation is set free from its bondage to decay" (Rom. 8:19). Such things are what God has done and is doing and shall do. Revelation is thus something done and to be done. It belongs to our future as well as to our present and past, and this is solely because God will continue to be God.

The most important *English* terms have already been introduced in the brief discussions of the Hebrew and Greek. Perhaps popular misconceptions of the very word 'revelation', require an even more thorough examination of the English vocabulary than of the originals. For, whether in Hebrew, Greek, or English, the purpose of the words is the communication of meaning in which authentic correspondence is established between their use as language and the realities which they serve as sign and metaphor. So we may conclude these linguistic matters with a quick examination of the English vocabulary of revelation.

In some sense or another, a sizable number of related English words mean 'revelation'—unveiling, disclosure, manifestation, communication, discovery. As words closest to the *theological* reality intended by the word 'revelation', the last two—communication and discovery—seem heaviest.

---

[4]This verb is also accompanied in the New Testament by other words of more or less similar meaning: ἐπιφαίνω (trans, 'to show'; intrans., 'to appear'; middle voice, 'to show oneself' or 'make an appearance'); δηλόω ('to disclose, indicate'); σημαίνω ('to show, make known'); φανερόω ('to manifest, make manifest'), and even χρηματίζω ('to reveal' as by an oracle).

Both words are two-sided; that is, in both a correspondence or interchange of some sort is implied.

Take the first one first. The root of the word 'communication', as a term for the biblical concept of revelation, gathers a cluster of important ideas to itself. Keep the word 'revelation' in mind as we look at a series of these just as examples. That is *communal* which is of, or pertains to, the people at large. It is the opposite of 'elite'. To *commune* means, with some intimacy implied, to have personal interaction or conference—so that, for example, eucharistic *communion* is something one *does* and *experiences* more than something one *takes*. It is not an instance of reification, of "thingification." The gospel is *communicable,* in the sense that it is capable, through rational discourse, of addressing free human persons and drawing free response that is also personal. This address response is essentially relational, only derivatively propositional. The Church as *community* bespeaks the harmony of the body of Christ made up of its multimembered people, identified as his not by a unanimous agreement in opinion but by the common character and goal that appear in all their diversity. They are one, but there is no erasure of individuality, no standardizing. One surely might say, no cloning.

Reflection upon this word-cluster helps us to say that 'communication', as a coordinate word for 'revelation', is the meaningful conveyance of truth—truth sometimes conceived as the energy of divine grace, sometimes as the meaning or power that emerges from the human relationship with it. If used as a synonym for 'revelation', it would be closer kin to acts than to ideas; and be recognizable more readily by experience or intuition than by discursive reason alone. It is accessible to all. The recognition and understanding of such communication arises through response and interchange at the level of personal freedom. This is holy ground; and in such precincts authoritarianism and creedal subscription are rude intruders.

So we see, the word 'communication' draws in its wake such ideas as 'accessibility to all', 'understanding growing out of personal relationships', 'responsible freedom', and 'individuality without individualism'. Grace and freedom are in the divine revealing; freedom and responsibility in the human response. All of these are involved in each, and all stand under what Emil Brunner always called "the category of the personal."

Whether in a religious or purely rational sense, revelation would seem to be inconceivable were not essential connection established between its giving and its receiving. There is never simply a voice, there is a hearing; not simply a disclosure, but also a seeing; not simply a message, but an embodiment of it in life. 'Communication' means that a common ground has been established by the revelatory-act because, through our response, the revelatory-act is established as revelatory-act-for-us.

As a synonym for revelation, the second word, 'discovery', is possibly an even better choice. The word 'discover', in its now older sense, meant 'to uncover' or 'disclose'. It expressed an action not limited to the subject but directed upon an object. 'Discover', in this transitive sense, would refer to an act of objective disclosing or uncovering. In this older usage, the syllable 'dis-' functions as a privative, that is, it reverses the meaning of the verb root which it serves as prefix; as it still serves to do, for example, in 'disavow' or 'dissociate' or 'disclaim'. Thus, if something were covered or hidden, to dis-cover it would be to uncover, disclose, or bring it into the light. "Discover" is also more or less synonymous with another word whose usage also is more restricted than formerly—the word 'betray'. One sees this sense illustrated in such a sentence as, "God's works betray his presence to us."

With a certain taste for Elizabethan and Victorian English, I have rather liked the use of 'discovery' as a synonym for 'revelation'. This is not simply antiquarian. It is due, primarily, to my understanding of the nature of the relationship existing between revelation and faith: God *dis-covers* himself to us; and we *discover* that he has done and is doing so. He brings himself into faith's view, with the result that we come to know him.

This is important to emphasize since, despite some instances to the contrary, the biblical texts consistently stress that he who reveals is also what is revealed—that it is himself that God discloses. The revealer and the revelation are indivisible, for the subject and the object of the revelation are one and the same.

Though much more is to be said of faith in the following chapter, this is why, in the Bible where it is the only proper corollary of revelation, faith is essentially relational in character. It has to do with the person's trustful relatedness with the divine Person and with other persons. I think this justifies us in saying that, by its very nature, revelation is essentially neither an aesthetic value nor a verbal structure. A response to revelation does not, in the first instance at least, take the form of admiration for an object. The only beauty celebrated as such in the Bible is the beauty of holiness. Neither is revelation *primarily* doctrinal in content: it never requires assent to true words. For faith no longer means, indeed, as Wilfred Cantwell Smith has shown, it never meant, what our language now means by a "belief."[5] Only in a secondary sense is revelation verbal in character. This is why revelation, in the Christian understanding, may be *associated* with but not *identified* with a book. Revelation happens between persons; it is the spiritual reality of God's self-disclosure that moved upon persons to write that book in the first place. The disclosure is completed in personal, which is to say moral, response. As entailing both knowledge and love, it is a spiritual event. It is the business of Scripture to witness to that event, that is, to point the way to the recovery or renewal of the experience in which the event was and is to be apprehended.

Revelation, then, is not a fact to be admired, not an idea to be accepted, nor words to be recited. Revelation is what is going on between God and persons on the ground of faith and between persons and persons because of God. This revelatory relationship is God's gift, and it is receivable only on the same terms in which it is given.

Reflection upon revelation as personal, as well as upon this language and its limits, reminds us that our subject is much more theological than linguistic in character. In revelation we are faced with the very stuff of theology; namely with personal meaning and moral claim. 'Communication' and 'discovery' have to do with our own reality as rational and moral agents—our 'selves' are involved in this matter. This is why openness to the truth of revelation is synonymous with readiness to follow where it leads. Only in the actual following is the openness confirmed and the knowledge established. This openness and this experiential knowledge is one facet of what we mean by faith; and the opposite of such faith is never doubt, which is an intellectual problem; it is apathy or fear, which are moral. The life of faith limps from craveness of will and failure of vision; the finiteness of our intellects is never the real problem. This is why Augustine defined faith as *adhaerens Deo* "sticking to God"—and why Simone Weil wrote that "in regard to thought of this kind, knowledge and adhesion are a single act of the mind."

We must move forward now to ask, with proper seriousness, "What has God dis-covered that we have discovered? Where has his presence been

---

[5]W. C. Smith, *Faith and Belief* (Princeton: Princeton University Press, 1979) esp. 105-27.

decisively or persuasively asserted? What is given and received, as T. S. Eliot says,

> . . . in a lifetime's death, in love,
> Ardour and selflessness and self-surrender.[6]

In a ridiculously simple way the New Testament addresses these questions by putting forward the narrative of one life, Jesus Christ. The story is succinctly told, but its interpretation is not simple. As Paul Scherer used to say, "The lock of the universe cannot be picked with a hairpin."

2. THE REVELATION OF GRACE AND ITS ISSUE IN CHRISTOLOGY

This story, which is not literally the same as the history, states that Jesus' appearance in the world results from an act of God (Lu. 2; Mt. 1); that after the fashion of our kind, he grew up physically and morally (Lu. 2:52); that his teaching was about the rule of God (for example, Mk. 4); that his proclamation of God's rule, or kingdom, struck his hearers as astonishingly fresh (Mt. 7:28-29); that his acts of healing were viewed as powers (the Synoptics) and interpreted as signs (John); that he gave special concern to the excluded and dispossessed, and seemed to think God did too (Lu. 16; Mt. 25); that he encountered conflict with the civil and religious authorities of his time (Mk. 11f.), and was executed by crucifixion at the hands of the Roman state (Mk. 15); that, almost immediately after his death, his followers declared him raised from death (Mt. 27; Jn. 20).

This is the straightforward, compact story told as a witness to revelation and, in one sense, as the bearer of it. At this last point, namely the resurrection, what has been said historically of Jesus merges with the superhistorical. Indeed, I should suppose that all history is always merged with the superhistorical. The reality of resurrection and its power, apprehended through trust in God who acted in it as the power behind both death and life, became both the point of departure and the rallying focus of their later—rather sooner than later—interpretation of the story. From their interpretation of Jesus' life and its victory, which was the one faith of the first Christian community, grew the full-blown theology of the New Testament.

---

[6]"The Dry Salvages," Canto V, in T. S. Eliot, *The Complete Poems and Plays* (New York: Harcourt, Brace and World, Inc., 1962) 136.

In the New Testament there is one faith, but it comes to us in a variety of theologies. How does one state succinctly the apostolic interpretation of the story? It can be done, I believe, by stating first their common agreement as to what had happened to them—that is, their confession of what God had actually accomplished in their case through this life, death, and resurrection of Jesus Christ. What God had accomplished in their case through Christ was what they meant by revelation *par excellence;* and it became, as we have said, the lens through which all else was viewed. Next, we can briefly examine the primary confessional form which expressed their response to the revelation and defined its warrant. Illustrations of this could involve the exegesis of the whole New Testament. I shall comment upon only one confessional form, and show how Paul, in his own fashion, gave it warrant in the Christological language of the first chapter of Colossians.

What had happened to them was that their sins had been forgiven and their lives had "been hid with Christ in God." The certitude of the forgiveness of sins—and with it the gift of new life in joyful freedom from guilt—is the heart of the early Christians' response to the life and death of Jesus Christ. The cross for them, paradoxical as this may seem to us, became good news. But for the cross, they would not have been Christian at all. The death of the cross not only crowned a life that had been self-giving from the start; it also disclosed the radical love that had produced the creation itself. The resurrection was God's vindication of such a life-in-death, and was viewed as the conclusive overthrow of the dominion that death had come to hold over the human family through sin. Reconciliation and forgiveness, freedom and immortality were, for faith, the result of Christ's cross. Around it, as a center of spiritual health and moral power, a new human condition-and-possibility was established.

This joyful freedom allowed these first Christians no easy amnesty from their sin and guilt. Redemption from sin was a reality laying moral claim on the redeemed: for the freedom of grace is freedom for the good, the freedom of filial obedience to the perfectly righteous Father, the freedom not to sin. To be sure, sin is less a reality than is grace. It has force but not ground, for sin is against reality. It is *anomia,* an affront to both order and reason. Its root is prideful self-centeredness; its fashion is freedom *from* God; and its public badge is what Carl Jung, remembering the prideful assertiveness apparently endemic to our kind, called our "God-almightiness." This is the nature of our plight. This is our alienation from God and our need for forgiveness.

Sin, then, if less a reality than grace, is almost as heavy. More than a misfortune has overtaken us. Sin is the distortion of our own selfhood, the flawing of the divine image in our kind, the breakdown in ourselves of a center of health; and because it is an offense against the divine love it is also an assault on the divine order. In God's world it will not finally work. This offense we have activated from within. It has had our consent. Rarely have we been as concerned for its unworthiness as for its disadvantages; and our struggles against it would not readily bring to mind the fiery duel with the dragon in the Valley of Humiliation, which left Bunyan's pilgrim wounded but able to continue his journey.

It is just here, where the early believers saw grace working through faith in the victory over sin, that revelation appeared most proximate to their existence. I believe it might be here, as well, that traditional theology serves us best.[7]

In Jesus Christ, as the sinless son, God reckons with our sin. It is precisely this sin in ourselves—*mea culpa,* my own sin, my own great sin— that prevents our seeing its involvement in the agony of the Cross. It is the same sin that prevents awareness of what we owe to Christ as the crucified Savior. Conversely, it was the absence of such sin in himself that enabled Christ to see sin for what it is: a dreadful violation of the divine love, and therefore the great destroyer of true humanhood. In empathy with our lot, and for our misery as sinners, he gave himself. This identification of Christ's own life with the divine antipathy towards sin and with the divine love for all laboring under its effects, is what traditional theology has meant by atonement. The New Testament celebrates Jesus Christ; and the reason for this is that the death of the cross encapsulates the spirit of his entire life of identification with sinners and outcasts. He bore our sins in his own body on the tree (1 Pet. 2:24). He involved himself, when he might have done otherwise, with the moral disablement and spiritual alienation traceble to our apathy and disobedience. As fellow-traveler with us, he endured the power and issue of our sin which is death: *Ecce homo.* Behold the man, indeed; *Ecce Agnus Dei qui tollit peccata mundi.*

---

[7]The next six paragraphs owe much to James Denney, *Jesus and the Gospel* (London: Hodder and Stoughton, 1909) 393-411; and to his *The Doctrine of Reconciliation* (London: Hodder and Stoughton, 1917) see esp. 91-120, and my reference to Denney in the "Acknowledgments" of this book.

Such grace actually happened and, so far as I can see the matter, this is supremely what early Christians understood to have been and to be the revelation of God. This is the light in which all else is viewed; and as it is all traceable to God's sheer grace, so, for the New Testament, is it all defined by Jesus Christ in whom God was present reconciling the world unto himself and not reckoning unto us our trespasses (2 Cor. 5:19). Viewed under the aspect of the eternal love, this forgiveness is completely *gratuito;* seen in its historical actuality, it is invariably *propter Christum;* our appropriation of it as salvation is always *sola fide.* To receive such grace, through the exercise of trustful obedience towards God, is the first line of what the New Testament means by responding to revelation.

Early on, the followers of the Way gave confessional form to what they had personally experienced of Christ as the revelation of God. They associated Jesus Christ with their worship of God. God's love in him had met their sin as forgiveness. Christ's love for his own, even unto death, was God's love at work for us all. He was the Father's true Son. He had rescued humanity from destruction and renewed their strength. He had overcome their death in eternal life. He was their Savior. Their very worship of God was no longer separable from the obedience they owed to Christ and from the new life they experienced in him. He was their Lord.

With the substance of these last affirmations, it is possible to express the faith of the whole New Testament: "Jesus Christ, God's Son, is Savior." This confession was given vividness as an anagram in the Greek word for fish: ἰχθύς. This was the primary content of the earliest Christian confession. This is the substance of that faith that confessed that Jesus Christ is Lord.

Jesus was seen as the fulfillment and transformation of Israel's covenant hope: he was the Christ. In his filial obedience unto death, God is revealed as self-giving love, and Jesus is revealed as God's unique Son. His solidarity with sinners marks him our Savior; his solidarity with God, our Lord.

For biblical faith, "Savior" and "Lord" express less of piety than of stubborn conviction; less of doctrine than of simple recognition of reality. These terms are not primarily of devotional character, though the realities they bespeak move to devotion. They express tough faith. By calling Jesus "Savior," those first Christians gave voice to their sense of unrepayable debt for what he had undeniably done. He had delivered them from sin, and from death which is sin's issue. "New life and living hope were

theirs through the gospel'' (1 Pet. 1:3). By calling Jesus "Lord," those
first Christians expressed their sense of absolute obligation. To their faith,
he was undeniably Lord, and they *belonged* to him—they were no longer
their own (1 Cor. 3:23). Their confession was: Jesus Christ is Lord (Phil.
2:11).

This is the early Christian interpretation of the story of Jesus' life.
It corresponds to believers' experience of Jesus. His life is the seed, this
experience is the soil, and the Jewish-Hellenistic climate the environment,
out of which grew the whole New Testament Christology. The story thus
interpreted and thus experienced still justifies itself in the mind of faith as
the basis for reckoning the story as revelatory. In other words, biblical faith
is still a viable option.

The quest of the Church's thinkers for the rationale of their interpretation of Jesus Christ as Lord led to the development of the Church's
Christological thought. This theological development, with contextual cir-
cumtances giving it shape, expresses the heart of New Testament thought.
It seems to me that the unity of the New Testament lies in faith's immediate apprehension of Jesus as Savior and Lord, and its variety in those further theological expansions that seek to render such faith as understanding.
In the former, we are dealing with immediate experience, with basic religious attitude and commitment, that is, with a faith carrying all sorts of
theological freight; in the latter, we are dealing with faith's need to realize
itself as rational meaning, that is, with a theology whose transcendent content is inseparable from human faith.

It has already been said that these *religious attitudes* expressed in
the New Testament towards Christ seem fully consentient—one might almost say identical. There is one faith, just as there is one Spirit, one Lord
and one Body. The Christological understanding in which this faith was
developed as rationally stated knowledge varies, however, from author to
author. The writers of the gospels of Luke and John, for example, or of the
epistles Colossians and Hebrews, hold one faith. They clearly do not hold
one Christology. The biblical canon itself preserves and bears witness to
this theological diversity, and should be taken as warrant for ours.

This is a fact of some significance for all Christians, and, in our own
time, should be stressed as important. The movement of our time that points
up this fact as both important and timely is the resurgence of Fundamentalism. Fundamentalism, like Gnosticism with which it has certain affin-
ities even as it is very different, is a sort of "polar opposite" of biblical

faith. Fundamentalism's efforts to ensure uniformity of doctrine, for example, represents a misreading of the nature of biblical faith, a dissatisfaction with the diversity of the New Testament canon, and effectively denies that freedom for which Christ set us free (Gal. 5:1). It attempts, as well, to control the Spirit of God who blows only where he will (Jn. 3:8). This understanding of faith reads the Gospel as "approved doctrine," not as good news to a free conscience. It mistakes the one faith for one approved manner of describing it. It feeds on the fear of being wrong. Such ill-regulated minds are finally their own punishment, but, for the immediate future, need to be taken seriously by many who, hitherto, have been too sophisticated to notice them.

To return to the main line and repeat: The Father discloses himself in Christ as the true Son, and through him lays claim upon us for whom he is Savior and Lord. No critical stance with which I am familiar requires the surrender of this unmistakable apostolic interpretation of the life and death of Jesus. Neither are the data *totally* convincing which would make it ridiculous to view this apostolic interpretation as resting on Jesus' own intuitions of himself.

What we have here for sure is a life and its death, its impact upon other lives, and an interpretation of that life and death as gospel. This is surely what the first Christians meant by 'revelation', and it is the one root of the New Testament Christologics. These Christologies are faith's effort to provide warrant for the interpretation of Jesus' life and death as gospel—and there is little, if any, speculative element in them.

Nor is there some antecedent theory of incarnation which that life must illustrate or confirm. There is the life itself for whose actuality as revelation a rationale is sought: namely, that, precisely in this life, God was working to redeem the human family, and was disclosing himself as present in his work. For many there came a convincing experience of that revelation and redemption in Christ, a commitment to Christ on the basis of it, an intuition of that revelation and redemption as religious faith, as moral promise and moral claim. Faith's response was to nurture this experience as grace, to understand it as human and cosmic meaning, and to share it with the world as hope and joy.

In faith's attempts to disclose the ground and rationale of this moral redemption as experienced fact, and to state it for purposes of clarification and communication, it does begin to use some highly metaphorical—even mythic—language. Such attempts are reason's way of disclosing the ground for faith's identification of Christ as Savior and Lord. These attempts appear throughout the New Testament, but seem to me to be most potent in Paul and in the Fourth Gospel. One illustration from Paul, the first chapter of Colossians, puts it as comprehensively and compactly as any.

The apostle (in the mythic language just mentioned) has just reminded the Colossian believers of our great salvation: God has delivered us from the dominion of darkness and transferred us into the kingdom of his beloved Son (vs. 13). Precisely in that Son we have the ἀπολύτρωσις, the redemption which includes and is known in connection with the forgiveness of sins (vs. 14). That is to say, forgiveness is the result of our justification, and is as well its content.

Turning from such an effect, Paul begins to extol its cause (vss. 15ff.). His Christology takes off from the Christian experience of forgiveness which is our justification (vs. 14), and ends with the 'self-giving of Christ' which is its ground (vs. 20). The Christological terms appearing between verses 14 and 20 are altered in meaning—that is, they lose their grip on reality—if separated from the grace of forgiveness through the cross. So inseparable is Jesus Christ from the Christian experience of forgiveness, the word redemption is used as a metonym for Christ: he is himself called our redemption (1 Cor. 1:30). His redeeming work—coming to climax in the cross and being sealed in the resurrection from the dead—reveals Jesus Christ as κύριος, and thus he began to be called. Such a title represented, for their faith, a natural projection on a cosmic scale of their actual experience of God through that one particular life.

Here, then, is the way it all sounds when Paul, in Colossians 1, makes such a projection of the meaning of Christ.

> He is the image of the invisible god, the first-born of all creation; for in him all things were created, in heaven and on earth, visible and invisible, whether thrones, or dominions or principalities or authorities—all things were created through him and for him. He is before all things, and in him all things hold together. He is the head of the body, the church; he is the beginning, the first-born from the dead, that in everything he might be preeminent. For in him, all the fulness of God was pleased to dwell, and through him to reconcile to himself all things, whether on earth or in heaven making peace by the blood of his cross (vss. 15-20).

Paul's association of the exaltation of Christ as Lord with the self-giving for sinners on the historic cross reminds us that, where sin is unrecognized or minimized, the understanding of the Christian life itself is deeply affected. We do not extol a Savior to whom little is owed. The apostle sees redemption as reconciliation with God on the basis of forgiveness as our only justification. It is a liberation-at-cost. Paul saw it as involving mighty powers of good and evil, to describe which in intelligible form required risky metaphors and mythic ideas: a 'ransom' is paid; or a deliverance from satanic slavery is effected. When the New Testament uses the word redemption, ideas of emancipation, release, rescue, freedom, and even immortality hover in the atmosphere. When we speak of revelation, in the sense of the New Testament, this redemption in Jesus Christ is what we understand to have been revealed. This redemption by the cross is historic fact; it is also the vindication of a lost creation and the seal of an eschatological victory.

After the cross no Christian may any longer regard forgiveness as a sort of easy amnesty, cheaply declared by an indulgent deity to a well-mannered offender. It is at cost—to God and to ourselves. This is why repentance, along with any restitution made for sin, can never be meritorious; it can only be gratefully obedient and self-effacing.

We touch here what I understand to be the recurring motif of the Christian life: gratitude begotten of forgiveness and acceptance. This gratitude resonates in all good theology and echoes in any free ethics—for gratitude is the most nearly perfect answer we can give to grace. Karl Barth put it this way, "the only answer to *charis* is *eucharistia*. . . . Grace evokes gratitude like the voice an echo."[8]

To sum up: redemption is God's costly act of release and reclamation, and the human state effected by that act. Grace does this in such way that, though it is awesomely sovereign, it makes no abridgment of our moral freedom; and, though totally free, in no way diminishes our moral obligation. In it all, God makes himself known to us as who he is.

Such is the shape of the New Testament faith. In broad outline, it is present everywhere in the texts. However, the spontaneity with which it was and is confessed as revelation is all but matched—especially for moderns—with difficulties which challenge its credibility.

Three of these difficulties define the problematic of H. Richard Niebuhr's analysis—a generation ago—of the meaning of revelation.[9] The

---

[8]Barth, *Church Dogmatics*, IV.i,41.

[9]H. R. Niebuhr, *The Meaning of Revelation* (New York: Macmillan, 1941).

questions that he raised seem still to be crucial; his management of the questions is illuminating and (overall) persuasive; the conclusions arrived at throw light upon the whole field of theological concern. (Perhaps the most important way in which this is true, for our time, has to do with the way we manage the theological issue—and opportunity—posed by the fact of the plurality of religions.)

For these reasons—as a way of examining the questions inhering in our subject, and as preliminary to some constructive statements that follow—I have chosen to deal with the problems of religious knowledge and the limits of historical reason within the framework of Niebuhr's thought. This calls for our seeing Niebuhr in relation especially to Kant (the "practical reason" or the "reasoning heart") and to Troeltsch (historical method, and historical relativity). Further clarification, it is hoped, will follow upon our putting Professor Niebuhr into some conversation with Barth and Tillich.

3. REVELATION, HISTORY, AND KNOWLEDGE

In the preface to *The Meaning of Revelation,* Niebuhr formulates the crucial questions as follows: They are questions "about the relations of the relative and absolute in history, about the connections between 'scientific' or objective and religious history, and the perennial problem of natural religion and historical faith," that is, with what has traditionally been called the problem of natural and revealed religion.

The fundamental character of the questions is plain from the way in which all bear directly upon the way we reckon the meaning of history, of faith, and of theology itself. Affected by them all is any claim to the reality and possibility of religious knowledge.

The first question—the relations of the absolute and relative in history—poses sharply one form of the question of the possibility of knowledge, and I shall deal with it in this chapter. The second—the connections between 'scientific' or objective and religious history—will be discussed in the following chapter in relation to the experiential character of faith as implying objective as well as subjective content. The third question—the perennial problem of the relation of natural and revealed religion—raises, among other things, the issue of the definition of theology itself and will reappear still later.

With regard to the question of "the relations of the relative and absolute in history," it is appropriate both rationally and theologically to acknowledge that we have no access to a universal knowledge of things as they are in themselves. It is easier for religious persons to admit this when we are knowledgeable also about subjects other than religion, and if we are not defensive about the limits of our own theological reason.

We can have no universal knowledge of things as they are in themselves, for the good reason that no universal equipment for registering that knowledge exists. Every human knower has not only a unique psychology and logic with their undeniable limits; but one's very capacity to know— whatever its limits—is tinctured with one's inheritance from a particular time and society. Our metaphysics and logic, as surely as our economics and politics, are qualified by our time and setting.

The capacity to recognize this fact, and its importance for theology, is the bequest principally of Critical Idealism, which has convincingly shown that reason operates with a particular, not a universal, psychology and logic. Under the impact of historical and sociological studies, we now understand as well that our ethics and theology also are, *in part,* creatures of culture, that is, of time and society. Theology and ethics may think, and think truly, of the transcendent. But our thought of the transcendent is not transcendent thought. This is beautifully illustrated in Kant himself, whose arguments on the categorical imperative and transcendental dialectic would betray, to any intellectual historian, his time, place, and vocation as a late eighteenth century, German, academic. It is a historical and social reason with which we understand. History and sociology have impressed upon us the conviction, as Professor Niebuhr puts it, ''that our reason is not only in space-time, but that space-time is in our reason.''[10] Or in another place, ''all knowledge is conditioned by the standpoint of the knower . . . so that no universal knowledge of things as they are in themselves is possible.''[11] I might add that the very questions that it is even possible for our minds to raise are shaped and, to some degree, controlled by our particular historicality.

In such words one has heard echoes both of Immanuel Kant (1724-1804) and of Ernst Troeltsch (1865-1923). Possibly, from the theological side of this problem, Niebuhr was thinking also of Luther's doctrine of God as simultaneously revealed and hidden. Part of what Luther meant by *si-*

---

[10]Niebuhr, *Revelation,* 7.

[11]Ibid., 5.

mul revelatus et absconditus was that knowledge of God is never reducible to rational cognition alone. It is a moral knowledge that takes shape in the soul as the result of the successful struggle of faith with the *reliquiae peccati*. At any rate, it is sound, I believe, to recognize with Kant the temporal character of our experience and of the positive knowledge that rests upon it; and, with Troeltsch, the interdependence but not the interchangeability of religion and culture.

That their points of view did not carry Kant into agnosticism or Troeltsch into skepticism, should curb any too-eager haste in those directions. For, always haunting all our intimations of complete relativism is the recurrent conviction, seemingly independent of circumstance, of a transcendent reality unmistakably present to and in our finite experience; and never absent in the spontaneous impulse—rational as well as ethical— to reckon with that transcendence. Kant's way of reckoning with that transcendence was the formulation of his doctrine of the practical reason. Troeltsch's way was to develop a view of religion whose validity would not hang on the question of its absoluteness.

Paul Tillich (1886-1965), who appeared on the scene as Troeltsch departed it, managed the matter by developing a paradoxical understanding of the relationship of temporal experience to the transcendent which, in early and mid-career, he called "belief-ful realism."[12] Faith, according to Tillich, is the paradox of participating in the unavoidable tension that derives from our historical existence being qualified by Transcendent Being. It is "belief-ful" because it refuses to deny the "special-moment experiences" of transcendent meaning on the one hand; and is "realistic" because it refuses to discount the actualities of our concrete existence on the other. Faith would thus seem to be, for Tillich, both the courage in freedom to accept our historical existence vis-à-vis the Unconditional or Ground of Being, and the interpretation of this reciprocal relationship according to which the Unconditional or Ground of Being is acknowledged as both supporting our existence and defining its limits. It is in this interchange that knowledge is gained.

H. R. Niebuhr was sympathetic with Tillich's thought, indeed was an early translator of Tillich for American readers. But Niebuhr found 're-

---

[12]See Tillich, *The Protestant Era* (Chicago: The University of Chicago Press, 1948). 78. Discussed by Hans Frei, in Paul Ramsey, ed., *Faith and Ethics* (New York: Harper and Brothers, 1957) 32-35.

lational' rather than "ontic" terms more suitable for stating his understanding of God. He found helpful Tillich's early thought on *kairos* as the presence of the transcendent in history; as well as the idea of 'belief-ful-realism' already described. But he does not, like Tillich, identify God as 'being-itself', or accept that term as "the only direct, proper, and nonsymbolic statement we can make about God."[13] Neither would Niebuhr try, as Tillich had attempted, to transcend the dialectic of 'self' and 'other'. Niebuhr developed a faith/relational method for the understanding of history and for the knowledge of God. An adapted form of Kant's doctrine of the Practical Reason was one tool with which he did it.[14] This seemed necessary, Niebuhr thought, since 'being' and 'personhood' in God appear to be inseparable, as is learned in God's confronting us as a 'self'.

Personhood in God cannot be understood simply by symbolic correlation with 'being'. The knowledge of God is based, for Niebuhr, on a unique and concrete relation activated and sustained through faith as participation in God's actual presence. Both the uniqueness and the existential quality of this faith rest upon the reality and uniqueness of the activity, essence, and perfections of the Divine Person. This understanding of God as objective person (and not merely as 'being-itself'), and as self-revealer actually known to faith, is inseparable from but never identical with the conditions of our own historical existence. We do know, though we know only in part.[15]

The thought of Karl Barth (1886-1968) also interested and challenged Niebuhr. For both men, God is really *God*. He is God both in his reality and in his sovereignty. Both Barth and Niebuhr see the anomaly of talking about God if God is not existent or sovereign as God—if he is not "there," so to say, as really God. Neither man is afraid of personalistic language, or even the language of analogy. Niebuhr's impressive and moving discussion of 'the deity of God'[16] is closer—in temper much closer—to Barth's understanding of God's otherness and God's humanity than to Tillich's 'Being beyond being'.

---

[13]See Frei, in *Faith and Ethics,* 77-87. I owe much to Frei's discussion.

[14]Cf. Niebuhr, *Revelation,* viii. See also Frei, in *Faith and Ethics,* 86n54.

[15]Cf. Tillich, *Systematic Theology,* 1:238-39; H. R. Niebuhr, *Christ and Culture,* (New York: Harper & Brothers, 1951) 238-41, 254-56; *The Meaning of Revelation;* and Hans Frei, in *Faith and Ethics,* 79-87.

[16]Niebuhr, *Revelation,* 101-39.

Barth and Niebuhr walk together not only in this ready acknowledgment of God's primacy as existent self, but also in an equally strong sense of our complete dependence upon him. More clearly than Barth, Niebuhr saw how our knowledge of God's presence and primacy as self is a radically conditioned—a historically and socially conditioned—relation. This relation is a 'given', but it finds no starting point which excludes ourselves.

Both Barth and Niebuhr believed that faith confronts an 'Other' whose intelligibility is more or less identical with his existence as person. Niebuhr, moreover, insisted that our faith knows what it knows not only in terms of its confrontation with the personal 'Other', but that our faith participates in that meeting as an active or even generative factor. Our own history and existence are included in the "givenness" of grace and revelation; both 'objectivity' and 'relation' are to be accounted for. Barth has held that, since the Triune God is "the primary and proper subject and object" of our knowledge of him, this knowledge "even as an action undertaken and performed by man . . . is objectively and subjectively both instituted by God Himself and led to its end by Him."[17]

Both men seem to me to be saying that, in attempting to explain living-faith-in-God-as-a-form-of-knowledge, human beings cannot resort either to an 'analogy of being' or to any scheme of meaning based on causal antecedents and consequences. Barth's way of explaining it is to treat our knowledge of God as a form of his knowledge of us. As Barth sees it, our knowledge of God, from inception to end, is a form of God's knowing us; and "this is in consequence of the fact that God Triune does not wish to know Himself without Himself giving us a part in the grace of revelation."[18] This "giving us a part" takes the form of our election: the divine faithfulness which alone is for us the only ground of certitude and confidence. God is the object of knowledge for our faith only because he wills by this means to make himself available to us as who he is.[19]

It is not of first importance for us to note that this is not Niebuhr's way of speaking, yet he is, I believe, in basic harmony with it. I think Niebuhr would not cavil at Barth's emphasis on the Trinitarian circle of God's

---

[17]Barth, *Church Dogmatics,* II.i,204-27.

[18]Ibid., II.i,204.

[19]Ibid., II.i,205-207.

love of self and its inclusion of ourselves. Niebuhr's actual emphasis falls, however, not on Trinity and election-by-inclusion-in-the-divine-love, but on the way in which God's revelation in Christ was ''an event that represented a 'surd' in our comprehension''; an event, as Hans Frei put it, that effects ''an ingression into the flow of time which causes a revamping of the whole process.''[20] Since no adequate measurements already existed in human experience for gauging this event, it is, in this sense, a miracle; and it is the impact of the event, working through a faith shaped by God's Spirit, that creates the tools of its own interpretation. In other words, Niebuhr here has chosen to reckon with the meaning of Christ, and our knowledge of God, as more a historical than systematic problem.

Let me pursue the historical matter for a moment with reference to another of Barth's ideas. Though he did not customarily focus on the relations of the relative and absolute in history, Barth has spoken to this problem in a rich variety of ways.[21] I mention here only Barth's view that the transcendent world and the historical world are, in a sense, indirectly identical. Our true life is life in God, and it is of God and from God that we have true knowledge. The Transcendent impinges upon our temporal lives so that, through our faith, we are reconciled to God and become heirs of eternal life—that is, we come to know his gracious and happy election of us. Eternal life is neither an alternative for, nor goal of, this life. Eternal life is the reverse side of this life; it is our present life as God sees it. To repeat, our knowledge of God is primarily a form of his knowledge of us. History is the continuum in which our faith is exercised dialectically: that is, as a form of moral and contextual knowledge but not as a form of rational or cognitive certainty. We know truly; but what we truly know is not yet fully manifest.[22]

---

[20]Frei, in *Faith and Ethics,* 105.

[21]One of these ways reminds us of one aspect of the thought of Horace Bushnell (1802-1876). Bushnell had declared in *Nature and the Supernatural* (1858) that nature and supernature are coordinate, not antithetical, factors in the one divine order. Cf. Alan Richardson, *Dictionary of Christian Theology* (Philadelphia: Westminster, 1969) 41.

[22]Carried within the shell of this argument is the kernel of Barth's ethics and eschatology. The ethics is developed, even from the years at Münster and Bonn, and is carried through in somewhat altered form in each major section of the *Dogmatics.* The eschatology is hinted at throughout the *Dogmatics,* but was never developed systematically, since the great man died before volume 5 could be written.

While all these claims to true knowledge of the Transcendent are arguable, it does seem to me that the readiness of some thinkers—on the basis of historical relativism—to assume the validity of agnosticism as obvious stops short of the real question. One of the commonest reasons for this assumption has been the recognition that our minds are stamped with a historical and social character. There is no direct access to the divine being for culturally relative persons. Pietism has sought to bypass this limitation with intuition of the Spirit. Mysticism attempts it by minimizing or denying the gulf between the human person and the divine. Fundamentalism avoids the problem by claiming as inerrant a collection of biblical texts.

That there is, for our kind, no direct access to the divine being, has been the real strength of agnosticism. But the crucial question is not whether there is direct access, nor whether the mind's categories are stamped with a historical and social character. That they are so stamped is undeniable— so who should wish to deny it? The question, better focused, is whether socially and historically conditioned minds, with no direct access to divine being, are meaningfully addressable from around or beyond ourselves. It requires no logician to recognize the difference between saying ''there is no absolute knowledge,'' and saying ''there is no knowledge of the Absolute.'' It is not demonstrable, but neither is it ridiculous, to say that one may know truly of the absolute what cannot be known absolutely. That is to say, any knowledge of the absolute is necessarily qualified; it is not necessarily unreal. Christian faith affirms that this qualified but real knowledge is mediated through historical experience and is a knowledge within history of the more-than-historical.[23] This being so, it surely brands as singular any leap from the generally accepted premise that all knowledge is historically and socially mediated, to the conclusion that in history and society no knowledge is mediated at all.[24]

Having now driven in the enemy's pickets, let us not suppose we have routed his army. For, believing—or believing not—in the reality of such mediated knowledge is certainly not the same as demonstrating either. It appears, indeed, that neither is demonstrable. In both, a stance or a position is *assumed.* This is for us a forced option, and neither position can

---

[23]See how Karl Barth justifies our knowledge of God in a letter to a correspondent, *Letters, 1961-1968,* 217 (letter 222).

[24]Cf. Niebuhr, *Revelation,* 13.

be guaranteed by history or social experience. It is impossible to be sure of the reality of religious knowledge on a discursive basis; on the same basis, it is equally impossible to know of its absence or impossibility. Knowing, or not-knowing, we all live and die by some structure of beliefs and values whose assumptions are not demonstrable.

These perspectives on religious knowledge are powerfully affected, as we have seen, by the question of the relations of the absolute and the relative in history. Let us accept, with Niebuhr, historical relativism as a fact. Should we not join him also in rejecting agnosticism as its consequence? This rejection of agnosticism could rest basically on two supports: one, the human mind's capacity for valid knowledge beyond the limits of pure reason; and two, the distinction in knowledge between validity and absoluteness. In other words, we have worked our way back around to Kant and Troeltsch. I have pursued the first of these points, in the main, because the second, in a somewhat altered form, will reappear in the discussion of theology and religion(s).

4. TWO METAPHORS IN AN ATTEMPT AT CONSTRUCTION

We must come now to some constructive statements about what we mean by revelation, and I propose to focus upon only two images or ideas: (a) the coming of light, and (b) the doing of love.

These affect the believing person both in his understanding and, for want of a better word, in his existence. Revelation illumines the understanding. It also remakes the person. Both the cognitive and the existential are included, and, as well, the universal and the historical moment.

a. The coming of light

The revelation can be described as the arrival of light in a dark place. But eyes accustomed to the dark are not ready for the light. It is not that more than light and eyes are needed if we are to see. It is that our eyes must become accustomed to the light; and that they require proper "spectacles" with which to put objects into clearer focus. Or, to use another figure, we possess the power of perception but we do not understand. For we see things *through* our eyes, not with them. We see things *with* our understanding, and it is our understanding that needs illumination.

That this is so is due to a practical necessity of fact, not to any necessity in principle. It would hardly be meaningful to call God the actual governor of our lives as persons, had he not so placed us towards himself as to make our knowing him a possibility. We have had all along, as it were, the equipment for the knowledge of God. This is clear from the fact that even after responding to revelation through faith we continue to recognize ourselves as who we were before. Apart from revelation, however, our equipment for the knowledge of God is able to register only those images of truth that we more originate than receive—so that that knowledge of God produced by our own equipment is largely a projection of our imperfect knowledge of self. Only God's self-disclosure to us can reverse this inversion. We know God by God's revelation of himself to us. It is knowledge of God that conditions and corrects our knowledge of self. All this is congenial with Karl Barth's argument, all those years ago in the *Prolegomena,* about the possibility of our knowing God apart from faith: namely, that theoretically we *could,* but actually we *cannot.*[25] To move from *could* to *can* is a journey short or long—for who can clock the timeless?—but short or long, it is of prime importance; for the road from theoretical "could" to effectual "can" passes through actual "cannot." All this is of a piece, also, with what Jonathan Edwards taught in the *Treatise on the Will,* "that while all men have natural ability to turn to God, they lack the moral ability—that is, the inclination—so to do." So closely related are our dark extremity and God's opportunity with the light.

So, an invitation into the knowledge of God is not on the basis that we have a capacity for the light (which, it seems, is true), but on the basis that we actually are in the dark, unless God—who is seeking to do so—shine upon us.[26] He does this, in the realities of grace and mercy, which we Christians associate preeminently with Jesus Christ and the grace of forgiveness. That God has brought and brings light, that he has forgiven and forgives, that he accepts and includes the forgiven, is what we mean by revelation. This revelation, given and received, is the reality and possibility of our knowledge of God.

We need now to take note of a matter that not all Christians have noticed, and some have misconstrued: namely, that knowledge of God through grace is given at the *beginning* of the pilgrimage of faith—at the beginning as its possibility, not at the end as its reward. The great Puritans

---

[25]Cf. Barth, *Church Dogmatics,* I.ii,301.

[26]Cf. ibid., I.ii,308.

seem to have understood this as well as any. They knew, as Perry Miller has put it, that "in divinity the end is given first, and the fascination and terror is furnishing it subsequently with means."[27] It is the business of faith alone to provide these means for the subsequent expression and exercise in the world of this given end. The great problem for faith, therefore, is not that we once were 'miserable sinners', it is that we now are responsible 'saints'; not that once we acted ignorantly in unbelief, but that now we must walk in the light while it is day; not how to share in a future reward, but how to manage in this present life a glory already thrust upon us.

This life of responsible faith, then, is a life before us; and even radical repentance means not so much a torment over sin behind us as a turning to the possibilities of faith before us. The only torment which faith has a right to entertain comes not from living with the shameful or the uncertain but with the final—with the end that is given at the beginning. For, to pine over finitude and failure is a form of self-centered pride, an exclusion of the vision of grace. If our religious anxieties are not to be neurotic, they must emerge not from our ignorance but from what we know. Faith can manage the fear of the unknown; its only defensible hesitations come from awe of what is given us.

Both the reality and character of this gift remind us that religious truth, in this sense, is personal or moral truth. The matter is too massive to be managed by the mere correction of misimpressions or the satisfaction of religious curiosities. The dark corners illuminated by the divine light are not patches of ignorance needing new information, nor of religious curiosity wanting relief. They are burdens of a guilt which needs shriving, pangs of alienation crying for inclusion and acceptance, pockets of moral cowardice, and refusals of strength. Revelation is utterly serious about our moral redemption. With our lives as persons at hazard, with both freedom and faith at risk, religious curiosities can take care of themselves. In a *moral* universe, they are not terribly serious.

We learn this moral truth through our experience of God in Christ. Jesus did truth even more than he taught it. When he "so loved the world," it was something he was doing. He identified himself with the lowliest and lost. He gave his life in death. This is the way God is. This only is how he rules. Our experience of the divine rule is imperfect, in the sense that it is

---

[27]Perry Miller, "John Bunyan's *Pilgrim's Progress*," in Willard L. Sperry, ed., *Classics of Christian Devotion* (Boston: The Beacon Press, 1950) 81.

both impaired and incomplete. Our laying hold on it as revelation comes through a lifelong repentance (in the sense of Luther's first thesis), and an unremitting quest (as of Bunyan's frail pilgrim). Because of its "imperfection," our experience must always be subject to rational critique. Because it truly apprehends reality, even if imperfectly, it gives coherence, both real and potential, to all our understanding.[28]

Perhaps one stumbling block of Christian revelation is exposed at this point: revelation includes and utilizes the human reason. Thought is required. Not only is thinking very difficult work, but we are also quick to reject any intimation that we might not understand our own experience. Any really 'illuminating moment' is so self-evidencing—both entrancing the attention and enjoining the will—that we prefer to suppose its meaning is as obvious as its reality. We desire from it the sort of certainty some find in transrational ecstasy, authoritative dogmas, or infallible texts. This, I think, will not do: our personal history itself, our human reason and finite experience, are included in the 'illuminative moment'. Because of this difficult and wonderful fact, the *meaning* of revelation and anyone's *experience* of it never fully coincide. The reasoning heart—what Kant called the practical reason—must probe and assess the experience of revelation as earnestly and repeatedly as does the pure reason analyze the expression of anything capable of being believed, doubted, or denied. We are to "test every spirit"—including our own.

The use of a phrase like 'reasons of the heart' reminds us of values not compassed by 'reason alone'. Reason can probe what is received as revelation; it cannot produce it. This is a bit sticky, but almost any great theologian of Church history could help us here. I am thinking especially of the ways John Calvin and Jonathan Edwards gave such help.

For those interested in such things, reference is made (but no discussion offered) to Calvin's understanding of 'faith' and 'holy Spirit', laid out with great force in Book III of *Institutes*.

---

[28]Actually we exercise this potential all of the time, but with varying degrees of awareness and aptitude. Utilizing the mind's categories, we are accustomed to examining any experience we choose, as a means for clarifying that experience as well as for finding out more clearly what was in our mind. What H. R. Niebuhr called the "reason of the heart" engages in a similar dialectic with what God is saying to us: and, as he says, "it does not really know what is in the revelation, in the illuminating moment, save as it proceeds from it to present experience and back again from experience to revelation." Cf. Niebuhr, *Revelation*, 100. Cf. here also, Calvin, *Institutes*, III.ii,4.

As for Edwards (1703-1758), we may turn only to a sermon preached at Northampton, and published at the request of friends in 1734.[29] The sermon, really a discourse, has the delicious eighteenth-century kind of title: "A Divine and Supernatural Light, Immediately Imparted to the Soul by the Spirit of God, Shown to be both a Scriptural and Rational Doctrine."[30]

Edwards regards it as almost impossible to doubt that Scripture does teach revelation as being of God and from God. He sees the light, after all, as "divine and supernatural." Thus, in order to understand him, we need now look only at the nature of the light itself, as Edwards views it, and the relation of its apprehension to our own rationality—to our "natural conscience" as Edwards calls it.

The light we speak of is, according to Edwards, that very glory and excellence that good religion ("the things of religion") has always attributed to God rather than to ourselves. Our recognition that this is so is itself "immediately given by God, and not obtained by natural or outward means" (109).

In the experience of recognizing, however, the natural faculties are an active subject of this light; they do not remain passive. I take Edwards to mean here by 'natural faculties' what Coleridge, a generation later, meant by 'understanding' as the faculty of judging according to sense. These natural faculties are included within the revealing activity. They are affected by this light. The natural faculties (or 'outward means') become involved in the vision of the divine and supernatural light; but in the same way as "the use we make of our eyes in beholding various objects when the sun arises, is not the cause of the light that discovers those objects to us" (109-10). God thus makes use of our 'understanding' as means; but neither understanding nor Bible nor any other means should be understood as 'mediate causes' which "produce this effect" (110). Only the Spirit of God

---

[29]This sermon reflects the strong doctrinal interests also found in his sermon of the same year, "The Excellency of Christ," and in his first published work, "The Publick Lecture," preached in Boston in the summer of 1731, and called "God Glorified in the Work of Redemption, by the Greatness of Man's Dependence upon him, in the Whole of It." This marked the beginning of Edwards's fame as a theologian.

[30]In Clarence H. Faust and Thomas H. Johnson, eds., *Jonathan Edwards, Representative Selections with Introduction, Bibliography, and Notes,* rev. (New York: Hill and Wang, 1962) 102-11. Further references are to this edition.

produces the effect of our knowing of what transcends us. This sort of knowledge cannot be reached by the "natural conscience"; it is knowledge of things "above nature." It is, to use words of Edwards, "spiritual reality wrought in the soul and made habitual to the soul only by the Holy Ghost as the indwelling vital principle in the mind of the saint" (103-104). Such knowledge is not speculative or notional; it is true knowledge of the Good that "consists in the sense of the heart" (106-107). This means it is in the "sense of the heart"—that is, in the understanding and conviction of the whole person as rational and moral being—that true knowledge of the good is put together in unity of meaning and staying power.

Such an understanding of knowledge shows why Edwards always associates "knowledge of the heart" with "the will or the inclination" (107). It is the difference one recognizes between "having a rational opinion" that a thing is "excellent," and what Edwards calls "being heartily sensible" of the "loveliness and pleasantness" of it "to his soul." Such a soul, now illumined by divine light, experiences how God "removes hindrances" to reason, and gives positive help to it, making it reliable and fruitful (108). Still, the "evidence that they that are spiritually enlightened have of the truth of the things of religion, is a kind of intuitive and immediate evidence" (109). It is a fair inference from Edwards's words that though we do not, even through authentic participation in it, gain demonstrable certainty of the truth of our faith, we do gain something much more important: the moral certitude or conviction on which we can actually move forward with our lives. Fixed in the soul's view, this immediate, intuitive evidence cannot be doubted. It is what the trusting person sees, something he recognizes, more than something he believes.

A kind of unity is present in this mode of understanding; still a tension of some sort remains between the two modes of perception, the natural reason and the reasoning heart. By the very nature of the case the tension cannot, I believe, be resolved by reason alone. Perhaps, however, the tension can be relieved, though not removed, with appeal to an illustration from painting.

Rather than reckoning with the problem of revelation in terms of the capacity of either reason or faith to recognize it, I propose that we have a look at how, in human experience, reason and faith seem to interpenetrate each other. Instead of focusing upon the differences between the natural reason and the reasoning heart—or between the momentary and the transcendent which they are said to serve—let us consider how, for the artistic vision, they may be distinguishable components of a single reality that, when limned in light, appear to merge. Set in this perspective, an actual visual object may serve as the means for depicting, and possibly for recognizing, the invisible and transcendent. We shall use, as example, some Japanese artists in comparison with the French Impressionists.

Japan had been opened up to the West, with the encouragement of our own nation's gunboats, in 1854. Japanese crafts and arts began, almost immediately, to appear and become popular in Europe and America. The Oriental artists, Utamaro, Hokusai, and especially Hiroshige were the most influential. Their impact upon Whistler, for example, is well known even if their names are not. And for the French Impressionists, as they had come to be called, Camille Pissarro records, in 1893, the enthusiasm which the Japanese paintings had aroused in Monet, Renoir, and himself.

There are important differences among these artists, French and Japanese. For example, under the influence of Zen, the Japanese were noticeably more devout than the French Impressionists who were mainly agnostic. This difference in intellectual style, in mood, in focus of affection—everything which, I believe, the French language means by *sentiment*—was reflected in but not decisive for their respective works. But the more important point, for our purpose, is the way the Japanese used various conventional details as signs—as signs *in general*—of nature, persons, or manmade objects. The Impressionists on the other hand, never depicted anything *in general*, but only *in particular:* never *women* or *rivers,* but *a woman* or *a river,* and always *in a particular time and place.* A statement out of the French Academy has put it this way: "The Japanese artist transcended the ephemeral in search of a reality beyond time, whereas the Impressionists captured the 'fleeting moment'."[31] One was concerned for the Ideal; the other for the Experience. What needs to be noted, however, is that both are equally concerned for the Real. The Japanese saw the real in a universal that transcended time—an ideal to which all experience could gather and find a center. The Impressionists concentrated their vision of the real in the ephemeral moment. The former show the real beyond all erosion of time or circumstances, and the latter, in the overspill of one specific moment—a moment in which truth is seen and recorded, however much later moments may obscure it. Possibly the Japanese are more like mathema-

---

[31]*Impressionism,* by the editors of *Réalités,* preface by René Huyghe (Secaucus, NJ: Chartwell Books, Inc., 1973) 57.

ticians who have seen a transcendent calculus; and the Impressionists like musicians who throw their beauty into the air, only to find that it continues to ring in the mind after it has faded in the ear.

Religious thought, with its tendency to come at reality from a variety of angles, needs, it seems to me, the sort of counterpoise one finds in these two styles of art. For the stuff of theology is 'Reality, and the knowing of it'—that is, its true matter is God and ourselves. It focuses for us the intersection of the Real-beyond-time with our experience in the ephemeral moment. Revelation, of God to *persons,* would seem to be neither a body of ideal truths fully amenable to rational depiction, nor any intense momentary experience whose truth is universally recognizable. Should we not then call revelation a dialectical movement, in both truth and awareness of truth, between the transcendent and the momentary? In the interchanges of such a dialectic, it is possible, even when looking at the transcendent, to sense its kinship to ephemeral experience. Or, to say it another way, if the mind is nondefensively open to the overtones of the commonplace, it discovers that the eternal has already crowded in upon it with a transformational power that leaves nothing merely commonplace: a power that also expands reason into appreciation and confidence, that is, into faith. To render this truth as theology requires hard rational effort; to realize it fully in oneself would demand that awesome simplicity which Kierkegaard called "purity of heart."

This truth, too inscrutable for reason and greater than our hearts—too heavy for our wills—is mediated through an *affective* state that includes them all. I do not mean 'an affective state' in the sense of sentimentality, or any emotion whose chief value is the experience of itself. This affective state, adequate to religious and moral issues and from which neither reason nor faith is excluded, is compounded of attitude, thought, and judgment, as well as emotion; and takes its worth from the object to which it is directed. There is nothing giddy about it.

Positively, what we are talking about is very close to what Friedrich Schleiermacher (1768-1834) meant by a term he made famous: *Gefühl.* *Gefühl* means feeling, sense, the affective capacity for intuitive apprehension. Schleiermacher found this term useful in his effort to show that our humanness is neither wholly exhausted nor disclosed by knowledge and action alone. We do more with our world, with events and other persons, than perceive or shape them. We are not only knowers and doers, we are receivers and clients. Schleiermacher believed that the truth of what I have just said was the truth that 'the cultured among the despisers of religion' most needed to learn. For he was convinced, as Rudolf Otto put it, "that if one experienced the environing world in a state of deep emotion, as intuition or feeling, and that if one were deeply affected by a sense of its eternal and abiding essence to the point where one was moved to feelings of devotion, awe, and reverence—then such an affective state was worth more than knowledge and action put together."[32] The pregnancy of this idea becomes even more obvious when one remembers how, for Schleiermacher, "every finite thing . . . is a sign of the Infinite," and "every such moment of conscious insight" into the Universe, "a revelation."[33]

So, the reality of revelation, and participation in it through faith, not only illumines our understanding; it reorders it. This is already plain in what immediately precedes, but needs further specification.

Let's say that revelation, as the coming of light, both regroups factual data into new patterns of meaning for us, and also turns our knowledge of the known into wisdom. There are all sorts of factual data capable of being shaped into new patterns of meaning: data from astrophysics or cell biology, from anthropological data on life in a New Guinea rain forest, to interpretation of John's Gospel or the meaning of history. I shall speak briefly only of how revelation affects our understanding of history itself, even while we are participating in it.

We are born into a physical world we did not make, into a mortal existence we did not choose. We are aware of an uncertain future we can affect but not control. This is the sober setting in which we come to awareness of ourselves as selves. Years before we had ever learned to discern a value or choose a good, we had become aware also of others—of others like ourselves. People, that is to say, of similar mortal existence, similar questions and problems, similar fears and conflicts, similar needs and drives similar hopes and dreams. People who touched, sometimes intersected our lives, so as to become a part not only of what we know about the world, but even more of what we understand about ourselves.

As we grew in experience and knowledge, we began to be more aware also of how both their lives and ours are carried on tides of historical

---

[32]From Otto's "Introduction," in Friedrich Schleiermacher, *On Religion: Speeches to Its Cultured Despisers,* trans. John Oman (New York: Harper and Row Torchbooks, 1958) xix.

[33]Schleiermacher, *On Religion,* 88-89.

movement whose directions do not appear to wait upon our wills, sometimes appear absurd or even malevolent, and whose sense, if any, is not apparent. In a universe like this, who has not sometime or other, felt like an orphan or a pawn? We have all asked, as poignantly if not as memorably, as did Thomas Hardy,

> Has some Vast Imbecility,
>   Mighty to build and blend,
>   But impotent to tend,
> Framed us in jest, and left us now to hazardry?[34]

But the more one looks attentively even at such history as that, listening with respect to the voices of the past, one learns something—possibly about the inmost nature of history itself, certainly something of its possibilities and effects. Viewed with some humility, with no attempt at self-justification, it is possible, from the very way in which events appear to form their own connection, to catch a glimpse of both meaning and benevolence. Many have even confessed to seeing, in and over the historical scene, what one has called "something which resembles a human countenance, with a smile that is at once both severe and mild at the nations, who believe themselves to be going their own ways, but constantly go where they had never wished to go." This glimpse, to be sure, could be reckoned an illusion. It is, indeed, either an illusion or it is not. But whether it is an illusion, or not, does not depend upon our reckoning.

Many have viewed it as illusion. Those who have viewed it with nondefensive humility have more than once been infected with the suspicion that what has variously been called 'the rules of fate' or 'the laws of history', are much less like a system of rules, and much more like "the utterances of a Personal Will" which intends nothing but our true good, and against which, in the long run, "no other can prevail."[35]

In such a glimpse, the factual data are shaken out, their effects upon human existence in the world are partially traced, and new patterns of possible meaning begin to emerge. No pattern of meaning is universally self-

---

[34]From "Nature's Questioning," quoted in R. C. Baldwin and James A. S. McPeek, *An Introduction to Philosophy through Literature* (New York: Ronald Press, 1950) 11.

[35]Nathan Söderblom, *The Living God* (Boston: Beacon Press, 1962) 371-72.

evident. People differ in experience and outlook, and so do their perspectives on this flux of time and movement that we call history. The meanings we assign to it will also reflect, in some measure, the stance with which we began. These interpretive patterns, meanwhile, relate to some kind of norm whose claims to authenticity seem undeniable. The Christian faith has found and finds this norm in him who, in his incarnation has shared this history, and, in his resurrection, has transcended it. He was no phantasm; he took our human flesh and blood. "He lived," as Carlyle said, "on victuals." He is our brother; yet, in so many ways, he hardly resembles us at all. He saw back of the panorama of history into the Providence that controls it. For him, nothing was as truly present to history or to humankind as was God, the sovereign of both. Jesus saw that "human countenance with a smile at once both severe and mild at the nations" and called it "Our Father." What he saw in that face turned him away from the seeking of his own things. What he saw in God led him to empty himself. He took the form of a servant. He came not to be served but to serve, and to give his life for the many. He had seen that this is the way God is, and he would reflect his image. "Lo, I come; in the scroll of the book it is written of me; I delight to do thy will, O my God" (Ps. 40:7-8).

Jesus not only believed that God's reign was upon us, just around the corner, so to speak, with the powers of the end of the age already moving in and upon our history; he also called for a response to this fact that he regarded as both imperative and unavoidable. The very meaning of time and history was being revealed in a new and decisive καιρός—decisive, because it was of a piece with, and a harbinger of, the final disclosure of all things at the end of the age. The meaning of the whole reality that already is should have its conclusive vindication beyond history. No one was to make true sense of historical experience except in terms, as Erich Dinkler says, that also envisioned deliverance from history through a sovereign grace that is both the Alpha and the Omega of history.[36] And the early Christians believed that through Jesus' perceptions of history's meaning, and the manner in which he managed that meaning as a way of life and death in the world, God had made revelation of himself.

---

[36]Cf. Erich Dinkler, "Earliest Christianity," in Robert C. Dentan, ed., *The Idea of History in the Ancient Near East,* American Oriental Series, vol. 38 (New Haven: Yale University Press, 1955) 171-214, esp. 174-80, and 205-14.

It was the reading of this revelation through the eyes of Jesus Christ that converted and revolutionized, for those early Christians, their whole religious understanding. The vocabulary of religion was known to them before they encountered Christ, or called him Savior and Lord. Almost any one of them was literate enough to tell you what he meant by 'savior', 'god', or 'goodness'. Yet in the actual experience of actual revelation in actual persons, these words are transformed, they take on new meaning and force.

I have never seen this described more clearly, or more movingly, than in the words of H. Richard Niebuhr.

> The God who reveals himself in Jesus Christ meets no un-responsive will but the living spirit of men in search of all good. And he fulfills our need. Here is the one for whose sake every life is worth living, even lives that seem bereft of beauty, of truth and of goodness. The glimpse of his great glory in the face of Jesus Christ, its reflections in the darkened mirrors of the saint's adora-tions intimate a God who is good beyond all that is good and fair beyond all fairness. Yet the goodness that shines upon us through the moment of revelation is not the glory or the goodness we had expected in our thought about deity. The essential goodness of the Father of our Lord Jesus Christ is the simple everday goodness of love—the value which belongs to a person rather [than] the value we find in an idea or a pattern; it is the goodness which exists as pure activity. He fulfills our expectation of the intrinsic good and yet this adorable goodness differs from everything we had ex-pected, and puts our expectations to shame. . . . Here is goodness that is all outgoing, reserving nothing for itself, yet having all things. So we must begin to rethink all our definitions of deity and convert all our worship and our prayers.[37]

Such perception of God-as-revealed must work at once on the con-version and reordering of both our understanding and our values. In such experience, knowledge of data is turned to wisdom—the power ''to dis-tinguish things that differ.'' Meaning comes to be shaped by our vision of God as the center of all value. Both history and the world change through such eyes. We still see through a glass, darkly; but we do see, and we know the joy of seeing.

So now we have said that revelation both illumines our understand-ing and reorders it, even, in a sense, converts it. We are caught up in this

---

[37]Niebuhr, *Revelation,* 137-38.

as conscious participants, so that while stressing certain aspects of revelation as primarily cognitive, we were granting admittance to other than
cognitive concerns alone. Now, therefore, let us look more closely at the
existential side of our involvement with revelation, remembering also that
this will carry, in its turn, certain cognitive significance as well.

The word 'existential' is not intended to arouse in the reader's mind
one or more formal schemes of Existentialist philosophy—schemes that
readily yield to either theistic or atheistic interpretation. I mean more a sort
of viewpoint that, without arguing the meaning of 'uniqueness', or that
'existence precedes essence', simply ascribes importance to the reality of
'subjectivism' in the recognition of truth. This is not a surrender of the claim
to objective truth. It is rather the simple recognition that participation in
such truth involves more than the subject's thought: it involves his whole
existence as a knowing and acting and appreciating person. If the source
of truth lies beyond ourselves, which is my own conviction, its concrete
availability does not. If "dis-covered" by Another, it is "discovered" by
actual persons precisely like ourselves.

A bit earlier, I suggested two images or ideas as tools for clarifying
what is meant by revelation: the coming of light, and the doing of love. In
speaking of the illumination and reordering of our understanding, I have
been attempting to expound the image of 'the coming of light'. In speaking, now, of the existential, we shall move closer to the idea of 'the doing
of love'. I want to do this as briefly as possible in relation to three facets
of truth that can be described as the relief of guilt, the establishment of integrity, and the freedom to love. All of these would appear to belong to
any soul in the degree that it knows itself.

b. The doing of love

Earlier, it was stressed that faith in God through Jesus Christ was
born in the experience of forgiveness of sins. Here was the spring of the
joyful freedom from guilt as confessed by the earliest Christians. This was
celebrated as gratuitous grace (that's the only kind there is), and as the deliverance from bondage. This is the ground floor of any sanctuary in which
Christ is confessed as Savior and Lord.

This apprehension of revelation crystallizes from the experience of
personal deliverance through God's love in the form of active grace. This
is uniquely the work of *agapē* for nothing else reaches into the deepest re-
cesses of our existence as aliens and sinners. We cannot live well on charm

and manners alone. What is needed is deliverance through forgiveness from sin and guilt. This is not to throw out manners for morals, as if they were not in some way related. That there is some connection between them is suggested by the fact that it is as difficult to be always charming as always good. Even so, ethics and aesthetics are not one and the same, and either, pursued to its end, must reckon with the Source and Norm of both.

An aesthetic or artistic credo may have interest or charm. It can speak with much meaning and beauty, and often with insight. But more than charm is required if we are to speak of the *source* of the beauty, or of its *uses* other than delight. This is because we must reckon with issues that lie deeper than delight: shame, despair, guilt, alienation, death.

The reason why the early Christians, despite the paradox, came to view the cross as the supreme expression of God's love was that they viewed it as the way love dealt and deals with humankind's most vicious enemies: despair, alienation, guilt, shame, death. In this manner of dealing, God, who is Love, discloses himself to us as who he is, and, in the response of trust, persons participate redeemingly and knowingly in what God is doing.

With some help from Erik Erikson, and from a recent article in *Theology Today* by Donald Capps, let's look only at the problems of shame and guilt.

Erikson has written that "shame is an emotion insufficiently studied, because in our civilization it is so early and easily absorbed by guilt."[38] It is possible that too large a part or our spiritual malaise—specifically, too large a part of our inability to recognize love and to trust God in our midst— is traceable to this absorption of shame by guilt. For guilt and shame are different in kind; neither yields to the same treatment as the other. Guilt is both objective and substantial. It is an actual defection from the good, a recognizable distortion of reality, a known refusal of the human possibility. Guilt is what it is only in relation to the norm to which it stands in violation. It is always and first of all against God. One may even suggest as an important reason why people have guilt feelings is that we are guilty. "Against thee, thee *only,* have I sinned and done this evil in thy sight" (Ps. 51:4).

Shame, on the other hand, is subjective; it has no substance of its own. All its power is borrowed from the consciousness of guilt. Shame

---

[38]*Childhood and Society* (New York: W. W. Norton, 1963) 252.

derives from guilt, but it does not correspond to guilt. It corresponds to inward despair and moral paralysis. For shame is peculiarly one's own, as one's guilt is not. Its concern is only with itself. Shame certifies itself in those painful, often unexpected moments when, with reddened neck and face, we are revealed more to ourselves than to those whom we fear might see.

A neutoric conscience, religious or secular, will cherish guilt and refuse forgiveness; but it will deny shame and suppress it. Participation in God's love means, among other things, the acceptance of forgiveness and the putting away of guilt in an honest forgetting. That same love is what makes possible a recognition of shame and its exposure to our scrutiny. Not our denial of it, but strong reckoning with it as forgiven sinners is the proper management of shame. It is too yeasty to suppress, for a suppressed shame will leaven the whole of existence.

It is more than a religious or psychological curiosity that we are more ready to forget shame than guilt, when our health requires the opposite. It is a plain sign that we remain more concerned with ourselves than with God, with our own vindication more than with forgiveness. Voluntary amnesia is as poor a management of shame as rationalization is of guilt.[39] To rely on either is possibly more to fear love than to despise it. The grace of forgiveness and the courage to overcome shame are gifts of love in which God is revealed to us as being for us. Acceptance from our side of this grace and love creates conditions within us by which we see what otherwise we could not see, and acknowledge what otherwise we would deny. Forgiveness (as the way love deals with guilt) recreates and renews us from within. It makes our present fruitful through a reconstituting of our past. Memory can now live congenially with our present self-awareness. God's love makes even honesty tolerable.

Through revelatory acts of love in which we find relief of guilt, comes also *the establishment of our integrity.* The link between forgiveness and integrity is neither accidental nor disposable. I have earlier spoken of the Christian confidence, rooted in the Jewish, that God is disclosed to us in history and in "our history." The emphasis here is that, through God's being present to us not simply in our history but in the depths of our own existence, our characters begin to share his own integrity. For reasons

---

[39]Cf. Donald Capps, "Parabolic Events in Augustine's Autobiography," in *Theology Today* 40/3 (October 1983): 268.

I shall try to make plain, this leads into some remarks concerning the Holy Trinity. For to speak of either God's being or his integrity is, for most Christians, to speak of Father, Son, and Holy Spirit.

God, in the traditional understanding of the Church, which I hope I share, is one and triune: God *is* the Holy Trinity. Simply as language, the word 'trinity', like that also of 'integrity', carries some numerical overtones. The reality of God is surely not a study in arithmetic, the art of computing quantity by use of positive real numbers. It is mathematical at all only in the sense that theoretical precision is sought in understanding the relations that exist between magnitudes or activities. It is not a study in numbers.

God as Holy Trinity has been thought of principally in two ways. The first is in connection with God's gracious lordship over history in the revelation of his power as love—that is, in the story of our salvation. This, as I see it, is the perspective of the New Testament, which also has ample grounding in the Old. The second way is the gradually produced crystallization of the belief-ful reflection upon the mystery of our salvation, which the early Christians, from the very beginning, began to put forward as attempts at interpreting it. This second way of thinking about the Holy Trinity focuses not upon the economy of salvation but upon the three distinguishable ways in which God subsists as the one God.

The first line of thought draws attention to the divine grace: how God *acts* as gracious; the second, to the divine integrity which is its source: how God *is,* as the ground of how he acts. The former emphasizes the threeness in the oneness; the latter the oneness in the threeness. The first is the *story* of how the Creator-Father draws the world to himself in the Reconciler-Son, whose reconciliation is made effective in us as redemption by the Helper-Spirit. The second puts emphasis upon the way in which the three *personae* coexist in an uninterrupted flow of pure awareness and pure activity. This coexistence contains and exhibits what Karl Rahner has called the "only two fundamental acts of spiritual existence, knowledge and love."[40] The way in which the Father loves the Son and puts forth his word and purpose in him, so that, without reserve or resentment the Son perfectly performs the Father's will; the way the Spirit is recognized pre-

---

[40]Karl Rahner, "Trinity," in *The Concise Sacramentum Mundi,* 1764. Quoted in Richard P. McBrien, *Catholicism* (Oak Grove MN: Winston Press, 1981) 360.

cisely in the way he treats the Father's will in the Son as his only love—this is the heart of what we mean by the divine integrity. In what God is as Triune, in what he has said to the world in the Word made flesh, in what he has brought to pass in us in the power and freedom of his own Spirit, there is total harmony. No separation is allowable between his descriptive properties, his factual status, and his revelatory acts. Between what God is and what he purposes, between what he purposes and what he says, between what he says and what he does, between what he does and how he does it, there are no gaps, janglings, or discontinuities. Nothing is fractional, nothing is mixed. All is harmony, an unbroken continuity between reality and appearance, between potential and act.

If in God this integrity is the substance and objective possibility of our knowledge of him, in us this integrity is the condition and subjective possibility of our knowledge of self. In God, this integrity is a native simplicity; in us it is a moral goal capable by grace of progressive realization: capable, that is to say, if our integrity be fed on his. Here is the link, wouldn't you agree, between questions, on the one hand, such as "Who is God, and where in the world is he?" and, on the other, "Who am I, and what in the world is happening to me?"

I have been reminded of these questions, as well as of their interdependence, by the article on St. Augustine by Donald Capps already mentioned.[41] In this article, Capps has drawn his competence in pastoral care into conversation with the current theological fascination with story and narrative. With such people in mind as James Olney and Sallie McFague, Capps explores "the connections drawn between Jesus' parables, understood as metaphors of God's activity in the world, and autobiography, viewed as a metaphor of the self in the process of becoming." The parables of Jesus throw direct light on what God is up to in the world: He is busy including rather than despising the Samaritan, and through him is defining for the rest of us what it means to be neighbor (Lu. 10); he is waiting the return to sanity of his prodigal sons and showing patience to his self-righteous ones at home (Lu. 15); he is showing us how blindness to the Lazaruses at our gates creates a vast gulf between ourselves and them which no piety can cross and no miracle can mend (Lu. 16); he is teaching that the true name of refusal to invest our opportunities in God's plans for

---

[41]Capps, "Parabolic Events in Augustine's Autobiography," 260ff.

the world—whether ten opportunities or five or one—is neither prudence nor conservatism: it is moral default and enmity against God (Lu. 19). This stubborn-minded unfaith is also timid. It always justifies such default on the ground that reckons, as William James once put it, "that it is better to risk the loss of truth than the chance of error."

In autobiography, we attempt to assess our development in the light of our roots; to reckon worth in relation to potential and performance; to tell a story of hope or despair, of success or failure; to reveal who we are in relation to what we have been, and to see where we are in terms of where we intend to go. Every narrative of a life can only be a moral tale, and we find its commentary again and again in those matchless stories told by Jesus twenty centuries ago. His knowledge of God, his insights into our humankind, are mirrors in which we can learn who we are and what is happening to us. We are neighbor to every person in the world before ever we are white or black, male or female, Protestant or Catholic, Samaritan or Jew. We are the Father's beloved children, whether in a far country or back at home, whether sulking outside or attending the dance. We are the rich who see Lazarus and draw near to God; or failing to see Lazarus, develop inhumane hearts that would respond neither to Moses nor the prophets. No arm is long enough to reach from a neglected neighbor to God.

Who are we, then, we ask, and what in the world is happening to us? We are the silly and wonderful human race whom God for Christ's sake has created and redeemed. We are they who know God in his knowing of us. Ignorance of God is not absence of data or complexity of subject. It is not even absence of piety; it is indifference to neighbor who is Everyman. One cannot see God in Christ who cannot see Christ in Lazarus.

What I am speaking of here could be described as a "vision of the moral conscience"—of what Kant called the 'practical reason,' and F. D. Maurice the 'understanding.' But whatever the terminology, this seeing ourselves in God in the faces of all our neighbors is one side of what we mean by revelation. Self-knowledge can be distinguished but not divided from the knowledge of God. To have both is to have integrity.[42]

---

[42]To know integrity, however, is not to comprehend all knowledge or understand all mysteries. God truly draws us into the closest possible relations with himself, but our *self,* in this closeness, never ceases to be either finite or fallible. Hope of fulfillment in the eternal kingdom is based neither on a transcending of our mortality or an absolute assurance of doctrinal correctness. Our hope lies in our moral conviction of the invisible realities and in the strength of the divine hands which hold us.

Such integrity is born in a dialectical movement of faith with humility. We make no claims on God, and we hide nothing from him. We have no contract to trust God provided he can render a good enough account of himself. Rather, the knowledge of God, its reality and its realization, comes as Dietrich Bonhoeffer reminded us, not where we lay our claims before Christ, but where we place ourselves and our times before his claim on us. In this encounter, God gets his true opportunity of being heard when he speaks and to be actually present to us in Christ as his Word to us all.[43] In such an encounter, the words revelation, truth, knowledge, and faith are seen to belong together.

In what has preceded, we have, in a variety of settings, spoken to the question, "When, how, or in whom is the ultimate reality disclosed?" The focus of the attempted answer has found us speaking of God's presence in Christ as the living Word and obedient Son. In the midst of our eternal concerns, we set up a historic cross. We have attempted to say what is meant by knowledge of God, only to find that no language is adequate to that task. We are reduced to silence and to prayer. But not to inaction.

The knowledge of God is where, in our actual existence, we know the relief of guilt, and the establishment of integrity. It is where also we find *freedom to love in return*.

Numerous times you have already noticed, and more than once I have mentioned, the impossibility of doing justice in finite speech to a subject that has no limits. The linguistic boundaries of our knowledge of God, however, are less imposing than its moral limits. The proportions of our subject are defined less by its size than by its character. For God who is known is also God-the-mystery. God is known, but God is not explainable. This mystery of God is the mystery of inexhaustible meaning, not of unintelligibility; and knowledge of the divine mystery is closer kin to wisdom than to information. God's deity is in part exposed in the fact that the wider the circle of this wisdom, the broader the horizon of the mystery.

This mystery has filled us with questions that cry for solution but which are too much for human strength: questions of historical relativity, of appearance and reality, of the relation of nature to faith, of correspondence between our cognitive faculties and the transcendent. These are heavy matters; but none of them, perhaps, so difficult as the moral. These intel-

---

[43]Cf. Dietrich Bonhoeffer, *Gesammelte Schriften,* herausg. von E. Bethge, Band III (München: Chr. Kaiser Verlag, 1966) 307.

lective questions present problems we wish we could solve. The moral matters we would ordinarily prefer not even to face.

The last few assorted remarks have aimed to illumine what is now to be said of "the freedom to love." Nothing is more moral, more miraculous, more difficult; nothing more dreadful than love. Here we do not merely throw words in the direction of their object. Here we encounter the aweful Subject himself: *God* is love (1 Jn. 4:8, 16).

This love is tough and persistent. It is who and what God is. A part of God's unchangeability is surely his persistence as love. This *agapē* does illumine the darkness of our minds and warms the coldness of our hearts. But it also creeps, as quietly and inexorably as lava, into our unconscious—into our forgotten, but not wholly forgotten, memories. It recalls heights we have failed to scale, depths we have feared to probe, and possibilities of human community for which we have developed neither the taste nor the courage.

It is through these moral depths, and from the misty vision of those heights, that we humans take on transcendence. In the face of love, perhaps as much as anywhere, we know Conrad was right in insisting, through Marlow, "that man's actions are somehow related to his 'soul' rather than to his 'liver' and that there is considerably more to man than the 'facts' of his observable behavior."[44]

But if love has to do with matters of the 'soul,' if it is awesome and mysterious, it is also the concrete power of our transformation and liberation. Love is the essence of God's being and the possibility of our knowledge of him. It has the power to attract and to drive, but its chief characteristic is the power to multiply itself—not simply to replicate or duplicate itself. Love's power is the power to engender in us the same freedom to love in which love has acted upon us.

Love is never irrational; but it is more than the rational. In the doing of love by our kind, we are clearly going beyond the rational and cognitive, and are "doing" existence. The absolute uniqueness of each individual consciousness already carries us beyond the abstractions and formulae of the pure reason. Our spirits are free, and are only understandable as rooted in God's freedom for us. God has acted in sovereign and unconditioned freedom in the giving and the redeeming of our lives; for *agapē* is

---

[44]G. B. Tennyson and Edward E. Ericson, Jr., *Religion and Modern Literature* (Grand Rapids: Eerdmans, 1975) 226.

neither sentiment nor disposition. Such is his love, and such is the point back of which no rationale of freedom can reach.

We have been, and are being, freely loved by God. We are not automatons. We are not pipes through which grace flows. We are not wires on which an electric energy moves. We are not sunflowers which have no choice but to turn towards the sun. We are willing participants in what we are receiving—and we are receiving God's love as free grace. In this creative and redemptive relation, his love as power becomes a power in us. A response to God's free grace begets grace, and the showing of it to neighbor is done in that same freedom in which it was given to us. The gift of God's grace, coming from his free love, *is* our freedom to love God in truth as well as to love neighbor in more than word alone. All true freedom is either God's, or it is ours-as-gift-of-God. That this be known at all is a revelatory gift.

God's love alone is the one power to create in us this freedom to love, the freedom to see God in our neighbor and our neighbor in God. It becomes for us the power and freedom to see ourselves in relation to the whole world, rather than to see the whole world in relation to ourselves. It is the difference between looking only inward *at* ourselves, and looking at the whole spectrum of existence *through* our own unique minds as informed by grace. Only in the freedom of Love does the individual reach beyond himself, into the fullness of personhood.

Fascination with the self soon palls, for one's life is more than an elaborated case history. That it is neurosis is the least important thing about fascination with the self. More significantly, this fascination is a strangulation of the unrealized possibilities of *agapē*. Its nearly disastrous results are all around in view. It treats persons as maneuverable objects. It makes theology academic, or even fatuous. It is also a form of slow death to the arts—painting, writing, music—when contricted, self-centered, and essentially uninspired minds produce works that tell virtually nothing of the beauty of the world, the miracle of existence, or the glory of God. What they do tell us, painfully and vividly, is how the artist himself felt that day. No freedom is a power that is helpless to transcend itself, and no freedom that is helpless to transcend itself is a freedom at all. Is it not more an omen than a commentary upon our time that many university students know Ayn Rand and few have heard of Simone Weil?

The exercise of love—revealing the heights and plumbing the depths—is the power that makes us persons, enriches both our experience and our potential, and loads our words and gestures with imponderable meanings. The energies of love, love's acts, probe the guilt and fears that have been hidden under the smothering bushel of shame, and invite us to come out and walk in the light of the day. "Love," as Samuel Miller put it, "always unburies a smothering self."[45] Love is the power of the new creation. It is the way the world began. It is how it shall end. In this freedom of love, there is courage, to traverse the whole course of existence between the beginning and the end, simply because we are sharing God's life, and have been given confidence in him as the author of the whole.

My line of argument has worked its way, now near the end of this chapter, into a meshing with something from H. R. Niebuhr, from whom the thought of the preceding sentence was taken in paraphrase. I mean both Niebuhr's understanding of the inseparability in God of power and goodness, and of the way in which human persons enter the moment of revelation when we recognize that no power could be apprehended as God except as expressed in an adorable goodness.

Nowhere does revelation more clearly show its radical character in relation to our religious understanding than in its impact upon what we ordinarily mean by 'integrity' and understand by 'power.' God's love towards us in Jesus Christ, in the power of the divine Spirit, is not a means for coordinating or unifying our motives and values and actions so as to bring success to purposes of our own. One can receive love as succor only by adopting it as norm. God's love towards us in Jesus Christ, in the power of the divine Spirit, demands and creates our integrity as singleness of mind and purity of heart. Love turns us away from a pious concern for our own spiritual health and self-centered action to the will of God alone. No one can serve two masters—especially if one of them is oneself.

Revelation reorders, as well, what we understand about power in God and therefore in ourselves. Power, which is necessary to the very idea of deity, is worshipful only as its substance is the self-giving goodness we have called love. Listen now to this point in Niebuhr's own words.

> What is powerless cannot have the character of deity; it cannot be counted upon, trusted in; to it no prayers ascend. When goodness and power fall apart and when we have no confidence in the power of the good or in the good of the power our religion turns to magic—

---

[45]*The Great Realities* (New York: Harper and Brothers, 1955) 150. Most of my paragraph is shaped by Miller's.

to the exercise of our own power whose goodness we do not doubt.
. . . Deity, whatever else it must be to be deity, must be powerful
in its goodness as well as good in its power.[46]

The giving of our lives in confidence to the goodness of this power
and the power of this goodness is what the Christian tradition at its best
has meant by faith. In the unity of the goodness and power our own integrity is established, and in the exercise of the power as goodness is revealed
the source and norm of all freedom—a love that not only certifies itself to
us as what it is; but being what it is, invites us into the free quest of its grace
and bliss.

Surely many readers of these pages have a fondness for Asheville's
Thomas Wolfe. In *The Story of a Novel* (1936), which describes his book
Of Time and the River, there is a pathos-laden passage in which Wolfe is
revealing himself in relation to his work. "From the very beginning," he
writes,

> the idea, the central legend that I wished my book to express had
> not changed. And the central idea was this: the deepest search in
> life, it seemed to me, the thing that in one way or another was cen-
> tral to all living, was man's search to find a father, not merely the
> father of his flesh, not merely the lost father of his youth, but the
> image of a strength and wisdom external to his need and superior
> to his hunger, to which the belief and power of his own life could
> be united.[47]

In answer to this hunger there is very good news. This *image* of all
strength and wisdom and goodness, which alone can make the truth to
spangle and the heart to leap, is but an imperfect, and sometimes baffling,
reflection of a *reality* it cannot adequately mirror, the echo of a truth it cannot fully repeat. There *is* such a Father, a father who is so great, as St.
Anselm put it eight centuries ago, that he exists not only in idea but also
in reality. God our Father is the living deity in whom all power and all
goodness meet, and whose power and goodness flow in and out of our
everyday lives and relationships as revelation and redemption. Our faithful
experience of this objectively real God, experience which comes to us
through nature and historical event, Bible and conscience, science and art,

---

[46]Niebuhr, *Revelation,* 135.

[47]Quoted in Elizabeth Nowell, *Thomas Wolfe* (New York: Doubleday,
1960) 27.

family and other persons—this is what we mean by receiving revelation. Here, in this world, everyday, is where God is known. In him we find ourselves and our neighbor. Here the commonplace takes on transcendence, and *all* the earth is holy ground. And here, if we have grace to take off our shoes, our humankind—for whom all innocence is but a faded memory—are given vision of the consuming fire that does not consume, and strength to bear the unbearable weight of glory of Him whose name is simply, ''I Who Am.''

To enter, through commonplace experience, into such moments—moments of illumination and of love—is almost more than one can bear. It surely is more than one can fully describe.

Through my office window, now years ago, I watched across the street one day as half a hundred children from a kindergarten turned out from school. One of them was my youngest. It was winter, and the kids tumbled out into the playground in nearly identical fleece-lined jackets and hoods. They all looked alike. It took five minutes for me to sort out my own. There he was with his buddy, and with another I did not know. He brimmed with energy, mischief, and innocence. He was five years old, and Eden was the farthest East he had ever been. I watched him as he rounded the corner and headed for home.

This became for me a sort of holy moment. His joy and innocence provoked in me a scarcely bearable longing—among other things, a longing for an irrecoverable innocence I once had known—a simplicity, a trustfulness, a singleness of heart, which now seem so unessential to our sophistication. I thought of the private anxieties and social pressures that make it hard for the young to keep their innocence, the follies and moral forfeitures that keep their parents from remembering it. My tears found wills of their own, and I cried for want of other choice.

Then I began to recall that God has in store for our race something higher than innocence—even moral knowledge of himself.

Moral knowledge is more rugged than innocence. Equally beautiful, it is more awesome. And if such knowledge is sweet as innocence in the mouth, in the belly it is often bitter. For moral knowledge is given to persons who live only beyond innocence; it is received in a world both fallen and redeemed. This kind of knowledge, as Berdyaev reminded us, can be had only in exile from Eden. It presupposes that the bliss of Paradise has been already lost. As Kierkegaard insisted, such bliss is regained, if ever it is regained at all, only on the beyond-side of Dread. This kind of knowledge could never be merely delectable; it threatens and redeems one's existence.

For this knowledge has to do with God and persons, with being and becoming, with responsible discrimination between good and evil, with the coming of light and the doing of love. It has to do with the confession to God of our guilt and the exposure to ourselves of our shame; with the management of anxiety and the awareness of death. It has to do with the Living God, and with all that he is up to in the world. It has to do with ourselves and all others, and with what is the meaning of our lives. Given to us as grace, this knowledge is revelation; received in confidence and pursued in loyalty, it is faith; reflected upon both critically and gratefully, it is theology. Such knowledge of God is with us, but it is also ahead of us, calling us on. And before this knowledge shall have been turned to sight and bliss, our quest of its truth and mystery—as Bunyan saw so clearly—shall have led us pilgrims down many an awesome valley, and through that last river whose crossing is deep or shallow according to the measure of our faith.

Chapter Three

The Nature of Faith

Faith is never correctly described when it is initially defined in terms of intellectual belief. The belief that something exists is an experience of a wholly different order from the experience of relying on it. . . . Faith is an active thing, a committing of self to something, an anticipation. It is directed toward something that is also active, that has power or is power. It is distinguished from belief both on its subjective side and with respect to that to which it refers.

—H. R. Niebuhr

This chapter on the nature of faith appears between discussions of revelation and of theology. Faith is the appropriate human response to revelation, and is present in good theology. A brief characterization of faith as a biblical and theological idea may serve as an orientation to the subject, and get us on the way.

1. FAITH AS BIBLICAL AND THEOLOGICAL IDEA

The Bible characteristically sees faith as taking its character from its object: it is a recognition of God as *God,* a trustful and obedient commitment of life to his will and care. This faith has to do with God and others and ourselves; that is, with the relationships of persons. As personal, which is to say "moral," faith is never simply the acceptance of ideas that happen to be religious. It is closer kin to "the fear of the Lord" than to "beliefs about God."

From *Jesus* we learn faith as confident trust towards God as King and Father. It seems that, for Jesus, the opposites of faith were not 'heresy,' but disloyalty or unfaithfulness; and not 'doubt,' but anxiety or worry. Faith, as the recognition of our dependence upon God as Sovereign and confidence towards him as our Father, is an acknowledgment that God is simultaneously supreme and caring. He rules the world and he shows mercy to his children. The way he cares for his children is the way he rules the world, and the way he rules the world is the way he cares for his children. This is why faith experiences both awe and joy: there is no break between God's power and his goodness.

This basic viewpoint of Jesus, regarding the rule of God and the nature of faith, should, I believe, be accorded normative force in the shaping of our own understanding. It should go far, also, in determining our evaluation of the remainder of the New Testament teaching.

In the New Testament teaching, faith appears in a manifold richness. Both the setting in which it is presented and the distinctive viewpoints of the writers affect the shape of this teaching. A few samplings should suffice to illustrate such a statement.

In *Acts,* faith appears as a trustful reception, by Jews and non-Jews, of the Gospel message (Acts 2, 10), a faith in which all peoples are given both inclusion in the covenant and a new understanding of God's purpose in history (2:14-36); are given the grace of repentance and faith, by which they receive the Holy Spirit as a gift from God (2:38), and enter a common life of sharing and mutual support (2:44-46). In *Paul,* faith can be described as the only true corollary to the revelation of grace, a response evoked by God's Word and Spirit, by which we are brought into right relationship with God (Rom. 5:1). Faith's opposite is usually self-righteousness; it is never doubt. By faith we are equipped to deal, in freedom and joy, with the challenges and limits that life assigns as our lot (Rom. 8). The *Johannine* tradition views faith as a special form of knowledge (Jn. 1:9-13; 1 Jn. 4:1-12)—the appreciating of the character and authority of Jesus (that is, faith) being a virtual synonym for knowledge of God (8:24; 11:37; 14:10-11). In the *Epistle to the Hebrews* faith is considered almost solely in relation to hope (cf. 11:1), to an expectation of the full inheritance of God's promise, for which faith is, in some sense, a 'title deed.' As the whole of Heb. 11 shows, faith is the medium of such perception of God and of the ideal world (vs. 27) as enables the believer to endure all earthly trials (11:25, 32-38), to live in heroic detachment from the things of time and sense (11:7), and to know—as if from beyond knowing—that he/she is heir of a commonwealth no human hands have built (11:10). Faith is a chief concern of the *Epistle of James.* Some have seen this letter as a reflection of a moralism traceable to the church of Hellenistic Judaism. It is possible that a grain of truth is present in this reading of the epistle. It is also possible that such an interpretation presupposes a more distinct identification of Hellenistic Judaism than can be recovered from the sources, and sets out with a certain Pauline norm of evaluation traceable chiefly to Luther. The Epistle of James is not a profound reading of faith, such as one finds in Paul, but neither is it a "right strawy epistle" (Luther). I see great difference from, but not antagonism towards, the understanding of faith one finds in Romans or Galatians. James's great value—what makes it worthy of the canon—is its insistent reminder that ideas about God (in this case, monotheism) are not faith, except as they call out trust and determine conduct.

In such texts, the centrality of faith for the Christian life is unmistakable. Not even Luther has overestimated its importance. Faith is important, in Scripture, as the human answer to God's summons and calling—a corresponding movement from our side to God's initiatives of grace. Being such, faith is response to God's self-disclosure, as distinguished from acquisition of data-knowledge. Faith is our "yes" to God's address. So, from our side *everything* would seem to depend on 'faith': our knowledge of God and the joy of relationship with him; the development of our moral character; the capacity rightly to see ourselves, our neighbor, and our world; the strength to bear, with equanimity and endurance, the trials and burdens that belong to our lot; the power to fulfill our human calling under God.[1]

So much for a beginning orientation. Now, brief attention needs to be given to *the vocabulary of faith,* ending with notice of the important distinction to be marked between 'faith' and 'belief'.

The Hebrew root (אמן), from which springs the Old Testament word for 'faith', probably means 'to support or stay', or, intransitively, 'to be stayed or supported', hence, 'to be firm', 'to be one on whom another could safely lean', and so, metaphorically, 'to be faithful, dependable, trustworthy'. In the Hiphil (causative) forms of the Hebrew verb the regular metaphorical meaning is 'to trust, confide in, to believe in, to say Amen to'. The nouns אמונה and אמת, which come from this same root, carry connotations of firmness and faithfulness, and are closely associated with both trustfulness and righteousness. These nouns sometimes appear to mean, more or less, what the faithful Hebrew meant by "true religion."

---

[1]Cf. E. C. Blackman, "Faith, Faithfulness," *Interpreter's Dictionary of the Bible,* 4 vols. (Nashville: Abingdon Press, 1962) E-J:222-34, much of whose work I have woven into my discussion.

The two nouns are used with reference to God and human persons alike, but *in the religious sense* are directed to one object alone: God. This is why, in the Bible, these Hebrew words are so often associated with two of the most prominent of God's qualities: 'mercy' (חסד) and 'righteousness' or 'justice' (צדקה). Perhaps even God's love should be described as the doing of his righteousness with mercy. To associate oneself with this righteousness and mercy through a commitment of the whole self—a commitment in which the moral will is prominent—is ''to have faith in God,'' or ''to know God's love.''

To be sure, no one could desire or understand such a relationship except from the presupposition of 'believing' that God is existent, is sovereign, is self-revealing. But 'faith' means more, and in a sense other, than 'believing' that these statements correspond with fact. 'Faith' means to trust oneself to God, to live by confidence in God's sovereign power and with dependence upon his mercy to heal and to save. This confident trustfulness, informed by obedience, is what Jesus was urging upon his hearers when he called on them to 'have faith in God'.

This summary discussion of the vocabulary of faith may be concluded with a closer look at the language of Paul. The Apostle's teaching makes a distinctive use of the word 'faith', and gives large place to its importance and meaning. His use of this word is a primary clue to the whole of Paul's thought.

For Paul, as for the Old and New Testaments generally, the understanding of faith gives little prominence, as such, to human feelings about God. 'Faith' (πίστις) consistently makes objective reference to the *ground* of our confidence and hope. It is the one indispensable condition for the knowledge of God and for the knowledge of self in God's light. Through faith one *apprehends* (perhaps better, ''is apprehended by'') the Absolute or Transcendent; and, through the energy of that faith, is empowered to perform the right or the good.

In Paul's understanding of faith, the immediately religious and the irreducibly moral exist in a complete union. This is a major dimension of his thought. To have faith is to be ''in Christ,'' that is, to be in complete union with Christ's own life, his own integrity and moral purpose. As an attitude, faith is the recognition of total dependence upon God for all things that ultimately matter, and an obedient trusting of the self to God's mercy in a loyalty that matches that dependence. Faith is the means—the 'vehicle' more than the 'condition'—of our reconciliation with God. In gratitude (a chief motive of faith) we respond to God's self-disclosure in Jesus Christ, and enter into the undeserved mercy. Too many have not seen the Apostle's understanding of faith; perhaps still others have seen it and have stopped there. Paul does not stop there.

For Paul, there is a *moral reverse* to the divine-human relationship without which the *religious obverse* is a counterfeit coin. One does not have religious faith with the option of adding 'ethical activities' to it, if one feels so inclined. Rather, the relationship itself is expressed in a faith that as such is ethical and in an ethics that as such is faithful. The two, if distinguishable, are as inseparable as the two sides of a single coin. For Paul, as for the Bible, generally, there is no true faith apart from ethics, and no empowered ethics apart from faith.

It is the manner in which the Apostle formulated the common biblical understanding of this union of faith and ethics that marks his exposition as unique. Two points should suffice to make clear what is meant— and some acquaintance with Paul will forestall any impression of their being overly paradoxical. One, the *religious sense* of utter dependence on God and confidence in his power is itself, for Paul, a *moral fact*—and, with the disaster of sin in view, a moral concern. No experience of faith puts us beyond God's law or its moral demand. Two, God's righteousness is less the ethical standard for judging our moral performance, and more the characteristic way in which God acts, in grace, to reconcile all who have offended against him. The *moral character* of the good (God's righteousness) is essentially a *religious fact*—and, with the forgiveness of sin in view, a religious mystery. In no other New Testament writer is there a more unified understanding of the relation of religious faith and the moral good. It helps us to understand, for example in the Epistle to the Romans, why Paul's exposition of God's grace, shown in justification as the forgiveness of sins, focuses so steadily on 'righteousness' (δικαιοσύνη) and on 'law' (νόμος). Nowhere is the apostle's thought more radical; nowhere is his message more distinctively Christian.

Earlier, I promised not only to discuss the vocabulary of faith and Paul's understanding of it, but, as well, to point up *the important distinction to be marked between 'faith' and 'belief'*. Recognition of this distinction is fundamental to biblical understanding, and has important bearing, as we shall see in the following chapter, upon our undestanding of religion and religions. Surely no one has contributed more richly to the understanding of this distinction than has Wilfred Cantwell Smith.[2]

In his *Faith and Belief,* Smith has established, in ways that would be difficult to rebut, that the shift in meaning that, over the centuries, has taken place with regard to the English words "belief" and "believe" has been both massive and fateful (p. 105). One should describe the shift as massive because of the all but total change in the meaning of the word; fateful because of the theological misunderstanding it has engendered. Smith's studies lead him to conclude that "faith is not belief, and with the partial exception of a brief aberrant moment in recent church history, no serious and careful religious thinker has ever held it was" (p. 127). (The "aberrant moment" to which Smith refers is the period of the Enlightenment which effected a radical reshaping of the concept of rationality, one result of which, in the theological sphere, was a gradual identification of faith with "belief"—a word whose meaning across some eight hundred years had all but completely changed.)

The essence of Smith's research, for our purposes, reveals that this change can be put as follows. Literally, and originally, 'to believe' meant 'to hold dear'—virtually, 'to love'. Through a development, parallel in most ways with other Germanic languages, the Anglo-Saxon (or Old English) and Middle English verb 'to believe' was the metaphor standing for such ideas (and relationships) as holding dear, feeling affection for, regarding as valuable or lovely; as setting one's heart on, or to give ultimate loyalty to, to belove. Historically, the real issue in the use of 'believe' or 'belief' does not come to focus on the question of whether something is regarded as credible: it focuses rather on the quality of the allegiance that is being directed toward its object. In Wyclif (circa 1320-1384), the word 'believing', for example, is used as meaning 'obeying'. "One might therefore urge," Smith writes

> that "belief/believe" be dropped as religious terms since they no longer refer directly to anything of human ultimacy. . . . The modern world has to rediscover what "faith" means, and then begin to talk about that; it must recover the verb, to rediscover what it means to have faith, to be faithful, to care, to trust, to cherish, to be loyal, to commit oneself; to rediscover what "believe" *used to mean.*

----

[2]See his *Faith and Belief* (Princeton: Princeton University Press, 1979) esp. 103-104n166, and 108ff.; also 105-27.

When we do this, we shall have also largely rediscovered what the Latins meant by *credo,* and the Greeks by *pisteuo;* for a straight line of continuity runs from Greek and Latin into our English. Much of modern theological misunderstanding is traceable, it would seem, to the Enlightenment's re-direction of the word "believe" from interpersonal relations to theoretical judgments and (with its new understanding of rationality) from the existential to the descriptive. This misunderstanding has been further enhanced by post-Enlightenment translation of earlier texts in which much actual mistranslation (in the sense of misinterpretation) appears.

We have now spoken of faith as the human answer to God's call, a corresponding movement from our side to the initiatives of grace. This is why we reckoned faith a response to revelation rather than as the acquiring of factual knowledge. It is also why we speak of faith as being more a power than a principle.

When Luther spoke of faith as a *power,* as he often did, he was thinking of it as coming solely from God and existing solely for God's sake. God is both the Source and End of faith. Faith is a power because it is that in us through which God himself is present to us—that through which he makes his presence known and brings his own purposes to pass. Faith thus takes its substance from its Source and acts in keeping with its End. *It is the only corollary from our side to the revelation of grace.* Faith is this effective exercising of God's Word and Spirit in and with and through the faculties of the human person. Faith thus results only from the presence and action of the one God. It never arises from a power intrinsic to itself. This is why faith always celebrates God, not itself; it extols not the divine nature of our human capacities, but the human quality of the divine mercy. All of this is why faith is a power; it is the strong conviction, shaped within us by God's own Spirit, which makes trust in God efficacious. It discovers God as contemporary, and thereby unleashes into our lives and relation-ships the powers both of creation and of the 'end of the age'. This means that historical faith corresponds to eschatological reality and draws upon it. (compare Heb. 11:1)

This life of faith is a concrete fact, but it cannot be exactly defined. Part of the reason for this is that faith is more than a fact. It is also a possibility that present experience and the boundaries of history cannot fully contain. Where God becomes actively present through our faith, the boundaries are pushed back; the horizons become all but limitless.

At the same time, however, the enlarged vision is less ethereal in character than earthy and social. For when by faith we know the one God who lives, we see the neighbor/brother in a new way. This kind of faith is a living experiment with persons rather than a set of doctrinal conclusions. It works at making explicit in our relationships with our brothers/sisters on earth what is implicit in our relationship with our Father in heaven. This faith understands the inseparability of the second from the first commandment: there is no true love of God with heart and mind and soul and strength which is not, as well, a love of neighbor as oneself.

Faith thus means to receive grace as gift and to serve it as demand. It also means to pursue it as possibility. Life and the universe lie before it. Faith never means to receive supernaturally bestowed information regarding the age of the planet or the time of its final demise. It is never the pious capacity to believe in at least two miracles before breakfast. It is never a view of biblical inspiration that one adopts by an act of will. Faith means the ongoing correlation of life with the presence, purpose, and activity of the one God. It is an open quest. It calls for pilgrimage—a pilgrimage into both meaning and mystery. It receives as well as acts. Sometimes it is openness to the Transcendent Mystery; sometimes involvement in the struggle against evil. Always it is personal and moral: it is marked by resistance to evil and discrimination of the good.

Much of what has been implied in the preceding three paragraphs can be expounded in the form of three theses: (1) biblical faith is realistic; (2) biblical faith is monotheistic; (3) biblical faith is eschatological. Let us take a brief look at what this means.

Faith is *realistic,* in the sense not only that it focuses upon the Real, but also in the sense that it is something one is actually doing with one's life. It is not one kind of wishful thinking. It is not even an idealistic philosophy. Faith certainly is no form of self-delusion. Nothing entails a more direct engagement with life itself, including the hard facts and threatening limits by which we are confronted. Faith operates on the boundaries of our finitude and fallenness—where chance, conflict, suffering, guilt, and death threaten the existence of us all. It is the power not of abolishing but of mastering such limits. Faith is the way, through the management of such limits, that we become who we are.[3]

---

[3]Some will see the relation of this to Karl Jaspers, *Way to Wisdom* (New Haven: Yale University Press, 1966), esp. 17-27.

This reminds us that faith confronts not only the limits beyond us. It must deal as well with the sad actualities within us. Faith is the actual power to confront, without despair, the fact of our alienation from God and neighbor and self. It is to receive a forgiveness that leaves a believer strong rather than weak. Faith is the capacity to know, and so to learn, who we are—in our grandeur and honor, in our apathy and misery. It is even the discrimination to see the wrongheadedness that lies in taking either of these moral estimations of ourselves more seriously than the other. For the substance of faith is neither self-despising nor inward assurance. It has little in common with 'positive thinking'. Faith is a form of moral knowledge.

This person of faith lives in a tension between his 'being' and his 'becoming'. He neither despises what he is nor takes for granted what he is becoming. Such a person assesses himself by both the judgment and the promise of the gospel. He never assumes that he 'has it made'. But neither is it possible for faith to regard one's human insensitivity or moral folly as being so ultimate as the relentless grace of God. The believer can never despair. Yet he never believes that this inexorable grace of God is to be presumed upon. He never lets himself off. He appraises his own insensitivity and folly by both gospel and law. He has achieved a realistic understanding of his existence, the kind of faith Perry Miller has described as a "spontaneous intuition" of reality which is his "salvation."

Such a person is neither an optimist nor a pessimist. He is a solid realist. In faith, he is under no delusions of self. He knows promise and judgment, gospel and law, grace and rebuke, freedom and responsibility. *In this setting alone, he knows who he is.* He is saint and sinner, wretch and son of God; all, and at the same time. He is "in terror of the Almighty" even while knowing that "all power in heaven and on earth is on his side." He has arrived at his own identity. He knows who he is because he now knows that God knows who he is. He is the "he" whom God knows! Neither more nor less, in gratitude and humility, he is who he is. Having come realistically to know who he is, he is now given all of his life to learn what that means. He is justified by grace through faith alone. Aren't we all? Such, in essence, is what was meant in saying that faith is realistic.

The second thesis reads: faith is *monotheistic*. 'Radical monotheism' is a phrase brought into general use by H. R. Niebuhr.[4] The moral

---

[4]Cf. H. R. Niebuhr, *Radical Monotheism and Western Culture* (New York: Harper & Bros., 1960) esp. 11-48.

essence of this phrase appears in its denial of any distinction between the principle of being and the principle of value. Philosophically this means that to acknowledge all being as absolutely dependent on the One for its existence is, at the same time, to value all existent beings as taking their value from the One. Put theologically, this means that God who redeems is identically the same as God who created and creates. Put in terms of the everyday practice of the Christian life, it means that faith is both reliance upon God and loyalty to his whole creation. This faith, as Professor Niebuhr writes,

> is reliance on the source of all being for the significance of the self and of all that exists. It is the assurance that because I am, I am valued, and because you are, you are beloved, and because whatever is has being, therefore it is worthy of love. It is the confidence that whatever is, is good, because it exists as one thing among the many which all have their origin and their being in the One—the principle of being which is also the principle of value.[5]

Such faith has in it the quality Schleiermacher called the ''sense of absolute dependence'' upon God. It has in it, also, the burly loyalty of a Puritan martyr, or the gentle radiance of a Catholic saint.

This quality of faith in the one God, and in God as one, is what alone keeps the religious life from self-delusion and idolatry. Biblical faith apprehends God as God, and also as God-for-us. The word 'God', as a Christian utterance, is a confession of the deity and the 'humanity' of God who lives; that is, of God who is God in himself, and of God who deals with our lot as though it were his own. And, indeed, it is. We learn God-who-is through what God does who-is-for-us: that is, we know the meaning of grace as the condition for knowing the meaning of being. In the modes both of his being and of his gracious activity, God is and is known as the Sovereign Lord and Caring Father.

When Christian faith talks about God, it is testifying less to our puzzlement over the cosmic mystery, and more to our relationship with this more than personal Person. Faith is relationship; it is not simply a predicate of the God-idea. God is not a symbol for the gaps in our information, nor a name we give to our cosmic nostalgia. God is not a religious theory that one might find more or less plausible. God is the living Deity with

---

[5]H. R. Niebuhr, *The Meaning of Revelation* (New York: Macmillan; paperback ed., 1960; sixth printing, 1970) 32.

whom we have to do—on whom we are dependent for our being, and support, and our final salvation. The truth of this is only slightly related, if at all, to the question of whether we have found God plausible.

To believe in God, then, does not mean that we agree to a convincing hypothesis about the superhuman. Nor is faith the same as holding good ideas about God because they inspire courage or promise comfort. It means to have sought God and to have been found by him. As Carlyle Marney used to say, to know faith is to be "seized upon from behind." Grace, by definition, is prevenient. Faith, by definition, is a response to grace.

God's gifts are made available to us through faith. But faith is a way of trusting and offering allegiance to God himself. God's primary gift to faith is the gift of himself; faith is not a device for receiving something else we may want. (St. Bernard of Clairvaux warns against being more interested in "the gifts of the Lover" than in "the love of the Giver.") We trust God for himself not as a means to something other than himself. We trust God who is and who saves, because he is and he saves—thus certifying himself to us as trustworthy. Faith puts persons in a redeemed and redeeming relationship with the one true God.

Only faith may receive God, but God can be no more compassed by religious faith than by natural reason. He includes and transcends both. Awareness of this transcendence lies back of Calvin's description of faith as "the sense of the divine majesty and empire." It is why faith as a mighty power can exist only as a genuine humility.

Faith in God is a form of seminal certainty of which our theological systems are expansions or developments. This faith is engendered only by God's "gift." As Professor Niebuhr put it, "We are being thought, therefore we are. We are being believed in, therefore we believe." Our faith is the living response to the presence and act—that is, to the Spirit and the Word—of the actual God, the only One there is. It is a true response because of God's reality. God is—he is there, and here. It is a true response because it is a proper correspondence from our side to God's determining grace which alone evokes the response.

Two points for emphasis may be seen to accompany the foregoing affirmation of the deity and onliness of God. One, faith is truly informed by the Absolute but is conceivable only in relative terms. Even in the gift of grace—especially in the gift of grace—God remains the sovereign Lord. No Bible or creed, no church or sacrament, no cult or morality may substitute for God himself. Each of these potential goods is fully as much a possibility of idolatry as it is a means of grace. Second, really to believe in God as one and only is to derive our values through our convictions of this truth. The *goods* we actively seek in the world must correspond in character to the *Good* we formally worship in the church. God defines for faith both the final power upon which life is dependent and the nature of those values on earth that faith is free to cherish. Faith, in this setting could be defined as the recognition and exercise of the conviction that 'being' and 'value' are not, and are not to be, separated. It is the harmony of what we confess with what we prize. To believe in a multiple source of good is polytheism; to esteem as ultimate any value other than God is idolatry. To believe in the God of the Bible is not to hold some view of the inspiration of a book or the authority of a church; it is not credence, credulity, nor creedalism. To have faith in a Christian sense is, with reliance and loyalty, to invest one's life in the meanings and values that the one God has told us—through the life and death of Jesus Christ—are the things that matter.

Christian faith, then, is realistic and it is monotheistic. The third thesis affirms that it is also *eschatological*. Christian faith has to do with what is final. An eschatology is implicit in any Christian reading of "our life in God's light." This investment of life in true meanings and values, which investment of life we call faith, is always *in viā:* faith is a pilgrimage. It always is moving towards a consummation.

We move towards a consummation not only because God is greater than our faith; it is also because our 'being' reaches always beyond our 'existence'. We must *become* what we truly *are*. Our true being is greater than our actual existence. Through the quest of faith, the never-ending remaking of our personhood is in process. We are taught—both by the Bible and the testimony of our own unfinished characters—that there are loves that must lose their ulterior motives and side aims. There are heights of honor that must be scaled, and possibilities that must be actualized. There are truths to which humble exposure of the self is the only realistic means of access. There are values that must not be forfeited, and firm acts of will that alone can hold us on course. There are works of charity that must not be neglected, and great ideas on which to try our strength. There are horizons of meaning for which we must broaden the circle of our understanding and sensitivity. Surely, all this must suggest something of what it means to be growing a soul.

There is a great word in the Christian vocabulary that resonates to these facts and possibilities. Unfortunately our religious culture does not throw it into prominent relief. The word is *repentance*. Most of us are familiar with repentance as a godly sorrow for sin. This is important and no Christian may take it casually. It is also but a partial apprehension of a truth more fully orbed. There is more to repentance than godly sorrow for sin. Repentance must primarily mean a lifelong and lifewide reorientation of the mind, an open mind, a mind eagerly responsive to all life's mystery and meaning—a mind courageously ready to undertake the ongoing reformation of life. Repentance is that refinement of perception, adjustment of attitude, and fixing of the moral purpose that enable us to learn God's secrets from life, and to accept growth and change with a measure of confidence. It is more a laying hold on the possible before us than remorse over the failures behind us. Its final end is the Final itself.

I used the phrase "a *measure* of confidence." No one can face life, "all confidence and no fears." Openness to possibility poses threat to us all. Change is demanded, so courage is required. In such circumstances it is not difficult to understand how some decide that it is better to bury one talent in the ground than to invest ten in life's market.

Trustful repentance, however, finds courage vis-à-vis this threat because, in principle, it has already divined a final secret. God himself is the possibility and the goal of our change, and God is in our midst. A bridgehead from eternity has been established in "our history." Christ became what we are that we might become what he is (Athanasius). He has made our sins his that he might make his righteousness ours (Augustine). The Kingdom of God is in our midst. That kingdom is where we belong; as Francis Thompson reminded us, that kingdom is "no strange land." There is life in time, now, already, which, under God and in God, is life eternal. Faithful repentance is that power of the soul, that gift to the soul, which sees God as present, and which releases into our lives and present time the powers of the "end of the age." What is ahead is being already absorbed into what is at hand. The present is less pushed into the future than the future is drawn into the present.

The past, as well as the present, is involved in this eschatological truth. This has been described in a useful way by Paul Hanson. Hanson has shown how, in living religion, the past affects the present and the present the past. Faithful interaction with the issues inherent in the present situation not only confirms the tradition of faith, but amplifies and deepens it. The past and present interact: they qualify and enrich each other. Hanson shows how a genuine religious experience discloses this back-and-forth movement between the confessional heritage and these current interactions with life in the world. Faithfulness to the biblical witness, and to God who evoked it, works out a fruitful unification of past and present. In this unifying process, a sort of symbiosis is at work; the vision of God's kingdom and the realities of this present time are seen as inseparable. Together they constitute the one revelatory fact.[6] The truth of this, I might add, will help us to understand why the great prophets of Israel sound, at one and the same time, both like oracles of God Eternal and moral commentators on the day's news.

That this should be so stems from the fact that the realities of revelation belong not merely to history and the imagination: They are *living* realities. This is why "exodus" and "cross" are present as well as past. They are not lost in the past. They have become part of our present knowledge of God and of self. They are a part of *our history*. They are ancient events, but not even ancient events are merely ancient: we have no ancient understanding of ancient events, only a present understanding of ancient events. This understanding becomes the way we interpret our present selfhood or the purposes of God. It is never simply a remembrance of things past. It is the clue to the conscious and unconscious process by which we decide what we shall forget and what we shall remember, what we shall disdain and what we shall prize.

This interpenetration of faith with history, and of history with faith, defines biblical religion as forever different from all Gnosticisms and all Fundamentalisms. Gnostics believe not only that faith transcends history, but that knowledge transcends faith. Fundamentalists not only refuse to allow the presence of relative elements in past revelatory events and in the biblical record of them, but also absolutize some present formulation of their meaning. They attempt to conserve truth by preventing change. The Gnostic way erodes history, the Fundamentalist way sets it in concrete.

This faith looks forward as well as back, and it is important that we not neglect this truth. Our present is as realistically a part of the future as of this past. The great prophets of Israel had seen also this end of the human situation. Just as the present gains substance from faith's appropriation of the past experience, so does hope carry the present forward as realization of the future possibility. Faith, as hope-in-God-who-lives, has

---

[6]P. Hanson, *Dynamic Transcendence* (Philadelphia: Fortress Press, 1978) 31-33.

already begun to appropriate those powers that belong to the end of the age. Faith, in this sense, is a kind of realized hope, though as yet it is not sight. Time continues, but it has been fulfilled; its final goal has been already disclosed. Time remains as our opportunity and responsibility: but life now, in this fulfilled time, is lived from the perspective of eternity. Our future is *now* because, in true specimen, it has already come to pass. God has revealed himself. Christ as true Son has shown us the true Father. In Jesus Christ, present to faith, we human beings do have actual and saving knowledge of God. God in Christ is the most important *human* fact—for our past, our present, and our future. Faith, so to say, has conquered time, and God in Christ is with us every day. All strength for living in the present and all valid hopes of the future are fed on this *quotidianus adventus Christi.*

This kind of eschatology, as we see, both engages and anticipates the future, but it is never merely futuristic. God who is "the end of life for which we are made" actualizes himself in and through our present experience. So is eternity interjected into our time. God can be our future only because he is already our present. In him we have located our values and our identity; we can face any future convinced that neither need be lost. This is what makes it possible for us to live as "citizens of heaven" while remaining responsible on earth. It is also why dependence on God does not make us weak, and why true repentance does not destroy us.

Eschatological faith is not a species of escapism from the world or from responsibility in the world. It finds the reality of God in our incomplete and sometimes unreal lives. We believe in God who was, and is, and is to come. Even when in the dark, we can walk towards this light; faith is already on its way towards sight. Even when facing death we can confess this life; faith is already rehearsing for immortality. To continue on this way in openness and hope is to become caught up in meanings and powers that acknowledge no limits of time, space, or possibility.

Great truths of the Christian life are implicit in the foregoing description of faith. We list three that correspond, successively, to these three characterizations of faith as realistic, monotheistic, and eschatological. These truths may be remembered in the form of three *inseparable unions:* realistic faith discloses a union of the knowledge of God and the knowledge of self; monotheistic faith knows a union of confidence towards God as God and loyalty to him in the world; eschatological faith shows a union of the uses of time and the experience of eternity. Finally, however, each of these pertains to all; they are of a piece.

Thus far we have sought to state what we mean by faith. We have looked at the vocabulary of faith, and the uses of the word in the New Testament. We have sought to sketch a characterization of faith so as to disclose its role in the living of life. This exposition, however, is easier than the critical task that confronts it: Faith is beset with a second problem similar to the one discussed in connection with revelation.

The confession of divine revelation is faced with the question of the relation of the relative and absolute in history. Viewed subjectively, it is faced also with the problem of the connections between 'scientific' or objective and 'religious' history. The question of the reality of knowledge is prominent in both. Something needs to be done with this problem before pressing on towards positive conclusions.

2. GOD, FAITH, AND OUR HISTORY

The problem of history is difficult essentially because the transcendent has ''infected'' it, leaving no ''mere'' history. It is difficult also because theology cannot describe God as he is in himself, but only God as he is known through human experience. There is no 'outside' history, in the sense of there being a history to which we have objective access. The ordered thought by which we speak of God is filtered through a finite experience and shaped by a historical reason. One remembers Archimedes who declared that with a fulcrum and a long enough lever he could move the world—if only there were a place to stand! He was right, but, alas, outside of space and time there is, for our kind, no place to stand—whether in physics or theology.

For humans, including Christian believers, there is no neutral standpoint, no point of view unaffected by history and social experience. As Professor Niebuhr put it, the past offers us no religious or moral truth outside of some social setting; and it offers us no way of avoiding the use of our history in saying what we mean.[7] Theology must, for this reason, reckon seriously with history. But revelation is not history, and faith is neither history nor experience. How shall we proceed?

Perhaps to hold the mirror once more before the whole problematic with which we have been at work would give sharper delineation to that part of it that is before us now. We have tried to keep before us those crit-

---

[7]Cf. Niebuhr, *Revelation*, 40.

ical problems, treated as crucial by H. R. Niebuhr, that condition any serious study of revelation and faith and theology. These are, (1) the relations of the relative and absolute in history (which we had often in view in the chapter on the meaning of revelation); (2) the connections between 'scientific' or objective and religious history; and (3) the perennial problem of natural religion and historic faith (what has been often called the problem of the relationship of natural and revealed religion—or, in a different setting, the question of general and special revelation). We dealt with the first of these in relation to the reality and possibility of the knowledge of God. The third raises issues touching on the definition of theology itself, and affects our treatment of religion(s) and mission which appears in the chapter on "Theology and Religion(s)." The second, "the connections between 'scientific' or objective and religious history"—which is in part a methodological problem—concerns us primarily in relation to the way in which the experience of faith implies objective as well as subjective content. This second problem is the one presently before us.

Professor Niebuhr himself approached the question of the connections between 'scientific' or objective and religious (or internal) history from a somewhat Kantian point of view that recognizes the difference between the pure and the practical reason as these deal with historical understanding.

Whether the Kantian distinction is the best way to deal with this problem of "faith and history," I am not finally able to say—though I have large confidence in Mr. Niebuhr. I do believe, if one may say so before pressing on to the point presently before us, that we human beings are not given the option of dealing with or of understanding "mere history." There is sufficient reason for this, and the reason is not simply an epistemological one. It has to do with the very order of things; there is no *mere* history. The source and meaning and end of history lie in what transcends it—that is, in God. History is the temporal unfolding of the eternal purpose, as that purpose has been appropriated wisely or foolishly—which is to say, faithfully or unfaithfully—by our kind. Recognition that this eternal purpose clothes itself in human history led Abraham J. Heschel to say that, "the most important *human* fact is God."[8]

---

[8]A. J. Heschel, *The Prophets* (New York and Evanston: Harper & Row Publishers, 1962) 226. Heschel's thought, in relation to what I am talking about,

Professor Heschel's insight is full of deep truth, and it is, I suggest, the same truth that Christians have confessed as the doctrine of the Word made flesh in the human life of Jesus (Jn. 1:14). To confess this incarnation of the Word of God is to say that the Eternal has given human and historical specification of himself: "God was in Christ" (2 Cor. 5:19). To say "the Word was made flesh," or that "God was in Christ," is a confession of faith. Its truth is not demonstrable. Equally so, to deny this truth is a nondemonstrable confession of unfaith. Neither the denial nor the affirmation can be a statement of "pure reason." One might by pure reason reckon with a syllogism (though even this may be debated), but by pure reason one may reckon no more with history than with faith. Something more than pure reason is involved in the knowledge of anything in which human beings are active participants. In the knowledge of both history and faith, everything is affected by the quality of those images and values that power the decisions of the reasoning heart.

So much for this reminder of where we stand when the mirror is held before the whole problematic of history and faith and knowledge. Consideration must now be brought to bear on the more sharply focused question of the 'objective' validity of religious experience—*the question of whether faith is more than a pious psychologism.* For this, it should be useful to have some expansion—and, I hope, clarification—of what is meant by "religious history" (or "internal history") and by "personal experience."

"Religious history" and "personal religious experience" are not identical but neither are they unrelated terms. Nor, it should be emphasized, are they together unrelated to the whole of history and to experiences not usually called religious.

"Religious history" does not mean history of religion. It is rather that dimension of the general history in which the faith of a person or a group of persons has seen a revelatory meaning. It is that dimension of the general history which such a person or group has appropriated as his (its) own—a dimension in which transcendent meanings and values have been recognized and received as normative for the interpretation of the whole of experience. "Religious history" is the experienced meaning by which

---

can be found in ch. 25 ("Event and Experience") and in ch. 28 ("Conclusions"). See also the introduction, xiii-xix; ch. 1 ("What Manner of Man Is the Prophet?"); and ch. 12 ("The Theology of Pathos").

we shape the understanding of who we are, and how we are related to the whole created world and to all persons and things that inhabit it. Such history, as personal experience, is the principle or norm by which we assess what we find within—the choice of memories to be cherished as realities, of hopes to be nourished as realizable possibilties, of present experiences through which to interpret *both*.

This sort of experienced history is not indifferent to general history—indeed, it is the general history that is being interpreted by the experienced history. But experienced history concerns itself with more than the operation of recognizable causes that produce measurable effects. It finds us not watching a parade but marching in the band. When it talks about life it says "we," not "they." In this living pageant, deep repentance, an act of love, or a vision of beauty, has no more *actuality* than a closed mind, a selfish act, or an obscene imagination. Personal religious experience, however, asks questions that run beyond bare actuality. It asks about meaning and about value. It understands that one of the above trios of actuality stands judged by the other one; and it knows which is which. Both are actual, but one group has more *reality* than the other.

Meanings and values that have been internalized—that is, have been incorporated into one's selfhood by personal religious faith—relate primarily to subjects, and to objects only in the light of the primary value of subjects. Internal history crystallizes from faith's making normative, not simply descriptive, judgments—as for example, about the relative priority of subjects as compared with objects. It sees value not as power but as quality.

The case for this sort of faith, viewed as an ongoing internalization of meanings and values, is supported by both its inner coherence and its social merit. It makes sense, and it blesses people.

Faith is the human response to divine revelation, an internalization of grace and truth through the relationship established in this response. This internalization becomes the clue to the evaluation of historical events. This is simple; it is not simplistic. What is meant is this: faith brings to the complex and bewildering and otherwise unmanageable mass of fact and event, a basic principle of interpretation. The principle? That cannot be true, outside of God, which is answerable only to itself. Faith is never autistic: it expresses itself in a response of the whole person to God, and it makes itself intelligible in the world as unselfish sharing with other persons. Facts and historical events that violate this principle may express power as force;

they do not express power as worth for selves. They may be interesting or important, but their future, short or long, is measurable. Their strength is drawn from humankind's misplaced confidence that things are worth more than persons.

But does this clarification of what we mean by religious or internal history demonstrate its validity? I think it does not. Is faith more than a pious psychologism? I believe that it is. The truth of faith is separable from its demonstrability. Nonetheless, faith's claim to credibility is very strong— as strong as any stance that can be taken. Its validity, however, can be established on no grounds extrinsic to ourselves. In what sense(s), then, is faith more than an indulgence of one's fancy? A three-sided answer—carrying rational, moral, and aesthetic freight—is available to us.

First, the *rational.* Faith is not reason, but neither is faith without reason, nor reason without faith. Faith can be rationally exercised and discussed. What is more to our point, faith includes reason in its own action. Faith is, to be sure, recognition of that truth and light by which we respond to God; but this response to God is not simply a complex of pious feelings. Faith also is an intelligible way by which we reckon the meaning of fact, event and experience as seen in God's light. Faith is one style of ordered judgments of value and meaning. That such meaning is interpreted as transcendent in character in no way reduces its rationality. Faith makes sense of the world; it fashions rationally coherent definitions of truth and value. It lays hold on truth(s) that are rational and on truth(s) that are more than rational—truths that sometimes fire the imagination or incline the will before they convince the mind. Faith is one way of looking at fact and event.

As an antidote to rational*ism,* it is useful, also, to remember that just as faith is not without reason, so is reason not without faith. To say that the human race lives by faith is not to say that it lives without reason. Reason itself can begin only with an undemonstrable presupposition. Samuel Taylor Coleridge put this as tellingly as any. He writes, "Whatever we do or know that in kind is different from the brute creation has its origin in a determination of the reason to have faith and trust in itself. *This, its first act of faith, is scarcely less than identical with its own being.*"[9] On this basis, Coleridge treats this act of faith on reasons's part as the "realizing

---

[9]S. T. Coleridge, *The Statesman's Manual* (1853) 1:210-11, quoted in James C. Livingston, *Modern Christian Thought, from the Enlightenment to Vatican II* (New York: Macmillan, 1971) 89; italics mine.

principle, the spiritual substratum'' of the whole vision of reality to which reason addresses itself. In reason's determination to have faith in itself, in its confidence that the world actually corresponds to healthy perceptions of it, more than reason itself is at work. This fact turns us to the moral side of our contention that faith is more than indulgence of one's fancy.

Faith is *moral* in the way it conceives God as good—as one who does justice with mercy. It is moral in the way it defines values in terms of persons-in-relation. To speak of faith as personal in character is to regard it as also socially accountable. Faith is never a merely private good. When faith is spoken of as a subjective experience, we mean 'objective' experience of God and others *by a knowing subject.* Faith actually encounters the transcendent, but it does not transcend the historical and social context in which encounter with the transcendent becomes accessible to us. It is first of all an involvement with persons, not, as one friend of mine used to say, ''a very private matter.'' By faith we act as moral members of an intelligible society of persons.

The moral side of faith appears in two further ways: first, to say that God is good and that the creation ''bears the hand of the Creator,'' is to accept moral responsibility for what has gone wrong.[10] This discloses the biblical rationale for repentance. We must adjust our own spirits to the moral reality that beckons them and understand the life of faith itself as a moral vocation. In this vocation of faith persons may not be discounted or ignored. The creation is good; it may not be abandoned or denigrated. ''The fault, dear Brutus, lies not in our stars but in ourselves. . . . '' This face of moral faith has to do with *relationships*—to God, the world, and neighbor—which are distinguishable from ourselves alone.

The second way the moral side of faith appears concerns something within: the moral *attitude* with which we pursue the vocation of faith. We said above that faith is neither history nor experience. Now what must be said is that neither is faith enthusiasm nor assurance. Sometimes, faith is the spiritual empowerment to get on with living one's life when enthusiasm has departed and assurance is low. In those times it can be less the exuberance to mount up with wings like eagles, and more the stamina to walk and not faint (Isa. 40:31).

[10]Cf. Huston Smith, *The Religions of Man* (New York: Harper and Row, 1965) 260-61.

This inner attitude marks a *distinction between faith as psychological assurance and faith as moral certitude*. It puts premium on the latter. The distinction that needs to be drawn between "assurance" and "certitude" could be easier done were the English language, at this point, more helpful. Though commonly treated as synonyms, the words assurance and certitude, coming as they do from quite different roots, carry a different kind of freight. Assurance, as a word, comes from the Latin *ad-securum,* which means more 'free from concern or care' than it means 'safe'. It means more the *sense* of safety than being safe in fact. It points to an attitude or feeling more than to a condition. It is closer kin to a feeling of confidence within the self than to trust in an object; as such it stands opposite more to diffidence or timidity than to disloyalty or unbelief. Assurance, in this sense, is the psychological sensibilty or cognitive "certainty" that everything is all right. Perhaps it is this reading of assurance that leads Catholic theology, rightly as I believe, to disclaim it.

Certitude, the word I am using with a kind of special meaning, is from *certus,* a participial form of *cernere,* 'to perceive or decide'. These words 'perceive' and 'decide' draw the rational and moral, not merely the attitudinal, into clear view. Moral certitude points not to a subjective state of confidence, but to a moral conviction of the dependability of the object to which the confidence is directed. It is not sureness that one is safe or right, but moral determination to pursue and act upon the right that one sees, with confidence that the object of trust will keep one on the way, in season and out of season. Certitude, in this sense, is a near synonym of loyalty and faith. It is not the antonym of diffidence or timidity, though it is distant from them. Moral certitude belongs to their faith who do not give in to disloyalty or unfaith (or to diffidence or timidity), to cowardice or ignorance or duplicity, to "the lust of the eyes or the glitter of life."

Cognitive certainty is not given by faith; moral certitude is. Moral certitude is the gift of grace, responsibly exercised as trustful obedience, by which the moral vocation is carried through to its proper end. It is actually being held by that which holds us, until we begin to hold it. No one has seen this more clearly than the great Puritans. "How far is it to the celestial city?" Bunyan's pilgrims inquire. "Too far for any," the shepherds reply, "but for those who shall get thither indeed." On something like this, surely, Catholic and Protestant thought can find some common ground.

These rational and moral considerations, just discussed, should lend credibility to the claim that religious faith is more than an indulgence of one's fancy. To these may be added an *aesthetic* consideration.

Aesthetics, as reflection upon one kind of immediate experience, is neither an exact "science" nor a passing fancy. It reflects chiefly on the experience of the "beautiful" as an objectified pleasure. An aesthetic experience values its objects for their own sake, and reckons with them conceptually as observed from without, or intuitively as experienced from within.

George Santayana made a distinction between what he called objectified pleasures (which alone he called beautiful), and others that were only agreeable. By objectified pleasures, regarded as beautiful, he meant such pleasures as occur, for example, when the harmonious structure of a musical composition or painting corresponds so completely with the hearer's or viewer's absorption in it that the feeling of pleasure seems to emerge from the object rather than from the observer or hearer.

Beauty is thus a quality of the experienced object, and, as Santayana puts it, "is pleasure regarded as the quality of a thing . . . [so that] it depends upon the degree of objectivity my feeling has attained at the moment whether I say, 'It pleases me', or 'It is beautiful.' "[11]

We have been speaking to the question of whether faith is more than a pious psychologism, and have adduced rational and moral reasons in support of an affirmative answer. In suggesting an aesthetic reason in support of the same affirmative, I am arguing, not to Santayana's point, but in terms compatible with his, that valid faith exercises itself in such way that what is intuitively reported from within (with regard to faith's object) effectively bridges the gulf between what is subjectively regarded as satisfying and what is itself satisfying in an objective sense. In this experience of reality, the conceptual and the intuitive blend, as do the subjective and the objective which the subjective has encountered. (Perhaps one should say: as do the objective and the subjective which the objective has evoked.) In either case, faith recognizes that which is inwardly pleasing as inseparable from that which is objectively beautiful.

This is one style of faith's answer to revelation. The faithful spirit makes a passage—it is to be hoped, repeatedly and progressively—from

---

[11]George Santayana, *The Sense of Beauty: Being the Outline of Aesthetic Theory* (New York: Dover, 1955) 32, cf. esp. all of 11-33. I have also read the *New Encyclopaedia Britannica,* Macropaedia, 15th ed. (1985) 13:16-27.

sensation to perception, and from perception to recognition and judgments of value. It is reasonable, from the presuppositions of faith, to interpret this as a movement of the aesthetic sense into a creative coordination with the rational and moral. It is, in the degree of its reality, a realization, on the religious plane, of the Greek ideal of καλοκἀγαθία—a union of the beautiful with the good. In this sort of faith, observation, critique, and appreciation flow together, and faith is given effective power to recognize the numinous and remote as "objectively" present.

An observation with two illustrations is pertinent. The observation is that the more one responds agreeably from within to objects perceived as beautiful, the more those objects come to be conceptualized as bearing both an intrinsic and a more than intrinsic value. Look at Joseph Addison's fine hymn as the first illustration:

> Th' unwearied sun from day to day,
> Doth his Creator's power display,
> And publishes to every land
> The work of an almighty hand.

This is no flight into either the romantic or irrational. It is a quite sober sensibility, defensible both rationally and morally. In it, feeling *recognizes* its firm coordination with fact.

The second illustration invites us to look at our long evolutionary trek into our still distant "humanization." This fact of our long evolution confronts us with unanswered biological questions, intriguing anthropological problems, and all sorts of moral issues. On one level of discourse, we are talking of a study of our species, or even of the thought of Teilhard de Chardin. On another, we are looking at the ways of God with our kind. The *meaning* of the process at work, the wonder of the *telos* in view, the excitement of the moral will in response to the human implications involved—all this entails overtones of beauty and of meaning which evolution, simply as process, cannot evoke. We are dealing with the wonder and awesomeness of creation, and to think thus, if suprarational, is not irrational. Such a reading of life builds up rather than erodes the quality of experience. It enriches the potential for further recognition and growth in the world around us. It is a tuning in to the Universe around us, to its rhythm and call, a perception of reality that grows in the silence of the soul. To make this trek in faith, in loving response to our total environment, is to encounter the *reality* of existence, its meaning and mystery.

This is a sort of "Feuerbach-in-reverse." We are not projecting ourselves upon the universe; the Universe is rather beaming itself to our rational, moral, and asethetic "receivers." The more this happens, the more—not the less—do we sense the dependability of the connection between our intuitions of reality and our convictions of reality; the more also do we gain certitude of the value and goodness of our long human trek. Here come together, in one, the beauty of the world, the miracle of our human existence, and the glory of God. This is an aesthetics which is not weakened when response to beauty or mystery for its own sake becomes response to beauty or mystery for the sake of Another.

Rational, moral, and aesthetic arguments make credible but do not prove the objective validity of faith. That much must surely be conceded to the difficult question of how to relate religious history and experience to the wider objective history within which it takes place. These arguments do much, however, to support the view that faith is more than a pious psychologism.

By way of summary, then, consider the following lines of argument. They are not proof of the objective validity of religious experience, but are considerations that suggest that there is more than sheer subjectivity at work in all subjective experience. The first is logical in character. Subjective experience is, and should be taken to mean, the experience of time and value, of objects and persons, by a living subject. There is no way to provide an objective understanding of subjective experience from which the subject himself has been excluded. The second consideration is empirical. A theology of faith, which neither ignores nor absolutizes subjective history, can be as coherently stated and/or as rationally faithful to its own starting point as any other type of intellectual work. William Temple's *Nature, Man, and God* or Karl Barth's *Church Dogmatics* is as unitary and coherent as, say, Ludwig Feuerbach's *Essence of Religion* or Karl Marx's *Capital*. Such a theology of faith not only makes sense; it also is just as socially alert as Marx's interpretation of Feuerbach. The third consideration is moral in character. This kind of faith does not pose as perfect, nor does it make promises it cannot fulfill. It is carried forward by 'moral certitude' rather than by 'psychological assurance'. It does not claim cosmic knowledge of the cosmos, nor absolute knowledge of the Absolute. It seeks its own way and only testifies to others that it believes it has, in principle, found it. It is a way of doing with the life what is confessed as truth and value and beauty.

This short detour into apologetics has detained us only briefly from pushing on to a closer look at Jesus' teaching about the life of faith. This teaching is of decisive importance for our understanding of the nature of faith, and it is right that Christians should treat it as normative for interpreting the Bible as a whole. A point of large importance which I find in Jesus' teaching is the way in which he views, as indispensable, the junction of religious faith and moral behavior. Both are essential to each. The relation of each to the other is native not contrived, required not elective. For purposes of clarification, ethics and faith may be distinguished; on no legitimate ground may they be divided.

In order to see this union, let us turn, first, to three items from Jesus' teaching, two before and one after Peter's confession of messiahship at Caesarea-Philippi. These texts will illumine the way in which Jesus saw faith and ethics as inseparable. The chapter will be concluded with an application of this point of view—one in Christian social ethics, the other in theology proper.

3. JESUS' OWN TEACHING ON THE LIFE OF FAITH

One way to disclose the union of faith and ethics is to recall how, for Jesus, *commitment to God coincides with service in the world.* The personal and public career of Jesus discloses, at absolute pitch, the harmony of such commitment to God with his service in the world. His teaching then puts this truth of his living into memorable words.

Jesus appears in Galilee as a spokesman for God to Israel. He stood in the tradition of the prophets of Israel. This is clear both from his response to the Baptizer's call for national renewal and by the substance of his own earliest message: "The time is fulfilled, and the Kingdom of God is at hand; repent, and believe in the gospel" (Mk. 1:15).

The burden of what Jesus had to proclaim, both early and late, was the "Kingdom of God." The operative word in this phrase is the word "God." The Kingdom of God is something God *is doing*. It is God's rule, his reign. It is not a territory, earthly or heavenly, constituting a realm. God's Kingdom is God's active sovereignty. It is God himself being busy as king. Jesus came into Galilee preaching the good news of God the King— the good news that God is and rules, the good news of what he has done and is doing.

The content of this good news is succinctly given: "The time is fulfilled and the rule of God is at hand." God has ever been God, and God has ever been doing what God does. Jesus was announcing the reality, the arrival, the presence and the coming of the divine rule as a plain fact. God's kingdom is. God's kingdom is here. God's kingdom is coming. God's kingdom is coming because it is a real and inexhaustible fact: God just keeps on being King. It is as if God is eternally "up to something." He has been, and is, and shall be at work bringing this something to pass. There is in God's Kingdom, since it is God's, the quality of eternity.

Human beings, however, experience God and God's work in relation to time and space and occasion. God's entry into *our* time and place and circumstance is, *for us,* a new thing. This new thing confronts us as both threat and opportunity. It is what Professor Dodd called the arrival of a "zero hour" in the human experience.[12] What God is doing in judgment and mercy is an exercise of sovereign grace exerted over, with, in, and sometimes against, the will of the persons and peoples for whom and over whom and in whom and sometimes against whom he rules. But *from time to time*—note God's kindly accommodation to our temporality—the time itself is transformed into opportunity.

This gracious accommodation is scaled down to our size in many ways. Sometimes, in the very way that events seem to form their own connections, a sensitive ear can catch the utterance of a Sovereign Will against which nothing shall finally prevail—and one knows the reality of being addressed. Sometimes, from the silence come echoes of an Ineffable Word, by which our own words are charged with new meaning or else wholly redefined. Sometimes, by listening attentively to the voices of the past, the Great Tradition becomes suddenly the Living Presence, to miss whom in our current hurry is to die in the desert. Paul Tillich said that in such instances the *chronos* is turned into *kairos,* the piece of time becomes a moment of decisive opportunity. And it really does.

Jesus seems to have believed that God moves on a purposeful line which runs from creation through providence to consummation. Right then and there, through the act of his own proclamation of the kingdom, Jesus was saying that the consummation of God's Kingdom was, *in principle, and in actuality,* being disclosed. The "powers of the end of the age" were being unleashed, and faith would recognize them for what they were and

---

[12]C. H. Dodd, *Gospel & Law* (New York: Columbia University Press, 1951) 56. This part of the chapter owes much to Professor Dodd, and especially to these "Bampton Lectures in America."

are. Our human words and silences, our history and deepest intuitions, were being illumined and challenged, judged and fulfilled by the "End" that was their ground and norm. What God was up to, what the prophets had envisioned, what the psalmists had celebrated, was at hand. It was at hand both as fulfillment and as transformation. It was the 'realest' fact of their existence. The time had reached full ripeness. God's rule was upon them. Unless we be excluded from what God is up to, it is upon us too. Faith means to put oneself into step with what God is up to in the world.

That this good news of the Kingdom is, in Jesus' mouth, a call to ethical responsibility is clear from the shift in verb modes from indicative to imperative. Just consider the use of the verb "to be" in Mark 1:15.

Jesus announced the kingdom of God as a plain fact. This is one of the most impressive things about it. The first part of his Galilean message is a simple statement of what is. Everything is in the indicative. The time *is* fulfilled. The kingdom of God *is* at hand. The reality of God and of what he is doing *is* the point of departure for everything else. Before God commands, God *is*. All biblical imperatives rest upon the divine indicative. The divine imperatives are historical and social specifications, for our own good, of what is required of us by the being and character of the deity himself. This amounts to saying, I believe, that God is the substance of Christian ethics in the same way and for the same reason that he is the object of Christian faith.

Surely this makes us more ready to hear the second part of the early Galilean proclamation: "The time is fulfilled, and the Kingdom of God is at hand." This is the indicative. So, what now? So, "Repent, and trust in the good news." The verbs have moved from indicative to imperative. What is required of us is determined by who God is and what he has done and is doing and shall do. Of us is required a moral response to what is given in the divine being and rule. This is faith, and for our kind it requires change.

Some indication of the meaning of repentance has already appeared in this chapter. For now, let it be noticed only that to repent is laid as obligation (and possibility) upon all who would hear Jesus' message and relate themselves to the kingdom he announced as both present and coming. It is an imperative: repent.

This obligation to repent suggests the following. Examining our own way, we discover that we are not on God's way. This is disturbing. We listen to that imperative. We begin to hear those voices and silences from the past. We reexamine, and find new sense in, those past events that have all but put themselves together as patterns of meaning for us. We attend our own consciences and find no ground of self-defense. To repent is not to tell God how sorry we feel about everything. It is not even to confess how sorry we actually are. Repentance means, with moral purpose, to undertake a new course. Because this must be done, it can be done. It must be done as an ongoing process of moral and spiritual growth, a renewing of the mind. In some such sense we read Luther's first thesis: "The whole life of believers should be repentance." Repentance is the ongoing conversion of the intellect, the affections and the moral will, and it continues for as long as life lasts.

This ongoing repentance is of a piece with the second part of the command: "believe in the good news." That God is, that he reigns, that, in his providential rule, a ripeness of the time has arrived for us—this is good news. It is a new opportunity to unite our own experience and history with the eternal sovereignty. We can answer the divine call in Jesus Christ which now is coming to us in and through our own history.

Acceptance of this calling as our own unfolds itself as a moral pilgrimage (that is, as a continuing obedience to the divine rule). Our faithful response becomes our moral style. The rest of life can be fruitfully organized around that as center. In such way our minds are illumined with truth, and our moral comitments marked by ultimacy. Faith in God becomes our vocation as Christians. The end is given to faith at the beginning. This is why we can say that the calling of faith is now to work out what is given, to understand what is known, to speak what is ineffable, to discover what is already revealed.

All of this is one way of saying what the gospel is and is about; it is also no less a disclosure of the basis of the Christian's behavior. God is; and he makes himself known in Jesus Christ. Jesus Christ is both our savior and model. This is why we call him Lord. God in Christ is our light and our salvation. We find our freedom, we find out who we are, in this relationship. This is good news. In this relationship with Christ we discover also that we never are with God or never stand before God without all others being there too. This is ethical responsibility and opportunity.

This two-sided character of faith is what keeps the Christian life from being a form of private spirituality, or even a species of devout self-centeredness. This, too, is why we have public, corporate worship. The glad secret of the Christian way is proclaimed in the celebration with others of

God's grace. It is why "in honor we prefer one another." We celebrate with others God's grace; we serve others for God's sake. The worship and the service are not without each other, just as the individual believer is not without the Church. The Christian life is common life in the body of Christ. Christian faith is obedient trust; Christian ethics is trustful obedience. By faith, which is trust, we are free in God and subject to no one. By love toward God we are bound to God and subject to everyone. We may use this idea of Luther's to suggest that, on biblical grounds, "the life of faith" is an interchangeable term for the Christian's "moral vocation." So, we may say that what Jesus taught as fact determines what is heard by us as obligation and as possibility: God is; thou shalt. Imagine the gospel from the modes of the simple verb 'to be'!

The same understanding of the indivisibility of faith and ethics appears *in Jesus' teaching regarding the greatest commandment.* Faithfulness to God who is one, and loyalty to God as he is met in the neighbor, are inseparably united by Jesus' subjoining of a second commandment to the first.

In Mark's Gospel (12:28-33) the question of what is the first—that is, the greatest, or basic, or most important—commandment is addressed to Jesus by one of the scribes. Jesus' answer is, "The Lord our God, the Lord is one; and you shall love the Lord your God with all your heart, and with all your soul, and with all your mind, and with all your strength." This is the essence of true religion. Nothing in life comes before the fact of God and the claim upon all persons of his oneness and onliness. For everything in life, we are obligated ultimately to God alone. The mode of the first verb is indicative, "The Lord our God, the Lord is one." The second is imperative, "You shall love. . . . "

This answer of Jesus, radical as it is in itself, still carries a familiar ring. It was certainly an answer available to any thoughtful believer in Israel from the time of Hosea. It is quoted, furthermore, from Deuteronomy 6:4-5. It is compatible with various rabbinical emphases in pre-Christian Judaism.

Jesus' life is the clearest commentary upon this first commandment, but he also expanded the meaning of the first commandment with a second: "You shall love your neighbor as yourself (Lev. 19:18). There is no greater commandment than these." Matthew's version (22:39) says that this second commandment is *like* the first. We may take this to mean, I believe, that the second is of a piece with the first, derives from it because it is implicit in it. This surely means that just as God is never with us to the exclusion of our neighbor, so neither are we with God where the neighbor is excluded or ignored. A disciple of Jesus, then, is one who does religion as love of God in the neighbor, and who does ethics as love of the neighbor in God. Anyone wishing to add something more to this, *in principle,* should weigh what Jesus goes on to say (Mt. 22:40): "On these two commandments depend *all* the law and the prophets." If Christian ethics is a grateful response in faith to the rule of God, it is also obedient acceptance of those obligations and limits that are defined by the neighbor's need.

Excluded from this Jesus-kind of faith is that most disastrous of modern heresies: that true religious feelings may operate independently of ethical duties. "He who does not love his brother whom he has seen, cannot love God whom he has not seen" (1 Jn. 4:20). God's holiness (what he is), God's righteousness (what he does), God's mercy (how he does it) hover over the whole, not simply the religious part, of our human life. God is the God of all the earth that doeth right. Responsibility to neighbor is present in all true worship of God.

This God of all the earth is not only King but is, and is to be called, our Father. This perception of faith seems, in Jesus, to be immediate. For Christians it is a perception of faith based upon our experience of God in Christ. In the way in which God is bringing his will to pass in Jesus Christ, he is revealing himself to us as our holy Father: as *our* holy Father, not simply as *my* holy Father, nor as the holy Father of *each-of-us-one-at-a-time.*

Let us tighten our grip on this truth lest it escape us. Religion for Jesus was not primarily individualistic. Love never is. Neither was it primarily mystical, a private affair with God. It was recognition and response to God and to what God is doing for all of us in this world. Jesus saw clearly—so clearly that he marveled it was not evident to all—that God is our Father. We are not alone, God who is transcendent over us is present with us, "the holy One in our midst" (Hos. 11:9). He is with us and for us. Our very knowledge of him is but our imperfect apprehension of his knowledge of us. Faith in God is participation now, in freedom and responsibility, in the rule of God who is our Father. This is the eternal life. It is commitment to God with heart and mind and soul and strength. It is not less commitment to one's neighbor than commitment to God. It is love of God through love of neighbor. It is "faith active in love" (Gal. 5:6). It is faith as ethics and ethics as faith. The doing of "liberty and justice for all'' is the prime *religious* activity, just as the loving of God is the original *moral* fact. This is how we have no other gods before God. The doing of justice with mercy is how God loves and rules the world; it is also the model for human faith.

The foregoing passages from the New Testament highlight the union of religious faith with moral obligation. The separation of commitment to God from service in the world, or of service in the world from commitment to God, is, finally, the death of both.

In a similar way, the moral character of faith is shown in the way *faith's characteristic features fully correspond with the motives of ethics*. Numerous options are available for showing this correspondence. Space allows two, and surely *agapē* and *discipleship* are as useful as any for the task.

If one should choose but a single word with which to compass everything pertaining to the Christian life, surely that word would have to be *agapē* (ἀγάπη), love. There is nothing in either faith or ethics but has its ground and norm and end in *agapē*-love. For "God is *agapē*" (1 Jn. 4:8, 16). *Agapē* is the eternal good-will from which come creation, providence, and redemption. "God so loved" that he made the world, redeemed the world, now upholds the world, and will see its salvation, through to consummation. *Agapē* is the reality that God is called or named. God is not called holiness (though he is holy), nor justice (though he is righteous), nor mercy (though he is kind). But God is called *agapē*. This is the absolute substantive; other terms are adjectival to God who is *agapē*.

If one ask, "What is *agapē*?", the difficulty of the answer arises not from a haziness of the subject so much as from its novelty and massiveness. For God is love so overwhelmingly that while God is love, love is not exactly God. Dietrich Bonhoeffer reminded us that love does not define God, but God defines love. God defines and converts our very notion of love itself. So we ask, and repeatedly must ask, What is love? The answer, equally religious and ethical in character, is "Whatever God is doing!" *Agapē* is God's work throughout time and space, nature and history.

This *agapē* is not, and never has been, abstract. In Jesus Christ as the Son of God's love, it burns its way into our awareness and experience as grace. It is also present in all others who live by his spirit. God's work is an exertion of God's being. Love is something, therefore, through which what God is is expressed in what God has done, is doing, and shall do.

This *agapē* is love, but not sentiment; it is charity, but always more than alms. The love of God is his unconditioned commitment to our good, our salvation. This is at cost. It were more accurately described as relentless or inexorable than as affectionate or sweet.

Agapē is outgoing, unmotivated, uncalculating good will, which seeks the good of its object even at cost to itself. It keeps no books. Its only source is God himself, for it arises as the active determination of his own being and will. This is why *agapē* always comes to us. We do not engender it from ourselves. It comes from God. It comes only from God. But it does come! It comes *to us*. It is the active determination of God's will, but it addresses itself to *our* wills. This is why, as Professor Dodd observed, *agapē* can be commanded, as sentiments and feelings cannot. The first form taken by obedience to this command is neither emotional nor devotional. It is moral. Such obedience is the intention of the divine law and the goal of the gospel promise. It is also the only power by which we receive and keep them. We are capable of *agapē* at all only because we were first its objects. "We love because he first loved us" (1 Jn. 4:19). The eternal love which alone is the source of our life is as well its only support.

So *agapē*, the very ground for faith, comes always as gift and sustenance. But it remains with us as demand. It is more moral vocation than ecstatic vision; more ethical act than religious feeling. It sacrifices more than it glows. It is dead serious, for it is serious unto death. *Agapē* gave and gives itself unto death for our sins. This is why *agapē* is very heavy even while it is the spring of all joy. Because of it, "the darkness is passing away, and the true light is already shining" (1 Jn. 2:8). In this way, God's love—more accurately, God himself as love—is both the means and the content of our moral enlightenment.

Moral knowledge is not the same as information. Moral knowledge is knowledge as faith, as insight, as religious certitude, as confidence to act on one's *selfless* impulses without shame or guilt. It is a form of truth because it is a participating in the life of God himself. This is why, "little children," it is the only power in which we can successfully "guard ourselves from idols" (1 Jn. 5:21).

To speak of *agapē* has been to speak of God, for "God is love." But God is not to be spoken of except from our experience, since we who must speak are they to whom *agapē* has reached. There is an inseparability of God and ourselves in the giving and receiving of *agapē*. God is love. This is true in itself, and whether we know it or not. But *we* know it is true because "he first loved us, and sent his Son as a mercy-seat for our sins" (1 Jn. 4:10). Our very freedom in grace and our moral obedience in freedom are forms of God's love. The exercise of Christian faith and the motives of Christian ethics coincide in us for whom God is the known *agapē*.

This correspondence from our side with *agapē* is alone what makes religious faith a source of human good. Religion uncontrolled by *agapē* is a dangerous virus. Often in history it has sanctioned tyranny, engendered hatred and disturbed the peace. It has produced as many neurotics as saints. Only through the power of *agapē* is it possible for religion to be worship without idolatry, conviction without dogmatism, commitment without fanaticism, and mission without bigotry. For, through humble faith, the actual love of God comes even to our kind. It makes for his peace. It brings our life and work to rest more on his faith in us than on ours in him. So, here, now, for us, God is *agapē*. This wonderful God can be trusted. *Agapē* certifies that God-as-he-is (*Deus a se*), and God-as-he-is-for-us (*Deus pro nobis*), is one and the same. One meaning of monotheism, as well as of *agapē*, is that there is total correspondence between God-as-he-is and God-as-he-is-for-us. We can depend on this. It will never change. Love is as ancient and as new as God: it will outlast the world.

These remarks on *agapē* should have served to illumine the thought that the moral character of faith is shown in the way that its own features fully correspond with the motives of ethics. The same point can be further developed by a brief discussion of *discipleship*. The discussion of *agapē* has disclosed this correspondence from the perspective of God's being and God's gift. Discipleship draws attention more to our calling and to the exercise of our wills.

To be a disciple is to have put oneself under the discipline and tuition of a Master—one learns and follows, and, in the following, learns more. The disciples of Jesus found this far from an easy way.

At Caesarea-Philippi, Peter had confessed Jesus to be Messiah, that is, the Christ (Mk. 8:29). From this very time, much to the dismay of the disciples, Jesus identifies the Messianic King with the "Son of Man" who "must suffer and be killed." Their dismay at this kind of messiahship does not dissuade Jesus from his course. He even extends the implication of this identity to the manner of their own association with his vocation and example. As it is put in Mark 8,

> If any man would come after me, let him deny himself and take up
> his cross and follow me. For whoever would save his life will lose

it; and whoever loses his life for my sake and the gospel's will save
it (vss. 34-35).

Jesus gave the invitation to the disciples to follow him. He gave it to the
multitude. He gives it to us. But to accept the invitation is to encounter a
demand. Fellowship with Jesus is fellowship with his cross. This is tough
teaching. It must be more realized as a discipline than learned as a doctrine. For discipleship of this sort, the moral will must be girded up. The
imagination must be fired with the vision of God and the surrounding glory.
The conscience must undergo a continuing education. Patience-with-
strength and a terrible humility are required. Following Jesus calls for more
than good intentions: attention to Christian sanctions or motives must be
paid, and the development of the inner attitude given high priority.

So those disciples, Peter, James, John, and the rest, were under Jesus' tuition. They were trying, literally and figuratively, to follow him.
They were his 'disciples', which was possibly to be more 'apprentices' than
'students'.

But what were they learning from him? Not much new, so far as
actual content goes. The specific content of much of what Jesus taught could
have been learned from the tradition of Israel and contemporary rabbis and
doctors of the law. Virtually everything that Jesus is reported as teaching
has parallel expression in the literature of Judaism. This should not sur-
prise us too much when we recall that Jesus was not a Christian but a Jew.
He was expounding the faith of Israel. He was serving the God of Israel.
He viewed his own message in the perspective of the tradition of Israel.
He knew and used the Law, and the Prophets, and the Psalms (see Lu.
24:27, 44).

Yet something in this teaching is new, in degree if not in kind. In a
manner reminiscent of the historical Jeremiah or of the ideal Suffering
Servant, Jesus embodies his sermon. He gives his life hostage to his message. His life is itself his greatest and most convincing message. It fulfilled
and transformed the language of hope and faith. It enfleshed the divine
mercy, it enacted the divine righteousness. It fulfilled very time. ''Messiah'' can never mean the same again. God's righteousness is even more
than the merciful justice by which God puts things right; it is the divine
quest given human hands and feet. It goes in search. Even the lost sheep
of Israel—especially these—are precious to the Master. The disciple is
learning this even more from what Jesus is doing than from what he is saying. In Jesus, God is seen as loving the sinner, as including him, as ac-

cepting him in forgiveness. No one is an orphan in his sight. God is seen in Christ as going to the outcast where he is and establishing solidarity with his lot.[13]

Jesus' call to discipleship was to ministry of this sort. He was not primarily attempting to gain their agreement on a set of ideas, even good ideas about God. Jesus was asking them to share, as "witnesses," in his messianic ministry—the ministry of a messiah who had seen the Son of Man as Suffering Servant. This is why it is Jesus' life that, for Christians, redefines Israel's term Messiah. The term does not explain Jesus' life; his life redefines the term. To be a disciple means to follow him on such terms into the lives of others. The life of Jesus in its concrete self-giving for others becomes the objective standard for the devout service and ethical conduct of his followers.

This was the most impressive human example these disciples had ever met. They saw in it, however, more than impressive human example. They saw, in this human self-giving of Jesus, the character and action of God himself as the Great Giver. *This is the base-line both for Christian social ethics and for the New Testament Christology,* as we shall shortly see. In these historical and human acts of Jesus, so they believed, an eternal and divine freight is carried. The historical self-emptying of the Son reveals the eternal outpouring of the Father. This is the central article of Christian faith: *Immanu-El,* "God is with us" (Mt. 1:23, quoting Isa. 7:14). It is equally a central motive of Christian ethics: "Have this mind in [among] you which was also in Christ Jesus" (Phil. 2:5). Christian faith confesses the first; it is committed to realizing the second.

This is the true *imitatio Christi*—not replicating or miming an external pattern of action, but a determined *following in the way of.* To be a Christian never means less than behaving in the spirit of Jesus and walking in his light. John's Gospel (8:12) has Jesus say, "He that follows me shall not walk in darkness." Thomas à Kempis says of this text, "These are the words of Christ by which we are urged to imitate his life and virtues, if we wish truly to be enlightened and freed from all blindness of heart."[14] Can

---

[13]This is essentially the point Hans Küng is making in a section called, "The Distinctively Christian Element in Ethics," in *On Being a Christian* (New York: Pocket Books, 1978) 594-95.

[14]Thomas à Kempis, *Of the Imitation of Christ* (New York: Mentor-Omega Books, 1962) 17.

any Christian believe he was wrong? Such imitation means to take Christ seriously. The only substantial evidence that we have done so is honest behavior and compassionate acts. The concrete life of Jesus, as the man for others, is the Christian's standard for both religious faith and ethical conduct. For our own life in the world, nothing is more essential than the pattern and power of this life. The reason for this is quickly put. It is from the teaching and work of Jesus, his life and death, that we formulate our understanding of both social ethics and Christology: that is, *Jesus defines for us both the nature of our moral life in the world, and the way we confess our faith in God.*

It is possible to work towards an understanding of both social ethics and of Christology from a number of angles. Let us do it simply on the basis, I hope not too oddly, of a consideration of *money and its humane use.* This appears to have been large in the concern of Jesus; and Luke, among the Evangelists, gives it the largest space. Luke's gospel appears to assume as fact that, in any use of temporal goods, eternal values are always at stake; and Dale Moody has recently reminded us that one of the most important Christological texts in the New Testament (2 Cor. 8:9) appears in connection with an offering of money for the needy.[15]

The question of money and its use is a subtle one: money is so consistently a part of most things good. The Bible nowhere condemns money, and has little to say about the machinery of its production and distribution. But the Bible is deeply concerned about the *use* of money and is highly sensitive to the dangers of affluence. Money is a form of power. It is the power to bless or blight the neighbor—and, in our time, the power to bless or blight the world. Nothing is more often involved in the "spiritual life" than the right use of money. Luke appears to see the misuse of money, based on love of money, as the root of more sorts of evil than any other one thing. He understands Jesus to be teaching, and appears himself to be emphasizing, that in any use of *temporal* goods, *eternal* values are at stake. This is, for Luke, a chief way in which is affirmed the continuity of this world with the next. The use of money, as Luke sees it, flows into both ethics and Transcendence.

---

[15]Dale Moody, *The Word of Truth* (Grand Rapids: Eerdmans, 1981) 106.

4. MONEY'S INVOLVEMENT
IN ETHICS AND TRANSCENDENCE (LUKE 16)

Nowhere is this matter better illustrated than in chapter 16 of Luke's gospel. Two stories there, whose conclusions are in eternity, begin with the use of money on earth.[16]

The first story (vss. 1-13) is of the dishonest steward, or crafty bookkeeper. He had wasted his master's property and was being fired from his job. Unemployment, presumably, was as cruel then as now. What should he do? Neither digging nor begging suited his style. He conceived a clever idea. For part-payments from his master's debtors, he would receipt their whole accounts. Later on, when out of work, those who had been obligated to him by this act—those whose good will he had purchased with his dishonesty—would offer him the hospitality of their homes. His employer praised the rascal for his shrewdness, a quality not always found in the stewardship of those who belong to the light.

Jesus told this shady story to his disciples, and drew from it a daring lesson: ''And I tell you, make friends for yourselves by means of unrighteous mammon, so that when it fails they may receive you into the eternal habitations'' (vs. 9 RSV). As if to say, ''Look, it is only money. In itself, it has no ultimate significance. Its only real value lies in its humane use. All money is tainted with injustice. If you do not redeem it as a means to human good, it will destroy your present and empty your future of hope. Money is only a *potential* good; it is a *present* threat. Invest your money therefore in the true welfare of others, and when you lose your hold on life— as through death don't we all?—those in whose good you invested it will welcome you into the eternal habitations.[17]

---

[16]In what follows, I am taking over, and generally changing the use of, parts of a sermon by James Denney of Glasgow: ''The Rich Man's Need of the Poor,'' in *The Way Everlasting* (London: Hodder & Stoughton, 1911) 164ff. I am taking over Dr. Denney's interpretation of Luke 16 (often in his own words), and using it, in my own way, in connection with the Christian's moral involvement in society's problems (with particular respect to world hunger), and as one means of approach to Christological understanding.

[17]Charles Talbert, *Reading Luke, A Literary and Theological Commentary on the Third Gospel* (New York: Crossroad, 1984) 155, reads ''they'' in v. 9 as a circumlocution for ''God.'' (He refers to *Mishna,* Yoma 8:9.) This is very possibly correct, but it does not *materially* alter the point that I am making.

In this story at least, Jesus appears to be saying that God will let one's final account be settled on the basis of the recommendations of those in whose good he/she had invested while they were alive, and who have now preceded him/her in death. If they are not there to speak up for him the case is lost.

The edges of this truth appeared less blunted to Jesus than to us. For him, this was a sharp 'either/or'. He saw that one who could not generously administer some tainted money on earth could hardly be entrusted with the true riches beyond. We are less convinced than he. No either/or for us. We would likely appoint a ''task-force'' to study this complex problem. We should like to know the degree of contamination in the money; or how many of the constituency believed the rascal should have been praised even for his shrewdness; or whether the obligation to others was to be measured before or after paying tithes or taxes. For Jesus it was simpler: one cannot be servant of both God and money. God's claim on us, in the need of the neighbor, is absolute; our ownership and control of our own money is not. The use of our money through repeated involvement with our neighbor's need is, according to this parable of Jesus, the way our final account with God will have been built up.

A group of religiously privileged people, who were lovers of money, scoffed at this teaching (vs. 14). It was difficult for them, as it is for us, to believe that one's own good, in either earth or heaven, is an inextricable part of everyone's good. This response becomes the occasion for the second story in the same chapter.

Luke appears (ignoring the unexpected presence of vss. 16-18) to present the parable of the rich man and Lazarus as Jesus' answer to those who had scoffed at the moral he had drawn from the preceding story of the dishonest bookkeeper. Taken this way, ''the rich man and Lazarus'' was a reply to their disbelief that one's own good, in earth or heaven, is a part of everybody's good. It is a story of a man who failed to invest in *agapē* until it was too late.

In Lu. 16:19-21, an earthly, visible scene is sketched. This is followed, in 22-26, with a heavenly, invisible scene. Verses 27-31 are an apparently curious addition to what Jesus' point seems at first to require. But wait and see.

So, the earthly, visible scene (vss. 19-21). The rich man's life is sketched. Riches is the power to have for oneself whatever can be had with money—the royal robe of purple, the fine linen undergarments, the overloaded table. There is no denunciation of property. It is not suggested that the rich man had made his money unjustly, or that he had sweated it from Lazarus. The rich man's manner of living is depicted—nothing more. He had money, and he enjoyed for himself what his money could provide.

Next to this is sketched the condition of Lazarus the beggar. Covered with sores and licked by dogs, he desired to be fed with scraps from that bounteous table. How desperately he needed a friend. Yes, but how distant our viewpoint from that of Jesus! The real point of the story, for Jesus, is not how much Lazarus needed the rich man; it is how desperately the rich man needed, and would later need, the recognition and recommendation of Lazarus (the name means "whom God helps"). Remember, it is Jesus' point that the rich man has a great opportunity to make himself a friend to the poor man by investing himself—his concern, his money— in the welfare and blessing of this poor man. How much would Lazarus' testimony to his kindness have been worth to the rich man in the future! But no such kindness came. The rich man is there in his purple and fine linen. The poor man is there in his rags and sores. Nothing is done. That is all. But that is not all. The world being God's, the visible scene is never all.

In verses 22-26 which follow, the heavenly, invisible scene is unveiled. Now the rich man and the poor man have been ushered by death into the kingdom beyond death. Now their roles are reversed. It is Lazarus who feasts in a place of high honor—in the bosom of Abraham, at the great Messianic banquet. The rich man is in a hell of thirst and torment. More terrible still, from across an unbridgeable chasm, he sees at Abraham's side the man whom on earth he could have befriended and did not. The purple, the linen, the sumptuous food are long since rotted. He had invested all he had in what could not outlast him. Only persons outlast life, and there was Lazarus in whom the man of means and power had not invested a care or a prayer, a kind word or a penny. Now the rich man has nothing, and Lazarus needs nothing. The rich man's character—and, therefore, even his eternal state—had been shaped by this neglect of his poor neighbor on earth. Failure to invest in generous charity had determined his final lot. Jesus understood this to be God's verdict on such things, and that from the verdict there is no appeal. Were it possible to scare hell out of people, this just might do it. But this is not possible, and the story is not about hell anyway. Those curious concluding verses show why.

Versus 27-31 appear, at first blush, to go beyond what Jesus' point required: that we should by charity invest in those who will welcome us into the world to come—fellow human beings, neighbors, the poor, the refugees, the lonely, the hurt. These will give testimony to God that, while on earth, we had acted humanely towards them—that we had shown towards them a concern that accepts both inconvenience and expense, a charity that does not keep books. The case of the inhumane man, however, is lost. No one comes forward to recommend him to God. In the kingdom beyond death no one can be found whom he had befriended on earth. But the parable does continue with these verses. And it could be—especially for polite and sophisticated people—that its main lesson is to be found right here.

In this coda to the theme, the rich man appeals to Abraham to send Lazarus to warn his five brothers about all that flame and torment. It simply would do no good. This is the awesome moral fact, as we shall see. The rich man voices his appeal, ''Send Lazarus. . . . '' What should we make of this ungranted appeal? Is it a symptom in him of a vestigial good, disclosing a humanity at least towards his own brothers? Or is it a sign of latent rebellion, the rich man implying that God is being ''inhumane'' towards him? Probably neither. How, then, do these verses support the story's preceding theme, and reveal its climax? Surmise.

''So, that is final,'' we can imagine Jesus' hearers saying to themselves when he had finished unveiling the scene in the kingdom beyond death. ''It is final, but is it really fair? The rich man (they might continue) did not know about this unseen world. If he could have seen the reality of the life beyond death, as clearly as he saw his own heavy table or even the wretchedness of Lazarus, he would have acted differently. He should have been more plainly warned of the consequences of such 'inhumanity', and so should others be.'' It seems to be the answering of such thoughts as these that carries the story into these final verses.

The parable gives no further notice to the rich man on his own account. From here on he is used simply to pose the objection which, at some time or another, is sure to present itself to everyone—that the invisible world of which the story speaks is without hard evidence. God does not do things as plainly as he ought. People do not know about the invisible world (the objection continues), and if motives from it are to enter life and influence conduct they ought to be told about it by a witness it would be *impossible* to doubt: ''Let someone go to them from the dead.''

It was earlier mentioned that this is a response to which the intellectually sophisticated, especially the empirically oriented, are naturally prone. But it should not be lightly passed over that Jesus treats such an objection as moral trifling. "They have Moses and the prophets; if your brothers listen not to Moses and the prophets they will not be convinced, even if someone were to return from the dead." Such a witness would simply do no good. Signs and miracles amaze or pique, they startle or excite. They do not morally turn people about in their way. They do not make uncaring persons humane.

If we can still be inhumane with the Bible in hand and Lazarus at the gate, no revelation of anguish in a life beyond death would have power to change us. For if the character and will of God as disclosed in Law and Prophets, if the appeal of the beggar at the gate, do not make persons genuinely caring, nothing will. The reason you cannot scare people out of hell is that you cannot scare inhumanity out of people.

At this point we have arrived at a fundamental understanding of the nature both of the gospel and of the life of faith which it evokes: the gospel is never less than a radical humanism. Before we are through, we shall say that it is much more than a humanism—but for now, and for always, it is never less.

From this analysis of Luke's text, it is possible to trace out two lines of Christian truth. The first will carry us into what we commonly call Christian social ethics, with special reference to the tragedy of world hunger. The second will attempt to draw one line of theology proper.

a. The line of Christian social ethics

The gospel speaks to all issues that bear upon the human good. (It is never less than a radical humanism.) So desperate in character are some of these problems that we must, soon, either deal morally with them or number our days on this planet. Consider: Nuclear terriorism haunts our future, as more and more we lose rational control of weapons. The monster we have created, says George Kennan, our former ambassador to the Soviet Union, is "taking possession of our imagination and behavior, becoming a force in its own right, detaching itself from the differences that inspired it, and leading both parties inexorably to the war they no longer know how to avoid."[18] So far, we have thought of no better way to avoid

---

[18]This is quoted from the "House of Bishops Pastoral Letter, General Convention (Protestant Episcopal Church in USA), 1982."

such a catastrophe than to increase and improve our capacity to destroy each other. The end of this course, unaltered, is sudden and apocalyptic.

In our generation, for the first time, we have discovered that our very environment has boundaries—and that this environment is fragile as well as finite. As someone has put it, ''We have a foot or two of soil, a few miles of air and two or three miles of ocean.'' The capacity of an industrialized society to inflict major damage on the biosphere is a new idea. Much more scary, it is an established fact. That such a process of damage has already become measurable is ominous. The end of this course, unaltered, is a disaster in slow motion.

Our attention must be limited here, however, to a single problem: the exponential increase of world population and *the horror of poverty and hunger* that follow in its train.

Our earth's population increases each week by two million new people. And the story has hardly begun. Such increase in population creates problems of space and food, to be sure. But a morally earnest analysis of the human situation on this planet also involves the question of the quality of life itself, and demands a reordering of all our priorities. The problem is not simply how to devise morally acceptable measures of population control, or a system of distribution to the needy of earth's abundance. These issues are a bit further before us. The immediate problem is how to deal with the humanly brutalizing fact that, right now, one-third of all the earth's people are hungry, and a terrifying proportion of that one-third are starving. What are we rich Christians (and Jews, and Muslims, and Buddhists, and Hindus) going to do about a hungry world?[19]

The investment in the needy neighbor of moral goodwill and generous love is not optional to the Christian life. It is not something—for those interested in such things—that one might add to the cultivation of his ''spiritual life.'' It is an imperative of God's grace; it comes with the evangel itself. Let me push this as vigorously as possible: for Christians to treat any form of human need, in this case hunger, as something of lesser importance than what is often (and unbiblically) called evangelism; or for Christians to remain willfully ignorant of these ''little ones'' for whom Jesus died—this is to subvert the gospel of Christ. It is a way, at the most

---

[19]This recalls the title of Ronald J. Sider, *Rich Christians in a Hungry World* (Downers Grove, Illinois: Intervarsity Press, 1977). My discussion of world hunger is deeply affected by Sider's treatment of the subject.

decisive point, of rejecting the incarnation of the Son of God. This kind of religion does not recognize Christ in the face of the suffering poor. Religiously, it says of Christ that "the Spirit of the Lord is upon him"; ethically, it forgets that our reason for knowing this rests only upon Christ's having been "anointed to preach the good news to the poor . . . to proclaim release to the captives . . . to set at liberty those that are oppressed" (Lu. 4:18-19, quoting Isa. 61:1-2). It is an immediate duty of all Christians (and all people) to give generously and sacrificially to any publicly responsible agency—governmental or ecclesiastical—that is getting aid to the largest numbers with the least administrative red tape and administrative expense. It is also a duty to find out and refuse support to those individuals and agencies that get rich on the desperation of others.

Meanwhile, *three lines for active faith, in the face of world hunger,* may be briefly proposed. Each suggests something that can be done. Each needs doing.

At the first and simplest level, morally serious people (and surely this includes some Christians) could do more by way of learning about our world and its peoples. This could be done while disciplining ourselves to serve them. It is a relatively simple thing for literate people to study an atlas, to read a history of a country and its people, to learn something of a culture's domestic, economic, political, and religious structures. Helpful works, by novelists, anthropologists, historians, and sociologists, abound. Effective caring for lands and peoples is not unrelated to our knowledge of them. God has created the whole world, not simply the Christian's part of it. God has loved and loves the whole world, not simply those of the Christian's own kind. The Christian remembers—or should remember—that God does not love Christians better than he loves anyone else. God loves all alike—the Christian and Jew, the Buddhist and Muslim, the religious, the non-religious, and the irreligious. A Christian might be defined as one who, through Jesus Christ, has found this out and who is seeking to copy God who "so loved the world."

Surely some acquaintance with the lives of the millions in China, India, Africa or Latin America would transform general religious sentiment into moral concern and willingness to share. Population increase, as statistics, is one thing. Population increase, as people who need education, living wages, decent life expectancy, food, is another. It is people, not statistics, who hope, or who, in the face of hopes repeatedly blighted, fall into dehumanizing despair. More is here than economics and psychology.

For it is at this point that economics and atheism are most apt to coalesce. Despair is an effective atheism. It is the conclusion, arriving each time a person's last feeble hope is extinguished, that the situation is too desperate even for God to remedy. How God, in our dear Lord Christ, loves the hurt of the earth who can no longer believe because they can no longer hope.

Ignorance of the world and its peoples is one problem. A second and deeper: We who are affluent have an aversion to the hunger and hurt around us. We do not really *want* to see the needy. It is painful to recognize or acknowledge that they are there. There must be courage to see.

This brings us back to the parable for a moment. The rich man is not condemned for being rich. He is not called a bad man. It is not even hinted that he was undevout—or being devout, was hypocritical. He probably contributed to the "United Way." But he did not really see Lazarus: his hunger and need for food, his loneliness and need for acceptance. The rich man simply did not see him, and Lazarus was there to be seen. Unable to see his poor neighbor, the privileged man's own personhood was fatally diminished. In every oversight of the poor, the vision of God is dimmed.

Albert Schweitzer has told us that this parable was important in his decision to invest his life in Africa. Already he knew that one cannot reach from a neglected neighbor to God. The gulf that stretches from a neglected neighbor to God is too wide for piety to bridge or for miracle to mend. Participation in the life of our neighbor, who is also our brother, is a form of participation in the eternal life. Actions, and their effects, carry from the earthly life into the kingdom beyond death. The scope of one's eternal life, in the perspective of this parable, is not unrelated to the size of one's earthly "neighborhood." If I cannot see my poor neighbor, I cannot see God; for, in this world, God is wearing that poor man's face. And if in this neighbor, I do see God, so in this neighbor, I also see my brother. For true neighborhood is a form of brotherhood; and true brotherhood, seen through the eyes of Jesus, is interpreted by Fatherhood. The spirit of brotherhood, which is the fulfillment of the Second Commandment ("Thou shalt love thy neighbor as thyself"), is rooted in the spirit of sonship to God, which is the fulfillment of the First ("Thou shalt love the Lord thy God with all thy heart and mind and soul and strength").

Learning all we can about our world-neighborhood, and guarding ourselves from the temptation to avert our eyes, will set us on the way. The way, however, must be taken. It must be followed at cost, as well as entered upon. Both personal discipline and public effort are required.

Discipline, I suppose, is never a popular word. It hints in common English at ideas such as "punishment," "enforced obedience," and the like. The word, in fact, is more positive. It means instruction that molds, strengthens, brings to maturity, and, in these senses, corrects. The words "discipline" and "disciple" are from the same root. A disciple of Christ is one who is being taught; is being brought towards maturity in the nurture and instruction of the Lord (Eph. 6:4); is being trained in righteousness (2 Tim. 3:16). Sonship to God and endurance in the demanding life of faith are the goals of such discipline (Heb. 12:7). The example of disciplined endurance, in the face of hostility against himself, is a part of Christ's bequest to us who follow him (Heb. 12:3). Through the lessons of such discipline, we learn to reorder our priorities, arranging all things secondary to serve things primary. For us affluent Christians, this is where the water hits the wheel.

Nowhere, it seems, does popular religion stand in a plainer state of self-contradiction than in its relation to the uses of money. *Money, as money, never reaches beyond the realm of means; but money, as means, reaches into the realm of ends. Both ethics and the Transcendent are involved.* Means are, by definition, the means to ends. Like the Sabbath, money was made for persons, not persons for money. Could any Christian, in principle, disagree? But the practice, rather than the principle, is our problem.

In practice, under heavy and often unconscious influence of our culture, we surrender to the claims of money and property over the rights of people. Morally, we must ask first, not "what are my rights?", but "what are my neighbor's needs and what can I do about them?" Plainly the Christian must not injure anyone. He may not even avoid opportunity to do well towards all persons. But in a world such as ours, he must go quite beyond either of these. He must seek out proper ways of making the largesse of the world available to human need wherever it is found. It is something that can be done. It can be done by disciplining our own lifestyle, as well as by witness and action in the public sphere.

These remarks, let it be remembered, are appearing in a discussion of the nature of faith. One form faith takes is Christian social ethics. Were the discussion before us on Christian social ethics as such, we should need to talk of such things, among many others, as our own intake of food (with some remarks on the subject of sensible diet), the uses of resources (such as energy), sexuality, the stewardship of money, and political action. For the real question for Christians is not really "Did I contribute to the United Way, or to the Church?" Not even "Have I tithed?" The question is, How am I investing my life, and its resources, in those divinely prized human values that outlast life itself?

Surely this much may be said. We affluent ones need to reduce our own intake of food; to become morally superior to what we own; to learn to distinguish between what we want and what we need. We need to recover the capacity to follow our generous impulses by getting out from under the burden of being always overspent. Just this much would free up almost limitless amounts of funds for aiding the world's hungry.

Beyond this, Christians could challenge notions regarding property rights and the use of resources which, though accepted in the public sphere as just, are without moral foundation. Consider some of these near-blasphemies: that God, being concerned for "souls," has nothing at stake in the extremes of poverty and wealth; that since property is legitimate, persons are absolute arbiters of their own; that rights of private ownership take precedence over the right of access by the poor to such resources as are necessary for the earning of a just living. The grandchildren of today's economic reactionaries will be as bewildered that their grandfathers justified such obviously immoral ideas as are we that our grandfathers justified slavery.

We must respond to these urgent issues in our time, or we shall learn, the hard way, something of the awful justice of God that Abraham Lincoln discerned in his. In the terrible carnage of civil war, Lincoln, like an Isaiah or Jeremiah, knew that "the Almighty has his own purposes." In his second inaugural address the president reminded the nation that it was impossible to understand what was happening to it, if the Almighty's purposes were ignored. In that address, he left us, as Bruce Catton noted,[20] one of the great questions for all persons to ponder: "If we suppose that American slavery is one of those offenses which, in the providence of God, must needs

---

[20]*The American Heritage Picture History of the Civil War,* narrative by Bruce Catton (New York: American Heritage Publishing Co., Inc., 1960) 591-92. A similar insight, coming a century earlier, is expressed by John Woolman in a letter to a friend. See *The Journal of John Woolman,* ed. Janet Whitney (Chicago: Henry Regnery Company, 1950) 40-41. P. T. Forsyth saw as clearly as most how the tragedies of history may carry the judgment of God. He saw more clearly than some how these judgments belong to our salvation. See *The Justification of God* (London: Independent Press, Ltd., 1948) esp. ch. 10.

come, but which, having continued through His appointed time, He wills now to remove, and that He gives to both North and South, this terrible war, as the woe due to those by whom the offense came, shall we discern therein any departure from those divine attributes which the believers in a living God always ascribe to Him?''

If we consider, in our turn, that poverty and economic exploitation have continued through God's appointed time, that these are evils which he wills now to remove, can any believer in a living God be surprised at divine judgment on human resistance to their removal? And cannot the morally sensitive, aware of our reluctance for justice and our fear of the cost of mercy, already catch the utterances of a Sovereign Will against which nothing shall finally prevail? As awful as is the thought, for life and for theology, could the predicted ''wars of redistribution'' somehow express the will of Him who answers moral folly in acts of terrible righteousness? God's love for all does not tolerate injustice for some.

This tracing of faith's line into Christian social ethics may be followed with the tracing of a second—into theology proper.

Thus far we have said quite a lot about humanity—humanity both as people, and as concern for people. We have insisted that faith in the gospel never entails less than a radical humanism; we have enforced this thought on the conscience by a moral consideration of world hunger and poverty.

It appears, very clearly to me, however, that Christian faith has to do with more than a humanism—and, in a sense, with other than a humanism. In the Bible, precisely where we learn that when persons are abused God is wounded, the human is not the ultimate value. The highest value, and the transvaluation of all values including the human person, is God. As those who cherish the biblical faith, our concern for persons derives directly from our involvement with God's concern for persons. We can love persons, we are to love persons, because God loves persons. We learn who the person is, and what he needs, from God in Christ. This stream of humanitarian concern takes its rise in God's own heart.

The central concern of the gospel is for the *humanum*. This seems, rather clearly, to be beyond dispute. But what the gospel says about man, for man, even against man, and to man begins *beyond* where even the highest humanisms can reach.[21] The gospel talks with us first about God

---

[21]See Karl Barth, *God Here and Now* (New York: Harper and Row, 1964) 101.

whom we know in his knowing of us. So, our thought on the gospel must not only lay bare our ethical responsibility as affluent believers in a world of need; it must reveal a truth, which the Church too easily forgets, about our Lord himself.

b. One line of theology proper

In biblical documents, witness is given to God as *God*—to the deity of God if one may put it so. God is holy, which, while meaning much more, never means less than that he is high above us, other than us, and not dependent upon us. He has the source of life in himself and is its perfect 'form'. In one manner of speaking, God the transcendent does come to us "directly from above," just as Karl Barth used to say he does. He is God and not man.

But he does come! He is the Holy One above us; but he is—as Isaiah and Hosea were both to say—"the Holy One in our midst." He is full of loving-kindness—he cares. He is actually *in our midst*. Barth himself, in the earliest years, was less ready to emphasize this than Hosea and Isaiah had been. The religious climate, he thought, tended to expose this truth to consistent misunderstanding. Perhaps he was right. But once he began to stress the divine presence as strongly as the divine sovereignty (and this was much earlier than was popularly perceived), he did it with fascination and with power. "God is *God*," he says, "but God is God in such a way that he also has the characteristics of humanity. . . . God's very *deity*, rightly understood, includes his humanity."[22] The God of eternity, as well as of the covenant-history, is characterized by both deity and humanity.[23]

Barth all along was right that Christian faith must resist all kinds of theology that are reducible to anthropology—to a doctrine of man. But neither can theology be understood as a doctrine of God, period. The later Barth saw this clearly, and decribed theology, at its best, as a "theanthropology," a doctrine of God and man, of the communication and com-

---

[22]Eberhard Busch, *Karl Barth, His Life from Letters and Autobiographical Texts* (Philadelphia: Fortress Press, 1976) 424.

[23]Cf. Barth's address in Aarau in September 1956, "The Humanity of God," (Richmond: John Knox Press, 1960) esp. 42-52. Already in *Church Dogmatics* I.ii,173, in "The Miracle of Christmas," Barth had said that "incarnation asserts the presence of God in our world, *and as a member of this world,* as a Man among men" (emphasis mine).

munity between God and man. So Barth says, "God alone is *God*. But God is not alone. A real conjunction of God and man has taken place in Jesus Christ. In Jesus Christ man is affirmed and taken seriously in his existence . . . man is over against God, but his independence is respected."[24]

In such theology man does not become God, but God does become man. "The Word became flesh and dwelt among us" (Jn. 1:14). The *humanum* is never swallowed up in the divine abyss; but is, by the incarnation of the divine Word, carried into God's life. Here the person is "discovered" (in both senses) in his true humanity. God's grace is shown in the fact that although he does not "need" this person, he does not will to be without him.

Our significance as persons derives from this fact. God likes us. He is for us. His delight in Jesus Christ is delight *in our own kind at our best*. The Son of God was the one true person. Our status as human rests on God's happy choice of us in his Son. This delight in us all defines the reason and nature of our responsibility to neighbor. It is God's work of grace on our behalf, encapsulated in the man Jesus, which is the ground and norm of the communication and community between God and man. In Jesus of Nazareth in Galilee, the *Theos* and the *anthropos* come together.

The Church tends usually to get this backwards. We formulate a high Christology—"begotten of His Father before all worlds, God of God, light of light . . . begotten, not made; being of one substance with the Father"—and suppose that a Christian is one who gives credence to these words. To confess Christian faith, however, is not the same as bragging on Jesus. It never has been. Faith means to see, by grace alone, that the *human concerns of Jesus' life* which drained his strength and compassed his death are what God is concerned about. It is to affirm that the energies which Jesus spent so freely on behalf of others were not other than God's own presence and power at work for us all. And also it is to know in one's bones that really to believe this is, according to the measure of our faith, to act the same way. A Christian believer is known not by what he says about religion, but by his manner of embodying God's concern for people. We know the deity of Christ, his God-ness, not by a creedal statement on the two natures in the undivided person: we know the God-ness of Christ

---

[24]See Barth's essay, "Evangelical Theology in the 19th Century," in *The Humanity of God*, 9. (I first ran across this in Busch's great biography of Barth, 424).

by what he did and does and shall do for the broken and hungry who lie at his gate.

The man, Jesus Christ, who sees the broken and hungry who are easiest to ignore—the Jesus Christ of this very sort—is the revelation of God. He is at the same time the revelation of our own true being and moral duty. He is the revelation of God; that is, his kind of self-giving for others is and discloses what God himself is always up to. He is the revelation of our true being and moral duty; that is, we truly are sons of our Father in heaven, when we can see Christ in the face of our neighbor. To serve God is to act in self-giving goodwill to that neighbor. Faith in God, working through self-giving love of neighbor, is the one credible confession of the basic revelation of God in the reconciliation of the race. This reconciliation, shown and effected in the life and death of Jesus Christ, proclaims itself both as revelation and as mystery simply by taking place. There is no glory of the gospel that outshines its "happenedness."

Let us wind down this discussion of the nature of faith with a last return to the parable. We have seen, in ways that seem true to this portion of Jesus' teaching, that our welcome into the kingdom beyond death must come from those who have preceded us there, those in whom we have invested our disinterested goodwill. What we have done for the hungry or thirsty, the homeless or naked, the sick or imprisoned, we have done for the King.[25]

On the basis of this truth, two things, in effect, have been said: that faithful service of others is love of God whether we name it that or not; and that the true confession of Christ's deity and Lordship—that is, the confession that God's presence among us in Christ is both real and sovereign— is made not by reciting even great historic creeds, but by Christlike service to our poor neighbor. By the incarnation of the Word of God, Christ himself is present in that neighbor.

We may conclude the discussion with two implications of such thought, which your own imaginations may already have taken up: the reality of Lazarus, and the knowledge of God.

Incarnational faith produces no cult of peace of mind, no exemption from the human conflict. It is not the absence of haunting problems, of torturous temptations, of human pain, or of appearances of cosmic absurdity. Believing people, like others, suffer and die. Lazarus is real.

---

[25]Cf. not only Lk. 16, but also Mt. 25.

The reality of Lazarus is marked by tragedy compounded with misery. He is poor; he is hungry; he is illiterate; he is a dreadful nuisance to all who are ''successful.'' He is easy to ignore, for he is hard to see. He is easy to abuse when he is seen, and finds it hard to fight back. But even in his misery he has a glory. He is God's creature, made in God's image. He really knows this whether he understands it or not, and in the short run he would be less miserable if he did not know it. But there he is—child of God and heir of freedom. His ultimate glory lies in being the object (and subject) of *agapē*. What we do with the fact of Lazarus reveals, perhaps more clearly than any other one thing, who we are.

As for the knowledge of God, not even with good hard data could we make God evident. Data can help to clear up certain human and theological perplexities. But theological perplexities have never been the same as religious difficulties. The question of God is clarified as moral knowledge only when the case of Lazarus is responsibly faced. Hence, a proposition for devout consideration. The proposition is suggested vis-à-vis the misconception, as I deem it, that though we know man, we do not really know God. The opposite, I believe, is the case: We know God; we do not know man, including ourselves.

We see man, but we do not know him: the upvaulting aspirations that take off from his spirit like rockets; the blind forces that flow like great currents in the unfathomable deeps of his being; the disharmonies that jangle between what he is and what he says, between what he says and what he does; the compulsive self-destructiveness that rages within him *sub limina;* the inexpressible yearnings that whimper within him like lonely violins in the wilderness of the Infinite. We do not know man. But we see him. He is our neighbor. He is our brother. In a profound sense, he is ourself. To ignore him is to overlook God. To wound him is to strike God in the face. We do not know man. But we see him. There he is at our door; and at that door, increasing millions of him are hungrier than Lazarus.

We do not see God, but we know him. He is beyond all our conceiving. His reality strikes dumb even the devoutest language with which we praise him. He is no more to be taken in by religious faith than by natural reason or aesthetic sensitivity. Even in revelation he remains both the sovereign and the hidden Lord. Still we know him. The ultimate heartbeat of this universe is the self-giving goodwill of God. For God is *agapē*. This is the secret of the whole creation, and we have met it, in its very essence, in our Savior. We have seen *agapē* with human boundaries but in divine fullness in Jesus. We have also seen it with divine limits and in only human measure in others. Except for knowing this, we could not even deny it.

To say all this is theology. It becomes faith which makes us whole when we wager our lives that in this world, in the presence of our plenty, God is wearing not simply Jesus' face, but, as well, the face of every Lazarus for whom Jesus died. Lazarus' face is the face that we are least apt to see; for his is the face that only love will notice—the poor, with no clout at all; the person who has nothing going for him that we could turn to our own advantage. He is just a poor man. But he has a glory: this face is the face of Christ, the very Lord who took to himself the nature and lot of Lazarus. We do not see God, but we know God. We know God in growing certitude and joy as we see and serve him in that neighbor. Lazarus's face is the face of God that can be seen.

Ignorance of God is not absence of data; it is indifference to Lazarus. The root of such ignorance of God is never lack of information. It is not even absence of piety. It is human insensitivity. One cannot see God in Christ who cannot see Christ in Lazarus. God have mercy: it is as awesome and as final as that! In the man Jesus who lived and died for every Lazarus—and for Lazaruses like us—God and all us poor men meet.

In the face of Lazarus, truly seen, we know God and find Christ in our world. This knowledge of God in Christ is the saving gospel through which all may find that liberation of faith to which the Holy Scriptures bear witness. For we come at last to ourselves, as well as to God, when we look in the face of Lazarus and see the face of Christ. This human path is wide open; when walked to the end, one is standing at the throne of God.

All this is why, fifteen centuries ago, St. Augustine exhorted us,

> Walk by Christ the man, and you will come to God. . . .
> Look not for any way except himself by which to come to him. For
> if he had not vouchsafed to be the way we should all have gone
> astray. Therefore he became the way by which you should come.
> I do not say to you, seek the way. The Way itself is come to you:
> arise and walk.[26]

This is the life of faith. In such a man-for-others, faithfully followed, we can see God himself, and walk in his light forever. It only remains to do it. It is never too late to begin.

---

[26]*Sermons* (de Script, N.T.), CXLI.iv,4, as quoted in Erich Przywara, *An Augustine Synthesis,* 329 (slightly modified).

Chapter Four

Theology and Religion(s)

As between religion and theology, then, the primary relation is the relation between immediate living response and reflective articulation and interpretation of that response. When such reflection begins, the character of religious experience is itself obviously modified. In some respects, it becomes less uninhibited and spontaneous, yet in other respects it becomes richer, clearer, and more stable.

—R. L. Calhoun

In this chapter we examine theology in relation to religion(s). We shall try to see theology as the servant of revelation and faith, and move to a consideration of it in relation to religion and the religions as accoutrements of faith. In the former part a sort of working definition of theology is drawn, and in the latter consideration is given to both theoretical and practical questions. Perhaps a good way to begin would be to establish connection with what already has been said.

In the chapter on Revelation, we claimed that there actually is what Jonathan Edwards calls a divine and supernatural light, immediately imparted to the soul by the spirit of God; that this is witnessed of in Scripture; and that it responds to rational analysis and reflection. It could be added as compatible with Edwards's thought but not developed by him, that this divine light has affinity for, but is not identical with, any historical religion. It is by faithful response to this divine self-disclosure that we come to knowledge of God and of ourselves as known of God. This light alone makes us to see truly the world, the neighbor, and the human good. It is revelation.

Faith, we also said, is not faith in faith. It is faith in God who is both the source and end of faith. Faith is the human response to God as revealed. The character of faith derives from its relationship with its unique and all-important 'object': the living God. Faith is a correspondence with God in kind, which principally means that faith makes it possible for us, in freedom and responsibility, to love God who freely loves us, and to love all beings and things that his love includes.

Serious trust in God as love discloses the closest possible relation between Christian faith and Christian ethics. This relation is native and permanent. In Christian understanding, faith and ethics appear actually as two sides of a single involvement. For purposes of clarification they may be distinguished; on no legitimate ground may they be divided. Faith is something one is doing with one's life; as such it corresponds completely with the Christian's moral vocation. It is a lifelong and lifewide response to God, whose nature and requirement are revealed in his action. It appears as both trust and trustworthiness. Christian ethics could be defined as 'faith active in love'. It is concerned with relationship, relationship with God and neighbor. This is the substance of what appears in the chapter on the nature of faith.

To recapitulate: Revelation is God's impact upon the human scene. Faith is human involvement in this revelation in humility and obedience, in such way that revelation is received as knowledge and experienced as love.

Theology concerns itself with both revelation and faith—for the both are finally as much one subject as two. Theology is ordered reflection on the action and nature of God. It attempts accurately to report and rightly to interpret God's disclosure of himself. It also seeks, complementarily, to elaborate the meaning of religious experience which comes through faith. Both—the creative disclosure and the faithful response—are theology's concern.

1. TOWARDS A DEFINITION OF THEOLOGY

Individual theologians, through history, have had their own way of giving accent to these two dimensions of theology's concern. The majority have viewed theology as primarily an interpretation of God's objectively real disclosure of himself to the human family. This line, with acknowledged fuzzy edges, would include such stalwarts as Thomas Aquinas, Martin Luther, and Emil Brunner. The other line, which has less of traditional history behind it, has construed its task as being what R. L. Calhoun has described as "the systematic elaboration of the content of religious experience." In this line a sharper focus is given to the human response in faith than to revelation as the objective activity of God. Theology is viewed as a *Glaubenslehre*, a doctrine of faith. This line sees it as the theologian's task to sort out the character and significance of this experience of faith. This line is anticipated in St. Bonaventure, is given its fullest and most impressive exposition in Schleiermacher, and reaches a sort of dénouement in John A. T. Robinson, the late Bishop of Woolwich.

A cautious suggestion: the two approaches seem best balanced in Paul, Augustine, and Calvin. In the work of all three these two sides are harmonized, not as in an arbitrary commingling of opposites but in what may be described as the natural conjunction of two ellipses in a single circle. To draw a picture of this with words should help to clarify the theological idea.

Imagine a circle in which is drawn one ellipse with its center common to that of the circle, and its long axis coincident with the horizontal diameter of the circle. Then, penetrating that ellipse, envision another whose center is also common to that of the circle and whose long axis is coincident with the vertical diameter. The large circle embraces both the horizontal and vertical planes. In theology, this mutual interpenetration of elliptical planes embraced by a single circle seems best managed in those three among the very great already named: Paul, Augustine, and Calvin.

Paul's hold upon the two sides of his theology is so equally balanced that it is impossible to conclude which is his dominant idea—God's objective act of grace in the justification of the sinner by faith, or the believer's being "in Christ." One emphasis elaborates the concrete givenness of the healing mercy; the other, the incorporation of the believer's present life into Christ's, by faith, through the presence and effectual working of God's good Spirit. Each belongs with the other.

Augustine, who is a principal father of everybody's theology, gives us the remarkable treatises on sovereign grace. Presented as God's objective and irrevocable work, grace embraces us as prevenient, unconditioned, and all but irresistible. On the other side, in his *Confessions,* which establishes the spiritual autobiography as a new genre of literature, his own life experience is probed in relation to God's calling and the reality of his presence in the temporal world. Yet, in an understanding such as Augustine's, the *Confessions'* examination of the psyche is not more, nor is it less, theological than the treatises on sovereign grace.

In Calvin's *Institutes of the Christian Religion,* which W. C. Smith suggests were better rendered as *Grounding in Christian Piety,*[1] we have

---

[1]Wilfred Cantwell Smith, *The Meaning and End of Religion* (San Francisco: Harper and Row, 1978) 37.

not only the awesome treatise (in Book I) on the sovereignty and knowability of the Triune God, but as well (in Book III) the even greater discussion of faith and the experience of the Holy Spirit.

It seems important that theology reckon in a balanced way with both the divine revelation and the human experience of it. These two ellipses interpenetrate each other. They belong in a single circle.

It would seem likely, in a time of both of intensified contact among the religions and of rapidly increasing scientific knowledge of the human species, that the human experience of God might be the handle on which, for many, the opening of theological dialogue could most hopefully take hold. A focus upon the horizontal plane of religious truth should not, however, lose sight of the vertical. Loss of the vertical is one way of describing what had happened in the thought of the bishop of Woolwich, who told us, perhaps less impressively than had Nietzsche, that God is dead. As a better guide for our time, I suggest the name of Jürgen Moltmann, alongside whose big books that expound with much clarity such truths as Church, hope, and spirit, should be placed also his perceptive and deeply moving essays in *Experiences of God*.[2]

Karl Barth has spoken of theology as the "special science" whose task is to apprehend, understand, and speak of God. God and his activity in creation, reconciliation, and redemption is the specific 'object' of theological understanding and controls theology's method as a 'science'.[3]

Christian theology is both catholic and evangelical—with lower case "c" and "e"—and neither, certainly, as the name of a church, denomination, or party. A theology truly catholic and evangelical will refuse to press any claim to its own correctness, whether as the only correct one among others or as one more correct than they.[4] This will be seen to have

---

[2]Jürgen Moltmann, *Experiences of God* (Philadelphia: Fortress Press, 1980).

[3]Barth, of course, is using the word 'science' in its European, rather than in the common American sense. In Europe the word 'science' is as appropriately used of the humanities as of the physical or life sciences. It means simply that, as a 'science', theology has a relatively well-defined scope and subject matter, a recognizable methodology, and that it participates in the universe of public inquiry and discussion.

[4]Cf. Karl Barth, *Evangelical Theology: An Introduction* (New York: Holt, Rinehart and Winston, 1963) 3-12.

considerable significance later when we look at the Christian way in relation to more easterly paths.

From the Catholic side, Richard McBrien of Notre Dame has a fine recent statement on the nature of theology, in which good balance is struck between the two sides of that enterprise. Theology, he says, "is that process by which we bring our knowledge and understanding of God to the level of expression. The articulation, in a more or less systematic manner, of the experience of God within the human experience."[5]

So. How are *we* to think of theology? It is the rationally ordered confession that God has spoken and we have faithfully heard; a confession that expresses love of God with the whole mind and which aims at clarity and mutual understanding. It is what Anselm meant by *fides quaerens intellectum,* "faith seeking understanding."

My own way of saying all this is that "theology is the *faithful and critical* attempt to state the reality of divine revelation as human meaning." Such a theology is flawed as confessional unless it is also critical; and as critical unless also confessional. Theology's scope is as high as God and as wide as humanity. Its point of departure is faith; its temper is nondefensive openness to truth; its aim is clarity in communication. My own theological line, which is most affected here by Karl Barth and H. Richard Niebuhr, proceeds as follows: God has irrevocably committed himself to us in Jesus Christ, in a sovereign grace eternally accomplished but historically known. So conclusive is this historial grace that it also controls the Christian understanding of both creation and eschatology, as well as of vocation and ethics.

Faith's job is the appropriation within time of this historical-grace-from-beyond-time. Revelation is given in the intelligible "event" of Jesus Christ, who, for faith, makes all other events intelligible. Theology aims at delineating this intelligibility. It does this on the basis of faith's appropriation of the revelation of grace, and in the service of faith's Object alone. Revelation depends upon faith in one sense, but faith depends upon revelation in all senses. Theology seeks to construe the nature and meaning of this dependence in relation to actual human existence in the world.

Revelation, which in the strictest sense is the primary substance of theological truth, remains stable even in the midst of our own continuous

---

[5]Richard McBrien, *Catholicism* (Minneapolis: Winston Press, 1981) 26.

change; its truth, however, is structured and clarified in relation to historical and human issues whose shape is always changing. The receivers of revelation vary greatly in their own identities and settings through time and space. Theology thus aims to give an account of what it understands about its own Object, and also to present itself as a form of truth worthy of consideration and confession by all peoples of whatever time and setting, including their cultural and religious heritage.

Within this overall description, theology busies itself with numerous more proximate objectives. Sometimes it will be aiming at the clarification of its own tradition; sometimes it will be in conversation with culture; sometimes it will be imposing structure on biblical exegesis; sometimes it will be speaking and listening to the faith of others; sometimes it will be formulating a rationale for some sort of ethical action. At its best it will sound more like a doxology than a thesis.

In attempting rightly to understand and to deal with such objectives, Christian theology will have begun with the Bible—its languages and religion, the history it contains, its own literary and redactional history as a definable collection of documents, the processes by which this collection of documents came to be regarded as Scripture, the distinguishing of what it has to say from the way it says it, how one is to understand the relation of the Bible's ''there' and 'then' to our 'now' and 'here'. This, I should judge, is the problematic that led Hans Frei to say, some years ago, that the task of theology is "to express, by means of our traditions, and present-day language, an understanding drawn from biblical exegesis."[6]

Theology must focus also upon the Tradition. The noticeably different points of view that the word 'tradition' historically evokes among Protestants and Catholics need be here neither our concern nor subject. We all simply need to realize as fact that, whatever the degree of truth in our religious understanding, it bears traces of those minds that provided for its transmission to ourselves. I am thinking here of tradition less as the whole of a religious faith considered as a complex of doctrine, cultus, ethics, and religious experience, and more as the hermeneutical transmission of the faith in postbiblical times.

Both Bible and Church—note, *both/and*—are forms of this living tradition of revelation and faith. Bible and Church being presupposed as

---

[6]Hans Frei, in Paul Ramsey, ed., *Faith and Ethics* (New York: Harper and Brothers, 1957) 102.

forms of a living tradition, it is clear that no theologian starts from scratch. We are not the first to whom God has spoken, nor the first to have written or spoken about what we believe we have heard him say. ''God spoke of old to our fathers by the prophets.'' In the fullness of time, he spoke more humanly in a Son (Heb. 1:1-2). He has been speaking ever since, and no culture or generation has been bereft of that witness.

It is important that we respect this tradition—these *sources* of our theological understanding. We must engage them and react to them—if critically and responsibly, also humbly and gratefully. Theology is nurtured on its sources; it has long, deep roots. Good theology is no fad. It does not hit the beaches with the frequency of surfers on the next wave. It will have pondered long the Law, Prophets, and Writings, the Gospels and Epistles. It will look long at the great tradition, and take seriously the Spirit's gifts to the Church through scholars, artists, and saints, through craftsmen, artisans, and laborers. We cannot live by their faith, but we must reckon with theirs when we formulate our own. And when we have formulated our own it should, despite, all changes of time or setting, be recognizable to an Apostle Paul or to St. Augustine, to Thomas or Calvin, to Richard Hooker or William Temple, to Dale Moody or Hans Küng.

It is the business of theology to listen attentively and humbly to the witnesses who have gone before us, and to attempt in our own time, and in our own way, what they were attempting in theirs. They are our heritage, and in a sense our future as well, for a theology without a past could have no future. One might say that a theology whose fathers are unknown is apt to produce a bastard offspring. We need to recall here, as important also for theology, T. S. Eliot's conviction regarding poetry: that the poet best serves his own time and craft ''when he consolidates his relationship to the poets of the past''[7]—that is, when he sees poetry as a way of celebrating and illuminating the tradition. Claims of originality are equally useless for poetry or for theology.

The nature of the theological task can also be illumined by a review of those questions that are central to the concerns of faith.

Religious faith shows, and the historical religions share, a concern for the fundamental human questions. What is the foundation and end of life, the

---

[7]T. S. Eliot, *Selected Essays* (New York: Harcourt, Brace & Company, 1950) 4. See also comments by H. Adams, *The Interests of Criticism: An Introduction to Literary Theory* (New York: Harcourt, Brace & World, 1969) 41.

transcendent good? (Who is God?) What is the meaning of history? (What is God up to and how may we know that?) What is the nature and possibility of our human meaning and worth? (Who am I, and what in the world is happening to me?) What should we do and what is the right way to do it? (What is the proper correlation between freedom and order?) What is our proper end? (What does life mean in terms of its final assessment?)[8]

The exercise of reason and imagination upon faith's concern for such questions creates a twin track upon which the train of theology runs.

Remember, it is faith's confidence that God has redeemingly disclosed himself in Jesus Christ. This event is taken by Christians as giving intelligibility to all other events, as being the key to those questions: Who is God?, What in the world is happening to me?, and What is the right thing to do? Faith's laying hold on the reality of this revelation turns its reckoning with these questions into an unending quest *in knowledge*. Theology aims to delineate this intelligibility, and to reckon rationally with this knowledge as both truth and mystery. It does so as service to God who is the object of faith; and it does it in a dialectic of conviction and openness that is always more but never less than rational.

In his *Radical Monotheism and Western Culture,* H. R. Niebuhr has reminded us of the role of the reason in the exercise of faith itself. He writes,

> Reason and faith are not exclusive of each other; reasoning is present in believing and one task of theology is to develop such reasoning in faith. . . . The second task for which theology, or part of it, is responsible is the criticism of faith, not as a subjective attitude or activity only but in relation to its objects. . . . Thus theology as disciplined development of the reasoning that permeates faith and as critique of faith must always participate in the activity of faith, though its ultimate concern is with God.[9]

The function of *imagination* in the doing of theology would seem to be as basic as that of reason. We do not see with our eyes, nor do we understand with our brains. We do both with our minds, which eyes and

---

[8]My reflections here are prompted by the reading of J. M. Kitigawa, "Primitive, Classical, and Modern Religions: A Perspective on Understanding the History of Religions," in J. M. Kitigawa, ed., *The History of Religions, Essays on the Problem of Understanding,* vol. 1 of J. C. Brauer, gen. ed., *Essays in Divinity* (Chicago: University of Chicago Press, 1967) 58.

[9](New York: Harper and Brothers, 1960) 13-15.

brains serve as physical organs. We see *through* our eyes, not with them. The mind we look *with* actively participates in the vision of what is seen. It brings something to the picture. Its power to image reality is surely one of its highest functions.

Lucy, Linus, and Charlie Brown might illustrate this for us, as they did in relation to another point in a recent sermon by my pastor.

They were lying on a little hilltop looking at the sky. Lucy, as you would know, is chairing the meeting. She is saying, "If you use your imagination, you can see lots of things in the cloud formations. . . . What do you think you see, Linus?" "Well," he says, "those clouds up there look to me like the map of the British Honduras on the Caribbean. That cloud up there looks a little like the profile of Thomas Eakins, the famous painter and sculptor . . . and that group of clouds over there gives me the impression of the stoning of Stephen. . . . I can see the apostle Paul standing there to one side." Lucy answers, "Uh huh . . . that's very good. . . . What do *you* see in the clouds, Charlie Brown?" Charlie Brown answers, "Well, I was going to say I saw a ducky and a horsie, but I changed my mind."

If theology requires Charlie Brown's purity of heart, it needs, almost as urgently, the imagination of Linus.

Reason and imagination combined, however, cannot cope fully with theology's ends, for theology itself is outmanned by its own 'object'. It can never have the last word. Like the long finger of John the Baptist in Grünewald's painting, theology can only point in the direction of the last Word. Grünewald's problem, embodied in the figure of John the Baptist, was posed by the intersection of the historical by the transcendent. In that painting, John the Baptist is pointing to a man with a name and address, Jesus of Nazareth; but he is also pointing to "the Lamb of God who takes away the sin of the world."

This is heavy mystery, and theology cannot fairly avoid it. Furthermore, even with the best reason and imagination in the world, this mystery could never be fully resolved. Quite apart from the divine mystery as a fact, any resolution of the mystery, through reason and imagination, is forestalled from our side by two other facts, one linguistic in character and the other historical.

The *linguistic* fact is that all levels of human discourse, especially the higher, are affected by a built-in component of ambiguity. It also appears that this is a scientific fact: the component of ambiguity emerges from an organic element. The *historical* fact is that history itself can give no historical accounting of the beginning that determines its meaning, nor of the end in which that meaning is finally disclosed. History carries an irreducible element of eschatology. Let me now try to illustrate these two rather simple ideas.

My comments on the first fact, the linguistic, derive from Huston Smith's *Forgotten Truth* and also from a use made there of Lewis Thomas's book, *The Lives of a Cell*. We shall come to that tricky little cell in a moment. The next two paragraphs depend wholly on these two books.

The linguistic problem is the observable fact that a built-in component of ambiguity appears in the highest levels of linguistic communication. This is true, for example, of words—which are symbols, as it is not true with numbers—which are signs. Numbers are completely unambiguous. As Huston Smith says, "4 is 4 and that is the end of the matter." This absence of ambiguity is why, in quantitative matters, scientific precision is achievable in uncanny degree. In qualitative matters, however, multivalent words do work that is beyond the capacity of monovalent numbers. For words are symbols, "and therefore by their very nature equivocal; their ambiguity can be reduced but never eliminated." Despite this fact, word symbols make connection with and throw light upon the higher reaches of the human spirit as numbers never can. "Poems cannot be composed in numbers."[10]

In *The Lives of a Cell*, Lewis Thomas is writing of ambiguity as the property that distinguishes language from other modes of biological communication. He writes, "Ambiguity seems to be an essential, indispensable element for the transfer of information from one place to another by words, where matters of real importance are concerned. It is often necessary, for meaning to come through, that there be an almost vague sense of strangeness and askewness. Speechless animals and cells cannot do this. . . . Only the human mind is designed to work in this way, programmed to drift away in the presence of locked-on information, straying from each point in a hunt for a better, different point." The truth of this fact will bear upon ideas found in a later part of this chapter.

---

[10]Cf. Huston Smith, *Forgotten Truth* (New York: Harper Colophon Books, 1976) 13-14. Cf. Lewis Thomas, *The Lives of a Cell* (Toronto: Bantam Books, 1974) 111. It seems to me that this point would remain largely unaffected were it determined that the element of ambiguity arose from an other than organic source.

For the moment, it is enough to notice that this scientific fact illumines what we have said of language's incapacity to speak univocally of the transcendent. It was likely also the unstated fact weighing upon T. S. Eliot's persistent consciousness of the limits of language, and upon Flannery O'Connor's habit of skewing or distorting her characters in the interest of disclosing their reality more clearly. Finite speech can, with some ambiguity, indicate or depict the infinite meaning; it cannot contain it. As Eliot himself puts it in the fifth canto of "Burnt Norton":

> Words strain,
> Crack and sometimes break under the burden,
> Under the tension, slip, slide, perish,
> Decay with imprecision, will not stay in place,
> Will not stay still.[11]

The *historical* fact, preventing the resolution of the mystery posed by the interpenetration of the historical by the transcendent, can be simply put: The historical can no more explain itself than it can account for the transcendent. The historical—as the instrument of interpretation—is commingled with the subject to be interpreted. There is no *mere* history. All historians participate in the history that we would study, and all history has been infected by the transcendent which is history's source and end. This is why, as I said, history carries an irreducible element of eschatology: as history, it can reckon neither its beginning nor its end. The meaning of history lies beyond history itself; it is one dimension of "the rule of God." History runs, as Tillich said, "toward the realization of the kingdom of God through and above history."[12] This faith is eschatological in the sense both that history itself, as a form of the divine activity, is never finished until it is ended; and because, for the finite mind, the ambiguities of history—as Reinhold Niebuhr used to remind us—can be conceived only in mythic and symbolic speech.[13]

---

[11]T. S. Eliot, "Burnt Norton" in *The Complete Poems and Plays, 1909-1950* (New York, Harcourt, Brace & World, 1962) 121. I am applying Eliot's words to a point that, in "Burnt Norton," he was not making.

[12]Paul Tillich, "Missions and World History," in Gerald H. Anderson, ed., *The Theology of the Christian Mission* (New York: McGraw-Hill Book Company, 1961) 281.

[13]Reinhold Niebuhr, *Faith and History* (New York: Scribner's, 1949) 125-26.

This forward thrust of the early Christian perception of life in the world and of its outcome in the Kingdom of God is a form neither of utopianism nor of futurism. The future, as related to what God shall bring to pass, is understood from faith's perceptions of what God has done and is now doing. Faith's concern is with God himself, and with the future only as with how God will bring to fulfillment the work of his hands. This forward thrust, therefore, moves towards neither the absent nor the unknown. It is a species of neither historical speculation nor religious curiosity. Faith simply confesses God as present and known through his gracious self-disclosure. Because God will continue to be who he is, the future is—in that sense only—predictable.

These remarks on history and language have been made as an aid to understanding why the mystery cannot be resolved. Perhaps they may also serve to remind that the continuance of the mystery is due to no failure of either reason or imagination. We fail the truth less because, with Wittgenstein, we can think only within the forms of prejudice-burdened language, and much more, as Kierkegaard knew, because we lack "purity of heart." And beyond all this—as Luther rightly saw and taught—God is simultaneously both revealed and hidden. God himself is the known but never comprehended Mystery, and only so may we reckon with him at all.

If such truths be taken now as the conclusion of reflections upon language and history, they may, perhaps, be taken also as a point of departure for understanding and appreciating religious diversity. For just as all languages combined could not tell God's story, neither could all religions together comprehend his mystery. As we turn to a consideration of this massive fact, the role of theology may appear with enhanced significance; it may, as well, require a refocusing of its powers to correspond to the realities of this present time.

The refocus, in theological study, seems already to have begun. It appears to signal a shift from those administrative and quasi-professional roles made prominent in theological curricula following World War II. It appears to be moving in the direction of contemporary reexamination of the data and the concerns that are central to Christian faith.

In 1982, for example, Vanderbilt issued a brochure titled "Questioning an Axiom: The New Program for the Education of Ministers at Vanderbilt Divinity School." The guiding concept behind this newly proposed plan of ministerial education came to expression in the phrase "the minister as theologian." The word "theologian" is not used there in a narrowly technical or specialized sense but in a general and, in many ways, a more traditional sense. Theology, they write, "names neither a set of doctrines nor a scholarly discipline, but the understanding, knowledge, and thinking distinctive to the Christian faith. Theology occurs when faithful people self-consciously and reflectively begin to understand the statements and symbols of faith and how they bear upon the world." This refocus, chiefly with the American scene in mind, could also find fruitful use in Christian approaches to non-Christian traditions. In our present world, faithful people must begin deliberately to reflect on the statements and symbols of *everybody's* faith.

The words of the brochure may serve to relieve a certain imbalance of emphasis, traceable in the generation now ending, on the minister as "professional." Implementation of the words should serve also as a timely antidote to parochialism in theology. Carried into the discussion of the topics of this book, such a theology should concern itself faithfully, reflectively, and openly, with such questions as, What—in our pluralistic world—does it mean to take God seriously as only, as one, and as living?, Who is my neighbor/brother?, What is the worth to God of this neighbor's inherited faith?, What does it means to witness? These questions are addressed, directly or implicitly, in what follows.

Everything said to this point seems to me to be straightforward and easily understood. Surcly, in my somewhat individualistic depiction of the nature of theology, nothing startling or even untraditional appears. The problems begin now to get stickier, not really because they are more difficult than what has preceded but because the terrain is less familiar. This will likely come into view as we begin, first, to recognize the fact of the plurality of religions as a problem for Christian (and other) theology, and when we attempt, next, to deal with the important matter (for Christians and others) of mission. Discussion of the former will lean a little more to the theoretical, of the latter a bit more to the practical.

2. THEOLOGY, FAITH, AND RELIGION

It already has been emphasized that theology concerns itself with both revelation and faith. That is, it attempts to illumine the meaning both of God's self-disclosure and of our human response. Theology does this in terms of all life's tenses, the past and present and also future. This is because it is the nature of revelation to be true, and germane in its truth, for all time and for all peoples. Revelation speaks in the name of God who was and is and is to come. In similar fashion, it addresses itself to all cultures and all patterns of language and thought.

Just as New Testament truth was formulated, for example, in the context of Hellenistic and Palestinian Judaism, of Graeco-Roman culture, and Oriental Mysteries, so that same truth can be restated—as both true and germane—in a secular society, or in the midst of the religions of the world. Here, attention is being directed only to the fact (and, for Christian thought, to the problem) of the plurality of religions.

The real problem is knowing what is the Christian word both to the world as a whole, and in relation to any given situation. This is more than a merely historical or academic problem.

We do not live in the Graeco-Roman world, or in the first century. Neither could the first Christians leave us a transcendent or absolute language—a language that perhaps could indeed have been called "God-talk." What they did give us, in a Bible both written by men and efficaciously inspired of God, was their testimony that the Christian word—the truth of God that both redeems and abides—is the Cross. The cross is the revelation of filial relation to God, expressed at absolute pitch as both trust and obedience. In this total self-giving of the Son, the Father himself is present, reconciling the world to himself and accepting his wayward children as his sons and daughters. This does not mean that all biblical images used in exposition of this truth must be lifted out of their time and context and taken literally in our own. It does not mean that to recite these biblical verses is the same as to communicate the gospel. What it does seem to mean—perhaps you will agree—is that the realities of filial trust and obedience must, and do, have centrality in any faith that would show continuity with the biblical witness.

This filial obedience becomes also the touchstone of a Christian approach to understanding other religion and religions. This sentence could well be underscored, for the humble spirit of such obedient trustfulness towards God will condition and shape our approach to others who differ from us, and will as well shape the answers to the questions that arise from contacts across religious lines. If the God of all is truly revealed in Jesus Christ, surely the revelation opens—rather than shuts—the door to a humble entry into the life and faith of others.

Neither the need for, nor the practice of, a cross-cultural interchange is foreign to the Bible. The Bible is in all essential respects an inspired report, from Israel and from the early Church, of divine revelation received in faith. In no way does this alter the other fact that, on the simplest level of description, the Bible represents a theological response—both positive and negative—to the cultural overspill of the ancient Middle East. Echoes, as well as substantive remains, of Mesopotamian, Egyptian, Canaanite-Phoenician, Persian, Hellenistic, and Roman origin are traceable in the Bible. Hebrew, Jew, Jewish-Christian, and Gentile-Christian have left their characteristic impress upon it.

Perhaps the crucial example, in the New Testament, of the reinterpretation of God's Word as gospel when carried into new contexts, is provided by the apostle Paul. No passage provides a better specimen of this process than Romans 1-3, of which we first give a running paraphrase.

a. The case of Paul in Romans 1-3

The apostle defines himself, in his new context, as serving the same gospel that the tradition of Israel had anticipated (1:1-2). He has complete confidence in this gospel as God's power for both Jew and Gentile—a power of salvation to everyone who is doing faith (1:16). This salvation is a being put right with God through confident trust towards him. It rests from beginning to end on faith, which is both the access to and the strength of our relationship with God (1:17).

The divine 'wrath' against the ungodliness and wickedness of men who suppress the truth (1:18) reflects, it would seem, the radical seriousness of God's will to save and his irrevocable opposition to sin as enemy of the human family. It bespeaks God's relation to unfaith, whether in religious or nonreligious form (1:19). Unfaith is inexcusable because knowledge of God's nature and power are clearly perceived from the creation (1:20). Human sins are thus signs both of the refusal of an accessible knowledge of God and of an erosion of the sinner's own integrity. These sins run the gamut from pride, ingratitude and idolatry, through sexual degeneracy, to violence and moral folly (1:21-32). There is standing ground for neither Jew nor Greek except on the integrity of his own performance before and unto God: God renders to each, not according to his religious or cultural heritage, his cultic acts or orthodoxy, but according to what each has *done*—"to every man according to his works" (2:6). God gives eternal life to both Jew and Greek who, by patience in doing good, seek glory, honor, and immortal life (2:7). To both Jew and Greek who obey not the truth, but obey wickedness, comes wrath (2:8), for there is no partiality in God (2:11).

Both groups then, regardless of heritage or affiliation, are in essentially the same condition (2:12-13), with Jews being judged not by the hearing of the Law but by the *faithful* doing of what it commands (2:13), and with Gentiles being judged by the measure of their *faithful* obedience to conscience, as a law written on their hearts (2:14-15). A final assize will disclose, for both, who has or has not truly kept the Law or obeyed the conscience (2:16).

The most distinctive mark of Israel's covenant, circumcision, is efficacious only if the law is faithfully obeyed (2:25), a true Jew being one on the inside—one who is circumcised in heart (2:29). Jews are in no better (and certainly in no worse) condition than Gentiles (3:9). *Outward* religion must truly reflect an *inner* love and obedience. In this sense no one is put into right relationship with God (is "justified") simply by doing outwardly what the Law of Moses or the law of conscience requires (3:20). Whoever is put right is put right without distinction to his being Jew or Greek, that is, without regard to his cultural heritage or his religious affiliation, on the basis of "the righteousness of God through faith of Jesus Christ unto all who have faith" (3:22).

These famous words have been subject to serious misuse from both sides of their meaning. They have been viewed as exempting ethical behavior from any essential role in that living faith that saves. The words have also been taken to mean that "believing" is the same as holding certain views or notions about Jesus, or the gospel, or the Bible, or the Mass, or apostolic succession, or justification by faith. This will not do.

Look at the words again: "the righteousness of God through faith of Jesus Christ for all who are doing faith." Let us first clarify "righteousness" and "faith" as theological terms, before attempting to illumine the apostle's meaning by examination of his grammar.

The righteousness of God (δικαιοσύνη) is more than a divine attribute or abstract quality of character. His righteousness is something God has done, is doing and shall do. It is a fundamental activity in which God, as who he actually is, unremittingly engages himself with the world. He does this in the vindication of right over wrong, of truth over lying and duplicity, of grace over sin—especially as this is seen in the free forgiveness (the "justification") of the sinner. This justification is both disclosed and effected in the faithfulness of Christ's obedience in the death of the cross. God's character pours into this activity and defines its quality. To be related to God's grace is thus to be brought into association with the righteous character and purpose out of which grace flows. It is this character and this purpose that we meet in the cross of Christ.

"The righteousness of God through faith in Jesus Christ" (διὰ πίστεως 'Ιησοῦ Χριστοῦ). What are we to make of the phrase, "through faith in Jesus Christ," as the RSV has it? First, the word 'faith'. Faith, here in Romans, is the recognition of utter dependence upon God for the realization of life's true end and ends, so that he who has faith gives himself to God in a loyalty that matches the dependence. Thought, feeling and will—the whole of the moral person—are involved. In the Bible, faith is never simply a predicate of the God-idea. God is not a symbol for the gaps in our information, nor a name we give to our desire to escape death. He is not a religious proposition whose authenticity it is our privilege to deny or affirm. God is he with whom we have to do, whether we have found him credible or not. Faith in God, therefore, is not the adoption of a convincing hypothesis about the superhuman. Nor is it the same as holding good ideas about God because they inspire courage or promise comfort. Faith in God means that we who have sought the True and the Good have in fact been found by him, have, through forgiveness, been put into right relation with him.

The apostle says that the point of intersection between God and the human family—the point where the human quest for God in spirit and in truth has been met by God's saving activity—is "faith of Jesus Christ" (or, perhaps, "that faith which was in Jesus Christ"). In 3:22, no definite article qualifies the word "faith," and no preposition precedes "Jesus Christ." To read the phrase "faith of Jesus Christ" as a subjective genitive—the "Jesus Christ kind of faith," or "faith of the sort which characterized Jesus Christ"—seems, in this verse, to comport best with the absence of the preposition and of the article. In that "Jesus-Christ-faith," God's righteousness (his saving activity) is effected and effective in all who are having faith (εἰς πάντας τοὺς πιστεύοντος), for there is no distinction. The primary emphasis in the phrase "faith of Jesus Christ" should fall, then, not upon the way *we* believingly respond to Christ, but upon the way in which *he* faithfully embodied and communicated the divine 'righteousness'—the way in which, through his faithful life and death, God's saving acts effect the free forgiveness of the guilty. In this reading, the phrase is seen as referring not so much to faith from our side towards Christ, as to faithfulness from Christ's side towards God. This reading of the text also allows the following words "in all who have faith" to be meaningful, where, on the other reading, they would appear completely redundant.

This rendering seems further confirmed at verse 26 where God is giving proof, through Christ Jesus as a propitiation or mercy seat (ἱλαστήριον) both that God is righteous and that he makes (or reckons) righteous the one who is of the faith of Jesus, or "the one who is of the Jesussort of faith" (τὸν ἐκ πίστεως Ἰησοῦ).

The reluctance of commentators to reckon "faith of Jesus Christ" as a subjective genitive is related, perhaps, to the feeling that such a rendering weakens the Christian sense of the essentiality of Christ's death for our salvation, or that it implies a reduction of our dependence upon and obligation to him as sovereign Lord. Were this verse (3:22) the whole of what the New Testament has to say of these matters, my proposed treatment of it would indeed leave this question moot. But Romans 3:22 is not the whole New Testament. Indeed, it is not the whole Epistle to the Romans. The New Testament, including Romans, rings with the confession that Jesus Christ is Lord. Except for such faith there would have been no New Testament at all. The question in Romans 3:22, however, is not whether the New Testament celebrates Jesus Christ as Lord; it is, What is the apostle actually saying in this particular passage?

What Paul appears to be saying is that just as God's saving activity (his righteousness) is revealed in the uncomplicated trustfulness and filial obedience of the "Jesus-Christ-faith," so it is effective in *all* who are doing faith—in all in whom the Jesus-sort of trustful obedience is present. This is faith, not as agreeing with some idea as to the meaning of Jesus' life or death, but as participating in the transcendent powers that his death both disclosed and unleashed.

It is unfortunate that the English noun 'faith' has no corresponding verb. We switch, in the verb, to 'believe'. This is unfortunate because, whatever may have been the original strength of the verb 'believe', it has come to imply, chiefly, the cherishing of a point of view or the holding of an opinion. Believing something to be 'a truth', or holding that it is a 'correct idea', was not originally and should not now be regarded as the meaning of 'believing' God. One "believes" God, or Jesus Christ, or the gospel—that is, one has faith or does faith—when he commits himself in kind to the faithful obedience of Jesus Christ.

This is why the gospel is a universal good. God is one and God is love; his righteousness in Jesus Christ is done on behalf of all. Jesus Christ's faithfulness, as human person, to the radical claim of that righteousness discloses and makes effective the grace of forgiveness for all human persons who trust themselves to it in kind—that is, to all who take Jesus' way, even unto death, as their own way. This personal commitment, being both deeper and other than involvements with culture and religion, gives equal access to both Jew and Gentile, since there is no distinction. For, since God is one, "he will justify the circumcised on the ground of faith (ἐκ πίστεως) and the uncircumcised through faith (διὰ τῆς πίστεως, 3:30). Cultural diversity bows to the divine unity and saving righteousness.

Such an analysis of Romans 1-3 is simpler than the question of what we are to make of its meaning for ourselves. How his own interpretation of God's saving righteousness defines, and in a sense redefines, the place of the Law is of prime importance in Paul's understanding. He asks (3:31), "Do we then overthrow (καταργοῦμεν) the law by this faith? By no means. On the contrary, we uphold (ἱστάνομεν) the law."

In his interpretation of his own meaning, throughout Romans 3, Paul is using the word 'law' in two quite different ways. He is marking a decisive difference between 'law' as a universal principle on the one hand (which could be truly obeyed in spirit only); and on the other hand, 'law' as a list of precepts (capable of being outwardly observed). The former, made known through both creation and conscience, is the "truth" of the Law of Moses and brings accountability to both Jew and Gentile, for there is no distinction. The latter—law conceived as a set of moral and religious requirements—was, in Paul's view, the way the Law of Moses had come to be popularly regarded in Israel, and was seen as hindering access to God's Kingdom for Jew and Gentile alike. He is in no way saying that divine revelation is absent from the Torah, or that Torah is only external in character, or that when one has faith he may cease to observe what Torah demands. Neither is Paul saying that radical obedience towards God is displaced by "believing" any one or any number of religious ideas. He is going behind religious forms and ideas to the moral and spiritual realities that underlie and give proper meaning to both Law and conscience. His principle does involve marking a distinction between the truth of the Law and the forms through which, in any setting, it may be expressed. It also includes a distinction between an outward or formal obedience and an obedience from the heart.

This, as I see it, is a principle of interpretation whose importance, for Paul, could not be overstated. So, as Jews, we do not trust covenant religion or legal observances; we trust God. We do not, as Gentiles, trust the impulses of our own innerness or the forms of our religion; we trust God. Faith, in either case, has to do with God in a more primary sense than it has to do with either religion or conscience. The apostle is certain that, in such faith, the Law is vindicated and given its proper due. Neither Law nor conscience is an enemy of or a substitute for faith; both summon to faith. "We do not put the law at naught, we rather establish it" (3:31).

Now these words deserve attention not only for Paul's sake but as well for ours. Is faithfulness to the text, in this case, simply to agree with Paul's understanding of the place of the Law in first century synagogue and Church? Or do we touch here upon something compelling in relation to our own time and calling?

Let us ask further questions. Should we not attempt in our time and place to reckon with Paul's vision in terms of our own faith and experience? Would this, or would it not, require *us* to mark the same distinction between knowledge of God through faith in Jesus Christ and a formal adherence to the Christian religion, which *the apostle* marked between being put right with God and a formal inclusion in the covenant? Just as there was for Paul the question of who is a real "Jew," so is there, for the contemporary Church, the question of who is a real "Christian." Paul saw that there were Jews who, at heart, were not "Jews"; and, more radically, that there were non-Jews who were—namely, Gentiles, who, through conscience, had obeyed the spirit of the Law and shown themselves "true Jews." Fidelity to the text, both here in Romans 3 and Romans 9:6-13, would seem to require, in our present context, that we recognize that there are Christians who are not "Christian," and that there are non-Christians who are (people of all religions and of no religion, who in trusting spirit and deeds of love are related to God as he was savingly revealed in the faith of Christ—people who walk in the Christ-way). For, if this Pauline vision suggests, in some, a religious form from which the reality is absent, so does it suggest, in others, a religious reality for which no "approved" form is present.

Does not this expand and open the gospel to all persons, for our time, as Paul expanded and opened the *truth* of the Law for his? And rather than to deny either Law or Gospel, is this not to allow to both a universal applicability? In such way, "we do not put the Law or the Gospel at naught, we rather establish it" as God's Word to all. This would be both an intensification of the meaning and virtue of the "faith of Jesus Christ" (as in

3:22) as historic act and fact, and also a universalizing of the access into that faith's reality and effects.

Such faith, as fact, belongs preeminently to Jesus as the Christ, the pioneer and perfecter of faith (Heb. 12:2). It properly belongs also to the inmost need and longing of every person by virtue of his creation by God in Christ. To exclude any person from his heritage as a child of God, *on the basis of his cultural or religious identity* (rather than on the basis of his relation to the truth of law or conscience), is to repudiate the law of creation and hold down the truth (see Rom. 1:18-20). Christian faith finds knowledge of God's eternal nature in the historical 'event' of Jesus Christ. In relation to the meaning of this event, Christians define the spiritual opportunity and the moral accountability of all, whether Jew or Gentile, Oriental or Occidental, male or female, white or black, rich or poor—yes, Christian or non-Christian.

This kind of faith may no more be separated from ethical responsibility in the world than it may be identified with any organized religion—including our own. In creation and in Christ all neighbors are actually brothers and sisters. Nothing human is alien to ourselves, nor is it of indifference to God.

We should now have before us the possibility of thinking realistically about religious traditions other than our own. I propose that we do this by stating briefly the relationship of faith to religion, and then the claim of our neighbor/brother upon our religious understanding—not simply upon our Christian charity, but upon our understanding of Christian faith itself.

6. Faith in relation to religion

The relation of revelation to faith and of faith to revelation has already occupied us through the earlier chapters. Revelation and faith are distinguishable; they are not separable. Revelation needs faith for its communication; faith depends on revelation for its very existence. Now, we ask, "What is the relationship of faith to *religion?* Let us approach the question by making a sort of initial circuit around the subject.

Faith is true faith because it participates truly—that is, creatively and redemptively—in truth. True faith is a form of knowledge, but it is not true faith because it has a corner on the truth. Faith also knows more than it comprehends. This is why, on one side, it is inseparable from the religious and theological forms that express it, and why, on the other, it does not correspond fully with them. For this reason, doctrine must be neither devalued nor absolutized.

Faith, as the way of doing one's life, may be intimately related, for example, to one's view of the person of Jesus Christ, to the meaning of tradition, or to the virtue of cultic forms. All these have played important roles in the history of faith. But faith does not exist in order to declare a certain kind of Christology, or to provide sanctions, for example, for the truth or necessity of apostolic succession, or to provide a defense for, say, believer's baptism or the transubstantiation of the elements in the Mass. Faith is true only in terms of its derivation from the truth, its continuing association with the truth, its service of the truth. It exists because it has been called into existence by the truth—by its proper Object who is also its Source. Faith is dependent on this Source. It is drawn to this Light. The light and truth image themselves in the 'believing' mind (the trustfully responding mind). In such light faith sees light, that is, it participates truly in truth. Out of this participation a true, but always qualified and incomplete, understanding crystallizes: a true and new understanding of God, self, nature, history, life. One should suppose that the more fully all of these— God, self, nature, history, life—cohere in the new understanding, the stronger the argument for faith's authenticity.

Faith's reading of reality shows coherence or integrity, as well as authenticity. If the integrity is genuine the circle of its applicability is capable of infinite extension. The whole universe is not too large for true faith. Faith has integrity if its Source and Object—the Image which has evoked it—is high enough to be above all, inclusive enough to compass the whole human condition, and accessible enough to be claimed by all. Such a Source and Object could be described as transcendent, universal, and utterly gracious.

The Image that evoked the early Christian faith—the Image which made faith much more noticeably a power than an idea—had such marks. Christian believers saw in Jesus Christ, in his life and death, the dominion of God over evil and death. The last enemies of the human race were crushed under the power of his sinless obedience unto death. They further saw, in his commitment to our need even unto death, the embodiment of the Father's love for all. As true Son of the Father's love, he was also amongst us as one of our own kind, accessible to all. All this, and more, lay in the early Christian reading of the cross. It was their recognition, in the deep places of their being, of the *divine* reality; and we, at least partially, miss the point if we view this early Christian experience as being primarily a form either of orthodoxy or of pious zeal.

These people do not appear as excessively pious, eagerly seeking out new images of meaning with which to adorn either their enthusiasms or their longings for self-realization. Those *images* of life and death and transcendence, which so characterize the pages of the New Testament, were forced upon the faithful out of the awesome *realities* of life and death and transcendence that their faith had truly encountered. Those realities transcended speech; they nevertheless required depiction.

Here, in the living faith of those early Christians and in their struggle to express the ineffable, the *truth* of Jesus Christ took on concreteness. He mastered them; so they called him Lord. They said that in him the divine Word was made flesh. He was affirmed as unique Son. It was said that in him the fullness of deity was pleased to dwell. Later Christians said— as at Chalcedon in A. D. 451—he is "truly God and truly man; . . . consubstantial with the Father according to his Godhead, and consubstantial with us according to his manhood." That he is "acknowledged in two natures, inconfusedly, unchangeably, indivisibly, inseparably; the distinction of natures being by no means taken away by the union, but rather the property of each nature being preserved, and occurring in one Person and one subsistence, not parted or divided into two persons." [14]

Such words are impressive and moving. The *truth* of Jesus Christ, however, does not lie in *our* confession of his deity, our confession of the incarnation of the Word of God, or in any creedal statement that attempts to define the relation of the two natures in the one person. Neither do persons come into saving faith (that is, into the reality of Christian existence) by affirming these statements as 'beliefs'. Faith entails theology, but theology is not faith. These confessions of faith, whether in Bible or creed, are images—time-colored and culturally shaped—that struggle without complete success to express the ineffable. The effort had to be made, as in every generation it has to be made, with such images and language as are available for the job.

The dependability of these faith statements does not lie in their being expressed in an infallible language, nor does their power lie in favorable comparison with other confessions of faith. Their truth lies in the Reality,

---

[14]At Chalcedon, October 22, A.D. 451; from P. Schaff, *The Creeds of Christendom,* vol. 2, *Greek and Latin Creeds* (New York: Harper and Brothers, 1919) 62.

experienced by faith, that first called them forth. The maintenance and perpetuity of the truth of such statements does not lie in freezing them in time-colored phrases to which dogmatic authority is ascribed. Their truth is maintained and perpetuated in the renewal of the experience of that same reality that had called them forth in the first place—and in a like-faithful effort to share their truth anew in language and image appropriate to present experience of the Spirit of God. The real focus of any disquiet about this should fix on the fact that we are threatened less by change than by hardness of heart.

This process of reinterpretation, done properly, never severs itself from its roots, but neither does it deify them. It seeks with Paul not merely to repeat, and surely not to abolish the truth, but rather to express and establish it.

The truth of faith is grounded in a divine reality transcending time and culture; the perception of it is cumulative and subject to progressive validation. No divine revelation can be fully experienced or explained. This will justify my dropping in someone's observation (which I can no longer identify) that good theology must not only say something which in itself is substantive and coherent. "It must also give promise of the inexpressible. It is a pointer to something beyond, something more, something not yet having official sanction." Fear of what, as yet, has no official sanction is one form of unfaith.

Not only do these last-mentioned truths give warrant to the necessity for each generation to reexplore the meaning of its confessions in the light of its own time; it also makes possible, for each generation, the reexamination of the times in the light of its own confessions. There is a stable element in truth, for God is God every day. Everywhere he speaks his Word through his work. Nevertheless, human faith experiences this stable element in individual and social situations which are always changing. In this interaction of person and context, a critique of the times occasions an enlargement of the understanding of the confession and the reexamination of the confession directly reflects itself in the interpretation of the times. In this way one can say that the truth of revelation is both unchanging and emergent.

The truth of the divine revelation lies in its unchanging Source, not in historically shaped formulae nor in ecclesiastical assertions made about God and other persons. To take God seriously as God is to confess a fixed point of truth above all tides of time. To take God seriously as Living should lead us to expect that revelation itself would penetrate our time, shape our formulae, and be continuing.[15]

This discussion of the timeless and the timely is one form of the question of the relationship of faith and religion, or revelation and tradition, and I shall conclude my remarks upon it by referring to a saying of Jesus, by citing a quotation from Friedrich Schleiermacher, and by examining a word made prominent in the early thought of Karl Barth.

Jesus told us that one does not put new wine into old wineskins (Mt. 9:17). He did not mention the fact that, were there need to do so, old wine could be safely kept in new wineskins. Jesus is talking about the relation of old and new, form and substance, in the knowledge of truth. *New truth cannot be carried in old forms; old truth can be carried in new forms.* The right care of both the new wine and the old wine is important, and a primary task of theology—Friedrich Schleiermacher thought it was of the essence—is how to manage this fact.

The wine-and-wineskin image comes from Jesus through the gospel tradition. Schleiermacher also is talking of the relationship of the truth to the language that carries it, but the metaphor is different. Each age has its own distinctive statements of truth—each is distinguished, as Schleiermacher puts it, by the '*letter*' (that is, by the right word, in the right place, at the right time), "and it is the masterwork of the highest human wisdom to assess correctly when human conditions require a new letter. For if it appears too early, then it is rejected by the still prevailing love for that which it was to have supplanted. If it formulates itself too late, then a fraudulence will have already set in which it can no longer exorcize."[16] A spiritual mind concerns itself for truth both as substance and as timely expression. It will not locate sanctity in age as such, nor will it take pride in its own timeliness. It will search for the truth alone, and for ever new ways to give it voice. It will ask both as to the actual text and of what the Biblical story is

---

[15]My earliest memory of encounter with this idea is from student days and the reading of Archbishop Söderblom's Gifford Lectures for 1931, *The Living God* (Boston: Beacon Press, 1962). Archbishop Brilioth's preface to this edition should also be read.

[16]Friedrich Schleiermacher, *On Religion: Speeches to Its Cultured Despisers,* trans. John Oman (New York: Harper and Row, 1958) 144. This quote is taken, however, from the translation of Albert L. Blackwell, as found in *Schleiermacher's Early Philosophy of Life: Determinism, Freedom and Phantasy,* Harvard Theological Studies, no. 33 (Chico CA: Scholars Press, 1982) 211.

saying in and to actual communities of faith who are responding to it. A theology setting out with a determination to be Catholic or Protestant, conservative or orthodox, modern or traditional, has already ascribed a secondary place to truth.

Schleiermacher's metaphor of a new "letter" (*Buchstab*) was employed in the interest of marking the continuity of the new with the old, and was proposed as a means necessary for preventing the expiration of the life of the spirit in language that had already died. He was essentially pastoral in this concern; he helps us to deal more clearly with the problem of communicating the gospel.

By discussion of a word made prominent in the early theological work of Karl Barth, I hope to illumine the line of the *partial* continuity of faith with religion, exposing one side of a truth that Barth himself may not have seen. The focus here is not upon the enhancing of the communication of the gospel (as in Schleiermacher); the focus in Barth is upon the more fundamental question of *how to understand the relation of revelation to religion itself.* It is one side of Barth's own way of dealing with the old question of "natural and revealed religion."

The Barth of the late 1920s and following saw only radical discontinuity between 'faith' and 'religion'.[17] In this, he is in some sense successor to the Hebrew prophets. He knew there is nothing good about religion as such. A "true religion" is as impossible to find as a flawless man. Whatever may be the proper role of religion in human life and society, in practice it is shot through with egocentricity, self-seeking and injustice. Its deeds of heroism are countered by baseness and moral duplicity. Fanaticism and hypocrisy, knowingly and unknowingly, parade as commitment and faith. Barth knew, like the prophets, that the human need was not to be more religious. Bad religion was destroying Israel in time of the prophets. In Barth's own time, bad religion, with so-called 'Christian' sanctions, was helping to create the Jewish holocaust. The human condition could not be saved by religion. No religion, in itself and as such, is true. Religion, as practiced in human society, since it acts as an instrument of self-justification or even as a device for avoiding God, should be viewed as "unfaith" (*Unglaube*). Religion—including Christian religion—must receive grace to be acceptable to God.

---

[17]Cf. *Church Dogmatics,* I.ii.297-325.

Barth had seen, as had Karl Marx a generation earlier, the complicity of religion with social injustices and with human exploitation at the hands of the status quo. Friedrich Nietzsche had realized, as Karl Marx did not, that the problem of religion is, in its basic character, theological more than sociological. Nietzsche reckoned religion's 'doing of good' in whatever forms, as, at base, a panic-stricken determination not to ask the question, What is the meaning of my life? Nietzsche managed the matter as an atheist. Barth had determined to deal with it from the perspective of faith. Nietzsche saw the abolition of religion because God was dead; Barth because he is alive.[18] These would appear still to be the realistic options.

All of this throws light on Barth's designation of religion as "Unfaith," as well as upon his assertion that revelation is the 'abolition' (the *Aufhebung*) of religion. It is possible that, with Barth's own remarkable word *Aufhebung,* we can move beyond his negative estimation of religion without losing its critical value.

The verb *aufheben* means, in its strictest sense, to 'lift up,' as in raising one's arm, or lifting a weight, or raising one's eyes. The word can also mean to 'keep' or 'preserve', though this appears to be a less common usage. To say *die Papiere sind gut aufgehoben* means not that the papers have been thoroughly destroyed, but safely kept. In a kind of metaphorical sense the verb is also used to mean 'raising', as in the raising of a siege or of a prohibition, that is, in bringing them to an end or terminating them. From this comes the meaning "abolish," in the sense that one might abolish a rule, annul a marriage, abrogate a decree, dissolve an assembly, or cancel a contract.

Aufheben thus may mean both 'to preserve' and 'to abolish'. Metaphorically, it can also mean 'to raise to a higher level', as, for example, in the sense of a Hegelian synthesis. This is the use found also in the seventh of Rilke's *Duino Elegies*. In the Elegies, which Erich Heller has called a "gnostic apocalypse," Rilke appears to say that the whole visible world is *aufgehoben*. It is *aufgehoben* (abolished), but it is not lost. It is transubstantiated by passing into the invisibility of true inwardness; "its most visible joy shows itself to us only when we transmute it, within [*wenn wir es innen verwandeln*]". The reality of the whole visible world is seen in terms

---

[18]See especially *Church Dogmatics*, I.ii.325-61. See also Erich Heller, *The Artist's Journey into the Interior and Other Essays* (New York: Vintage Books [Random House], 1968) 181-82.

of an inward perception or experience [*Nirgends, Geliebte, wird Welt sein als innen*]."[19]

When Karl Barth spoke of the *Aufhebung* of religion, he was not, like Rilke, talking about a certain style of spirituality—a way of appreciating and perceiving the world from the perspective of one's own innerness. He was recognizing the truth which W. C. Smith was later to point out, that, viewed "objectively," that is, externally, Christianity "can appear human, corrupt and absurd."[20] In this angle of vision Barth maintained that all "religion" including "Christianity" stands condemned. Revelation is the abolition of religion.

Barth never changed his mind regarding "natural theology," nor about revelation as the *Aufhebung* of religion. He had seen early and clearly that one does not say "God" by pronouncing the word "man" more loudly. He had recognized the prideful urges and self-deceptions by which, through religion, we beguile and stultify ourselves. Revelation, known in faith, is the "abolition" of religion: religion, like all other human urges and acts, stands under the judgment of truth. If, however, there was no "change of mind," there was, I believe, a shift of emphasis—an admission to discussion of issues earlier subordinated.[21]

---

[19]Rainer Maria Rilke, *Duineser Elegien—Die Sonette Orpheus,* ed. Katharine Kippenberg (Zurich, Manesse Verlag, 1951) 39 (this is from the Seventh Elegy). There is an English translation by David Young, *Duino Elegies* (New York and London, W. W. Norton and Co., 1978) 65; See also the Ninth Elegy of his translation, 83-84. Cf. also Heller, *The Artist's Journey,* 101-70, esp. 158-70. Cf. further John B. Carman's "Religion as a Problem for Christian Theology," in Donald G. Dawe and John B. Carman, eds., *Christian Faith in a Religiously Plural World* (Maryknoll NY: Orbis Books, 1978) 83-92; discussion pertinent to this same subject continues on pages 93-103, chiefly in relation to W. C. Smith's *The Meaning and End of Religion* (New York: Macmillan, 1963).

[20]W. C. Smith, *Towards a World Theology* (Philadelphia: Westminster Press, 1981) 100.

[21]That there was no substantive change of mind on these matters appears in Barth's steady continuance on the Christological line in his treatment of Providence as associated with *faith in God,* and not with a worldview or philosophy of history (in *Dogmatics* III); his insistence (in *Dogmatics* IV) that in any discussion of the *pro nobis,* the *in nobis,* and the *extra nos* of God's saving action, the *extra nos* must be most tenaciously maintained; his comments (in a letter to the pope) on the encyclical *Lumen Gentium,* that, according to his understanding of the Bi-

Perhaps *my* argument really changes the meaning of "religion" as Barth used the word. But I think not—at least not wholly. God must indeed forgive us our religion; but our religion is *a part of who and what we are,* and it is precisely this "who and what we are" whom God is redeeming and remaking. Our religion is accepted too—along with ourselves.

For does not religion, like all of life, stand under the divine promise as well as under the divine judgment? Are we not *simul justi et peccatores*? May not revelation/faith preserve religion by transformation, not simply tinkering with its frailties, but raising it to a higher level of meaning—converting its actuality into its potential and its potential into living truth? I believe that it can, that it does.

Clearly, theology is not, in the first instance, a report on the state and meaning of religion and religions. It is concerned for revelation and faith, disclosure and response. But if theology is concerned with revelation and faith it is, so to say willy-nilly, concerned for religion. For theology, religion, and faith interact: theology is the shape that faith takes when seeking understanding, and faith expresses itself, among other ways, in religion.

Religion then—we should be ready to admit—is not an intrinsic good. Too often it is a form in which, with religious language, we reveal

---

ble, neither the natural law nor the conscience could be considered as a *source* of revelation (a position cautiously approved by Cardinal Cicognani in the reply made on behalf of the supreme pontiff).

That there was a shift of emphasis, or an admission to discussion of issues earlier subordinated, is suggested by the fact (even in his discussion of the ethics of reconciliation, *Dogmatics* IV) that, despite his rejection of natural theology, he affirms that God is known (objectively, as well as subjectively) to the "world," and (in his discussion of the second commandment) commends the "struggle for human righteousness." Further, in stressing to the Roman pontiff (and Cardinal Cicognani) that there is a fundamental distinction between the revelation of God on the one side and the realm of nature and conscience on the other, Barth does agree that nature and conscience *co-determine* the form in which revelation is attested to us. This last point appears in a letter written just two weeks before Barth's death.

The reader could find guidance also for the pursuit of these matters by looking into Eberhard Busch, *Karl Barth, His Life from Letters and Autobiographical Texts* (Philadelphia: Fortress Press, 1976) 364, 445, passim; and in Jürgen Fangmeier and Hinrich Stoevesandt, eds., *Karl Barth, Letters 1961–1968* (Grand Rapids: Eerdmans, 1981) 357, 334, passim.

our secular values; and, in our invocations of God's name, manifest an interest chiefly in ourselves. But he to whom invocation is made is neither idle nor indifferent. He also knows our frame and remembers that we are dust (Ps. 103:14). Our self-estimations are distorted, but he moves to correct them. His presence and love serve to correct and rehabilitate even our imperfect expectations of him. Our self-seeking, our efforts at self-justification, are rebuked in the vision of one who for our sakes reckoned not equality with God a thing to be grasped, but emptied himself (Phil. 2:7). Repentance, not primarily as remorse for sin, but as exposure of the self to the divine grace and to the new creation before us, is as possible and real as it is threatening and promising. So, we begin ''to rethink all our definitions of deity and convert all our worship and prayers. Revelation is not the development and not the elimination of our natural religion; it is the revolution of the religious life.''[22] It abolishes, but also transmutes, and raises to a new level of meaning, the foolish and sometimes unholy gestures we had thought were our religion.

To find this true for our own religion is surely to be saved from either romanticizing another's religion or contemning it. The same hardheaded critique and warmhearted charity that we fear and welcome for our own must be brought with humility to bear upon all.

c. The claim of our neighbor/brother/sister

Perhaps the word ''dialogue'' suggests the form in which this interchange may best be carried on. A monologue is a recitation or address: one speaks and another listens. A dialogue is a conversation: each speaks and both listen. The spirit in which dialogue is undertaken is of decisive importance. ''A religious dialogue,'' Raimundo Panikkar has reminded us, ''must first of all be an authentic *dialogue,* without superiority, preconceptions, hidden motives or convictions on either side. . . . Dialogue listens and observes, but it also speaks, corrects and is corrected; it aims at mutual understanding.''[23] The religious dialogue must express the spirit of its own subject. Religious dialogue also, as Panikkar has stressed, is more than an exchange of doctrinal statements or intellectual opinions. The pro-

---

[22]H. R. Niebuhr, *The Meaning of Revelation* (London: Collier-Macmillan Limited, 1970) 138.

[23]Raimundo Panikkar, *The Intrareligious Dialogue* (New York: Paulist Press, 1978) 50.

cess of dialogue itself must be carried out in the religious spirit. In the dialogue, that is to say, persons must speak and listen as before God, and also one to another as those in whom God's face is to be seen.

Some years ago, in a characterization of the study of comparative religion, Wilfred Cantwell Smith expressed the spirit of authentic dialogue.[24] He writes of moving "from talk of an 'it' to talk of a 'they'; which becomes a 'we' talking of a 'they'; and presently a 'we' talking of 'you'; then 'we' talking 'with' you; and finally—the goal—a 'we all' talking together about 'us'." Such a view—visibly charitable, but even more realistic—postulates that we see ourselves as participants in one community, the human; and that the Christians see the Christian group and other groups as fellow participants in that one community.[25]

This seems to be humanly workable, and compatible with the Christian understanding of faith in God and love of neighbor. The Christian believes that, in Jesus Christ, God has found us all—has redeemed the world. Every person, for all are included in the great redemption, is therefore doing more in his religion than cultivating his own religious ideas or seeking to justify himself. With his very life, he is living on grace and participating in the common quest for knowledge of God and truth. This fact is earth's possibility of community. It is a *live* possibility of community; we must be hopeful. It is our *only* one; we must be wise. Henri Nouwen has said a similar truth with a different metaphor, "God is the hub of the wheel of life. The closer we come to God the closer we come to each other. . . . When we keep our minds and hearts directed toward God, we will come more fully 'together'."[26] Surely, on the basis of the *one* human quest, the inclusive love of God, and the authentic experience of faith, we can talk with each other about us. In our kind of world, Christians must view this less as an option and, now, more and more, as a compulsion laid upon us.

---

[24]In "Comparative Religion: Whither—and Why?" in *The History of Religions: Essays in Methodology,* ed. Mircea Eliade and Joseph M. Kitigawa (Chicago: The University of Chicago Press, 1959) 31-58. Referred to, in passing, in *Towards a World Theology* (Philadelphia: The Westminster Press, 1981) 101.

[25]Smith, *Towards a World Theology,* 103.

[26]Henri J. M. Nouwen, *The Genesee Diary* (Garden City NY: Doubleday and Company, 1976) 188.

Such an angle of vision should help us all escape from the (unconscious?) arrogance that religion so readily attracts to itself. We begin by believing we are God's people. We move on to mean that God is more committed to us than to others. From there the steps are short to the feeling that we are wiser or better than others, to the notion that grace makes us more praiseworthy than responsible, to the conclusion that we are right and others are wrong. For Christians, this is to forget that we stand under the promise of the gospel only as we stand also under its judgment. There is no transcendent reality or value to historic, organized Christianity, except as it embodies its own message of love of God and neighbor. Revelation abolishes such religion as refuses the judgment or the promise of its own message; it preserves and raises to a new level of meaning and possibility the religion which accepts it.

Revelation is the 'abolition' of all religion, Christian or otherwise, which does not love in truth. For ''Christianity'' saves no one, whether Christian or other. God alone is the redeemer in Christ. The Church is the servant of God's Word in Christ (Barth); or it is witness to the New Being (Tillich); or it is the community whose purpose is the increase of love of God and neighbor (H. R. Niebuhr); or it is the embodiment of what the Christian hopes is present as an unrecognized reality even outside of organized Christianty (Rahner); or it is that worshiping community that, through faith, receives God's act of justification of sinners as the truth about ourselves and also as hope for the whole world (Wainwright).

Enough has been said to justify one thing further: the Christian witness is never to Christianity; it is witness to God whom we have truly and savingly come to know in Christ. We have no commission to show our religion right and another's wrong. Our witness does not aim at urging more religion upon another person, or at correcting the kind he already has. We have no need or right to prove someone wrong. We are called to serve all, without distinction, for sake of Christ, and to tell all, as humbly as we can and as plainly as opportunity allows, why we are doing it. We tell persons of God's love, not of our religion, and we listen with respect and openness to their replies. The aim is the sharing of the blessing we know, not a gaining of their agreement with ourselves. We do not serve the one God of all by convincing Buddhists or Muslims that Christians are right, but by loving them as our neighbors/brothers for God's sake. And doing this latter, cannot we wait in trust and hope for God to teach both them and us?

They, also, have much that we need to hear, and, so to say, to "see." Read of the Tao, and how it carries the universal secret. It is beautiful and worthy, pliable and enduring, instructive and mysterious, but also free and accessible to simplicity. Gautama the Buddha would, by any informed count, be reckoned as one of the most remarkable men of all time. One can follow him into our psyches, and with his help come to learn that even the quest for happiness is a form of grief—for self-serving desire, which we Christians call sin, is the root of human misery. God must be very fond of Siddhartha. There are passages in the Holy Qur'an where Muhammad's prophetic sense of the onliness and mercy of God would resonate to any Psalm or doxology. Certain passages on the divine compassion, in the Bhagavad Gita, could be read in tandem with the book of Hosea or the First Epistle of John. That these traditions are precious to others can be understood even by one who historically views them from without. Even an "outsider" can partially appreciate and respond.

This openness to others requires no depreciating of the traditions of one's own faith. I am a Christian. God came and comes to me in Christ. He has spoken and speaks to me in the Scriptures of Old Testament and New. He has nurtured and does nuture me on the faith and worship of his Church, the one body of Christ. My life is hid with Christ in God; and by that name I seek to understand myself and others, as well as to interpret the meaning of our common journey as "riders on the earth."[27]

It is in terms of Jesus Christ that the believing Christian has come to construe the character of God, and to read God's presence in every person and thing that he has made. To be a Christian, then, does not mean to believe that Christianity is the best religion, nor that it is superior to Buddhism or Islam. It should mean that, by the life and death of Jesus Christ, we see all others with ourselves in God. This is why our concern for the faith of others grows precisely out of intellectual and moral involvement with our own.

This section of the "argument" in relation to theology and the plurality of religions may be both illustrated and brought to a close with a Christian assessment of the divine character and purpose. This will be followed by an inquiry into the meaning of 'conscience'.

---

[27]The title of the fine and sensitive "memoir" of Archibald MacLeish, *Riders on the Earth* (Boston: Houghton Mifflin Company, 1978).

d. The divine character and the human conscience

For the Christian, the question of how to relate to other religions should be less a question of strategy and program and more an exercise in theology and *agapē*. The Christian does not first ask, "What should I think of traditions other than my own?" He asks, "What do I know of God who has come to me in Jesus Christ?"

The Lord God, we are told, in six days made the heavens and the earth, and all that in them is. The climax of this creative activity was the forming of the human person: "male and female created he them." The creation continues in the rapidly expanding universe, and in the biological and social evolution of our kind. The numerical growth of the human family has been equally spectacular, and at present continues at an alarming rate. We cannot speak of what we know of God who comes to us in Jesus Christ without speaking also of God's concern for the creation and for this human family.

Attention has earlier been called to the fact that our earth grows heavier each week by the weight of two million new people. So exponential has been the rate of increase, that in the early twenty-first century there will be more living people than dead people on this planet: that is, more than one-half of all the people of all time who have ever lived upon this earth will still be living. As we saw, such drastic increase in population creates problems of space and food, of production and distribution, and we discussed the tragedy of world hunger in relation to the doing of faith in this world. Any serious attempt to see our life on this planet in the light of God forbids our viewing of this population increase as simply a problem of space and food. It also involves the quality of life and the possibility of human community. It is this fact that brings moral considerations to the fore and calls for rigorous theological scrutiny and assessment.

Why such words on population growth? Because the Christian confesses that God created this whole world, not just the Christian's part of it. He confesses that God has made all these people in his own image, and loves them without partiality or exception. Each one is included in the shame and grace of the cross. The Christian remembers that God's love to him is by virtue of his being included in God's love for all. For God does not love Christians better than he loves anyone else. He loves all alike—the Christian and Jew, the Buddhist and Muslim; the religious, the non-religious and the irreligious. A Christian could be described as one who has found this out, who defines the meaning of it in terms of what he has seen of God in Christ, and as one who seeks to "copy God," who "so loved the world" (Eph. 5:1; Jn. 3:16).

When one thinks of the hundreds of millions in China, India, Latin America, and Africa—in the traditional societies as well as in the developed areas—the irreducible fact is this: God made and loves them. His love of them is their true identity and worth. They are best defined as those whom God loves. This is who they *are*. He does not reject or exclude them. They may not be rejected or excluded by the likes of us. Their value, grounded in his love, may not be tampered with. They are one with ourselves. Their problems, needs and responsibilities, in principle, are as ours. Their sins need shriving as ours. Their almost infinite possibilities are as our own.

It is no more possible to suppose that God has no stake in the history of these people, their traditions and cultures, than to suppose that God does not love them. And further, to suppose a general condemnation upon them for their cultural identity and inherited faith, or upon their history apart from the gospel story, is to slander the God and Father of our Lord Jesus Christ. We did not learn it so from Jesus. As in the Church we find tares with the wheat, so also in the world we find wheat with the tares; and it is not our calling to divide them.

Jesus had unlimited compassion upon the multitudes who seemed to him like sheep that have no shepherd. He had harsh words only for the self-serving and deliberately wrongheaded (the New Testament calls them 'hypocrites'), and for the hard-hearted who by injustice and exclusion of mercy abused their positions of power and privilege. Not even in the Hebrew prophets does the vision of the terrible majesty, the invariable justice, the inexorable mercy, appear in such balance.

Jesus believed that God is for us, that he moves upon us by his good Spirit to draw our response of loving trust. He nowhere assumes, with a sweaty evangelicalism, that everyone is going to hell unless he can talk God out of it. In him, clearly, there is no denial of judgment and no minimizing of the human risk. He saw in God's love of all no ground of presumption. But always he saw the redemptive possibilities in judgment itself, and that none is condemned for holding membership in the wrong group.

Always, he saw, God is for us. We are in God's hands; always closer to light and grace than to our own breathing. This is why he could deal with our kind with such encouragement, and see even our perverseness as distortions of the good. Even true repentance for sin he saw as more reasoned and steadfast than feverish and harsh. The burden of the biblical witness, and a huge part of the historical witness of the Church, rides with this view of Jesus and his teaching. God is love; his concern is that "none should perish, but that all come to eternal life." This is the God and Father of our Lord Christ.

The promised inquiry into *the meaning of "conscience"* is now required, and I am aware that this is one of the most difficult subjects in moral theology. No exposition of it as a subject unto itself is required here. Let us rather establish a working idea as to our use of the word before relating it, first, to the fact of variety in human faith, and then to the question of what Karl Rahner and others have called "anonymous Christianity."

We begin the discussion of conscience with a distinction, formulated by F. D. Maurice,[28] between the empirical (or existential) self and the 'true' (or transcendent) self. This latter self, Maurice (1805-1872) variously calls the "I," "the true self" or "the conscience." Conscience, in this usage, is a synonym for the true self. It is not subjective conviction or scruple; it is "self-in-relation," the "I" who is a socially related person and who cannot be reduced to an "it." This "true self" is the relational possibility of knowing both God and our existential selves. Inasmuch as such knowledge belongs to our created condition and proper end, conscience could be defined as the possibility of this knowledge. Faith, as trustful relatedness with God, is what activates this possibility and makes reliable our natural reason, our feelings and sensations. This conscience is not primarily a subjective entity. It is that in which the true self and God share life together. I believe it could be called a sort of moral and spiritual horizon that is brought into view by the activity and insight of living faith. It is shared-life with God, but it does not forget that this sharing-self is dependent upon God for its being as God is not dependent upon this self for his.

These perspectives—they are surely insights more than perspectives—show why Maurice believed that the existential self cannot know

---

[28]See Maurice, *The Conscience* (London and Cambridge: Macmillan and Co., 1868). The same points of view reappear in his voluminous writings. Some of Maurice's thought on this (these) subject(s) is carried forward by H. R. Niebuhr's article, "The Ego-Alter Dialectic and the Conscience," in *The Journal of Philosophy* 42 (June 1945): 352-59. I am emdebted, for much of my understanding of Maurice, to conversations with my friend and sometime colleague, Guy H. Ranson, and to a close reading of his doctoral dissertation at Yale.

its true self without knowing God, and why all knowledge of God entails knowledge of the true self. It is also why, in the true self, knowing and existing are indivisible. It is why ethics is grounded in knowledge rather than in prudence. It is why the important question for human beings is, "What is true?" not "What will work?"

One further comment will bring into clearer focus both Maurice's thought and some of the perspectives of this book. I mean the way in which such an understanding of "conscience" marks a necessary distinction between conceptual and "personal" knowledge. Maurice indicates this distinction by his differentiation of the terms "reason" and "understanding." For example, "reason" may *reflect* on God the idea, on God the absolute, or God the void; "understanding" *knows* God as God the Lord, God the redeemer, God the friend. The "self" in this relationship does not cease to be either finite or fallible: but the relationship does make it impossible for the "self" to be fully possessed by finite things or find fulfillment in them.

In this self (this "conscience"), the sense of *oughtness* remains constant, and obedience to that sense of oughtness, exercised faithfully within the limits of one's earthly place and relationships, is what is meant by human knowledge of God. And knowledge of God is, in simplest terms, what is meant by saving faith. It appears that, for Maurice, this truth establishes not only the difference between reason and understanding, but also between belief and faith. Pursue this perspective, now, with some early Barth.

In 1928 and 1930, Karl Barth had lectured on ethics in the universities of Münster and Bonn. I cannot avoid mentioning that, in some ways, he seems to foreshadow sensibilities that found later expression in his lecture, in 1956, on "The Humanity of God." These lectures on ethics, published in English in only 1981, are still worth our time.

In paragraph 16, Barth discusses "conscience."[29] He was teaching that with conscience we are dealing primarily neither with natural self-consciousness, nor with the differentiation to be noted between moral values and biological drives. Neither did he concern himself with the role of the group in the shaping of the individual. Barth first comes at the word conscience etymologically: 'conscience' means '*co*-knowledge' (*con-*

---

[29]Karl Barth, *Ethics* (New York: The Seabury Press, 1981) 475-97.

scientia). In a Maurician sort of way, it refers to our co-knowledge with God. It is the divine gift to us in and by which authentic understanding of self and of God is arrived at. It bespeaks the submission of our wills to this divine will, the answer of our love to Love's invitation. In such co-knowledge there is true *freedom* of conscience, where our own voice is God's voice.[30] This is dangerous truth and carries Barth's *caveat* with it. But how can one avoid danger when taking seriously the divine command and the divine promise? It might be mentioned, at least, that the danger is reduced when this freedom of conscience is understood as faith through which to obey, and not as cognitive certainty with which to judge someone else.

We need remember that to speak of conscience, whether in Maurician or Barthian terms, is to speak of a 'universal'. Conscience is not a property of biblical religion; it does not *belong* to all of the religions combined. It belongs as such to all varieties of humankind. It is created and maintained by the intersection of the transcendent with the human; and we need soberly to learn, with T. S. Eliot, that to apprehend the meaning of this awesome intersection ''is an occupation for the saint.''[31]

It would seem, therefore, that the conscience is as everywhere present as is the Spirit of God. It is the living evidence of a relation that belongs to us by creation and calling. To show disrespect to the conscience discounts persons in both their historical actuality and human identity. The same disrespect, knowingly or unknowingly, sets God at naught. Indifference to the conscientious faith of other persons is, in degree, an indifference to God's presence and activity in and among them.

Possibly the above understanding of conscience can help us to deal with the undeniable fact of variety in human faith. It should further help us to reckon with the fact that people exist quite outside historic Christianity, who are trustfully obedient towards God and who do uncompelled acts of love to neighbor. It was the presence in such persons of what we are accustomed to call 'Christian' faith and graces that led Karl Rahner and others to speak of ''anonymous Christians.''[32]

---

[30]Ibid., 485.

[31]''Four Quartets: The Dry Salvages,'' in *The Complete Poems and Plays, 1909-1950* (New York: Harcourt, Brace and World, 1952) 136.

[32]Karl Rahner, *Theological Investigations,* vol. 6: *Concerning Vatican Council II* (New York: The Seabury Press, 1974) 390-98.

Rahner sees, on the one hand, how authentic faith is demanded absolutely and for which nothing else can substitute. On the other, he remembers the universal salvific will of God's love and omnipotence, the divine concern "that none should perish" (1 Tim. 2:4).

Out of this tension, Rahner came to the conclusion that, somehow, all persons, whether within earshot of the Christian message or not, must be capable of being authentic participants in God's life and grace—not merely "in the sense of an abstract and purely logical possibility, but as a real and historically concrete one." For Rahner, "this means in its turn that there must be degrees of membership in the Church, not only in ascending order from baptism . . . to the realization of holiness, but also in descending order from the explicitness of baptism into a nonofficial and anonymous Christianity which can and should yet be called Christianity in a meaningful sense, even though it itself cannot and would not describe itself as such."[33] This faith, wherever genuinely it is faith, is a response to the grace of God in Christ—"in no other name is there salvation"—a response directed and empowered by the Spirit of God. The same Spirit of God (which Barth and Maurice have seen as a sort of *alter ego* of the conscience) is the means and the "title-deed" to this person's inclusion in "the people of God."

All this, it seems to me, is compatible with a responsible use of the Bible, though I should prefer to substitute "saving faith" for "Christianity" in the Rahner quote. Rahner's argument comports, as well, with the moral recognition that God's inclusion of Christians is a part of his inclusion of all. "Our solidarity precedes our particularity," says W. C. Smith, "and is part of our self-transcendence. The truth of all of us is part of the truth of each of us." This conviction is why Smith adds, "Not them, not you, but some of *us* are Buddhist, Muslim, some Jewish, some skeptic, some confused. Some of us are Christian."[34] Being Christian would seem to mean, for Smith—and perhaps for others—that we have, through faith, joined the one human race whom God loves and for whom Christ died: that we see ourselves and others as fellow-participants in that one community. As Smith puts it, "The first step is to recognize the faith of other men.

---

[33]Ibid., 391.

[34]*Towards a World Theology,* 103.

Once that step has been truly taken, the next step is the recognition that there are no *other* men.''[35]

Unless we are to admit of a sizable difference between faith's view of another person as compared with love's view of that same person, Smith's words must strike the faithful conscience with force. Whether they fully or only partially persuade the mind, they must *affect* any use we may make of the phrase ''the meaning of mission.''

3. The Meaning of Mission

Let us come at this topic, The Meaning of Mission, by relating it to some of the ideas that have begun to come clear in these pages. This should lead us into some formulated idea of what we mean by the Christian mission in and to the world. Some theological rationale will then accompany and lend support to that idea. Discussion of good styles of approach to understanding across religious and cultural lines may conclude the discussion.

The first of the ideas bearing on the understanding of mission is this one: God is the creator and redeemer in Christ. He is the great ''Original''—the sovereign over all, in whose impartial love and saving activity all are included. Second, God's saving presence is seen amongst persons of all cultures and religions. This is certified in their trustful obedience to the Good, and in their unconstrained acts of love towards others. Third, the fact and function of conscience in all persons testifies to the presence and activity of God's Spirit. Fourth, the Cross, as the heart of the Christian message, reminds that true mission aims not at the achievement of success but at the disclosure of *agapē*. Fifth, awareness that we have no knowledge of things as they are in themselves conditions the religious understanding we have of both ourselves and others. We can speak only of ''what we have seen and heard and our hands have handled of the Word of Life'' (1 Jn. 1:1).

a. Religious understanding of ourselves and others

Before attempting a ''definition'' of mission, we should try to establish some sort of perspective from which to view the subject. For the above affirmations carry a hidden conviction too important to leave merely implicit, namely, that a fundamental distinction is to be marked between

---

[35]Ibid., 103.

the *reality* and the *forms* of faith. Not to be separated, the two are always to be distinguished. This, rather than any specific doctrine, seems to be the most important of those theological bequests that have come to us from the liberal tradition, and the roots of this bequest are planted deep in Scripture.

This distinction does not validate, but it does make reasonable, some positions taken in *Towards a World Theology,* by Wilfred C. Smith. Professor Smith goes well beyond the above indicated distinction to hold that, while faith differs in form from culture to culture, it does not differ in kind.[36] The argument is persuasive, and I am not yet ready to evaluate all that it entails. He means, to use his own words, that, "just as Christians have been saved by Christian faith, so have Muslims by Islamic, Buddhists by Buddhist" (168). Without the context such words might easily be misunderstood. Smith does not mean that persons are saved by Christianity or Islam or Buddhism. He means that all who are "saved" are saved by the same faith—as actual, trustful obedience towards the Ultimate Good—for there is but one kind of true faith. This faith becomes concretely real and effective (the argument continues), for Christians through the Christian gospel and tradition, for Muslims through the Qur'an and the Sunna (traditions), and so forth. None, including the Christian, is saved by his religion; all who are saved are saved by the one God on the ground of trustful and obedient faith. This salvation is viewed as the true work of God; and it is held that genuine faith in each instance differs from the others in form but not in kind. Christian theology itself, Smith notes, has not taught that there are different kinds of true faith.

Of the grounds on which it might be possible to defend such a perspective, two claim instant attention. Every friendly observer of people in non-Christian cultures has readily recognized certain lives that are endowed with graces we Christians claim for our own tradition: confidence towards the Universe, disciplined character, morally courageous and self-directed wills, outgoing kindness, loyalty to community wider than one's own. Through their own Scriptures, or traditions and custom, or personal vision, or conscience, God's Spirit addresses a saving word to them. No *saving* word has any other source. The other ground is an implication of Christian theology as such. It proceeds from reckoning Christ as the perfect clue to the understanding of God—the Christ who, as Smith says, re-

---

[36]Ibid., 168, 171.

veals "a God of mercy and love, who reaches out after all men and women everywhere in compassion and yearning; who delights in a sinner's repentance, who delights to save." And, "it contradicts the central revelation of Christ to say anything else" (171).

All these facts should make us both humble and grateful. They do not qualify us, as we have said, to prescribe for others a predetermined form of religious understanding and practice. This disqualification is made more obvious when we recall that even our true knowledge of God is qualified; when we further remember the fact of God's sovereign access to all persons through whatever religion or through conscience; and when we understand that all theology is too weak to carry the whole of its transcendent load.

This situation makes for humble readiness to listen as well as to witness. For, if our historical particularity and theological limits render it impossible to speak *for* others, they do not make impossible our speaking *with* them. It is possible for people of goodwill to search openly within their own traditions for treasures regarded valuable by all. Furthermore, the role of theology itself, as the *servant* of revelation and faith, reminds that the bonds of unity under God are, in character, more inclusively human than exclusively doctrinal. Truth is always more than any one intellective form in which it is conveyed. Here the whole circle of personhood is involved—that is, the actual lives of actual people who hurt and rejoice like ourselves, and whose true good requires more than a confidence of holding "pure doctrine." This more-than-rational humanhood that belongs to our kind, plus the derivative (if important) character of doctrine, appear to be the twin facts that lead Raimundo Panikkar to note a dual requirement for today's Christian reflection, namely, that it be both "loyal to itself and faithful to the world."[37]

In such light it would appear that a sensitive mission in the world of today and tomorrow must focus more on means and less on goals; more on understanding and service and less on expansion and success. Mission is not a sports engagement, now on offense next on defense. It is more like a colloquy where each is heard with openness and respect. Perhaps more,

---

[37]This is a principal theme in Panikkar's book. I know of no more vivid commentary on the tension between faith's being loyal to itself and faithful to the world than the novel *Silence,* by Shusaku Endo, a Catholic Christian and one of Japan's contemporary novelists.

it is like a meal that the Christian will prepare for his non-Christian brother—and also serve it.[38] In such a meeting, done in such a spirit, we come to understand our brother better; we come also *to understand better ourselves and our own faith.* Because of this, in such a context, to raise the question of what we mean by mission is, at the same time, to raise the prior question of what we mean by Christian faith itself.

Let us attempt to illumine this fact with two illustrations, before attempting a definition as such of mission.

Let's say an American Christian is living in a land predominantly Muslim—Jordan, Pakistan, Indonesia. The Christian's faith affirms that God is the sovereign Lord and that, in Christ, he has redeemed the world. Because the Christian believes this, he cannot not believe it simply because he lives in a Muslim country. But being in a Muslim setting does affect the way that the Christian perceives the meaning of Christ. Also, the style of witness here invariably would differ from bearing witness, say, in Massachusetts or Texas. The realities of the ''human situation,'' as distinguished from theological conviction alone, become visible. Points of contact which could be presupposed and understood by a Christian witness in Texas—the common cultural base with its possibility of easy understanding—are absent for the Christian in Jordan or one of the other countries. At home, familiar lines of experience and thought have interacted to produce the possibility of mutual understanding—a possibility easier to presuppose in a homogeneous setting. It is precisely the absence of this setting that makes communication more difficult across cultural and religious boundaries. It is what, also, calls for humility and patience in one who would witness across those boundaries. The truth of the Christian gospel is basic to this situation; but the human situation is also basic to this situation! Community, as well as truth, is at stake. This is one illustration of why the Christian witness must begin to ask not only, What does it mean to be Muslim?, but why he must also ask—with clarity and charity both at stake—What does it mean to be Christian?

The problem can be put in brighter light by appeal to a second illustration.

Shusaku Endo, a Japanese Christian, has been called one of his country's most important contemporary writers. His novel, *Silence,*[39] takes

---

[38]A figure used by H. R. Niebuhr, *Revelation,* 13.

[39]*Silence,* trans. William Johnston (New York: Taplinger Publishing Co., 1980).

its story line from the seventeenth-century mission to Japan by Portuguese Jesuits.

The protagonist of the story is a young priest, Sebastian Rodrigues. He is in Japan in the heavy times of the persecution of Christians by the Tokugawa Shoguns. Rodrigues has put up courageous resistance to his own torture. Then the government agents become more cunning. They put a group of native Japanese Christians to a torture that could end only in their death. One condition alone must be met to rescue them from certain death: apostasy *on their behalf* by Rodrigues himself. The missionary should show this apostasy by stepping on the *fumie* (a mirror) on which was shown the face of Christ. In his tortured soul, Rodrigues comes finally to reason that, "*for love,* Christ would have apostatized to help men." The agony of this dénouement arises from the bitter struggle in the priest's soul between compassion and fidelity—compassion for his suffering Japanese brothers, and fidelity to his Christian faith and calling.

This story dramatically highlights the tensions that inhere in committed mission in today's world. It touches upon the radical character of community as such, as well as upon questions of Christian truth that arise with equal urgency out of Christian commitment in the actual world. A principal theological question that arises out of Endo's largely historical story, for example, can be stated in connection with a question of my own regarding certain recognizable similarities between Buddhism and Christianity: for example, to what extent do human compassion and divine *agapē* overlap? Because of Transcendence, I have been unable to regard them as identical. Because of Incarnation, I cannot regard them as unrelated or entirely different in kind. It is not my purpose to treat of this question here— indeed, who is able to treat of it at all? But the question may be cited as a difficulty being forced upon anyone engaged in either serious mission or serious theology.

There are further complications: for the missionary stands in a shrinking world where the boundaries of the religions no longer correspond with geographical areas and national boundaries, where patterns of mutual understanding must be developed—if at all—across cultural lines, and where the word "Christendom" has ceased to have any usefulness as a geographical term. How, in this situation, does Christian reflection remain both loyal to itself and faithful to the world? At stake in our answer is Christian, and human, community. What, in such a world, does it mean to be a witness?

On the other side, it is not self-evident that Christ would have apostatized in order to help men. There is in the divine *agapē* a promise and a demand, a terror and inexorability, which are more awesome than death through persecution. Christ *died for our sins*. How, in view of this fact, does Christian behavior remain both loyal to itself and faithful to the world? Not less than Christian truth is at stake—truth more all-encompassing than can be stated by reason alone. What, in such a world, does it mean to be a Christian?

Willingness to reckon with the second part of this dilemma—how to be faithful to the world—does not come easy to us parochial Christians. The courage to consider it at all rests upon two aspects of truth that appear to be rooted directly in the Bible itself: one, in a world of which God is creator and redeemer, it would appear that loyalty to the gospel and faithfulness to the suffering human race could not be in final conflict. Such a view is encouraged, secondly, by the reminder that precisely in this irrationally sinful and much abused world of persons is where we *do* faith, hope and love; it is where we have the option to see God's presence in the need of our brothers and sisters or not at all.

Perhaps the world situation itself indicates for us both a change of focus or a shift of emphasis. We have tended, through most of Christian history, to do theology (or at least to learn theology) and then seek faithfully to communicate it. In the radically new circumstances of the present, it is time, perhaps, to do faith in the actual world, and to reflect theologically upon it. Such a shift of emphasis should serve as an antidote to narrowness and parochialism, as well as to free us from bondage to our own experience. Surely it is prideful to suppose that a reconsideration and enlargement of our present doctrinal understanding were the same as disloyalty to Christian truth or abandonment of the Christian gospel. No form of religious understanding can be liberating once it has been equated with the good news it is supposed to serve, and no loyalty to Jesus Christ is adequate that stops short of human solidarity with all whom he loved. It would appear that this is a distinction we need quickly to learn.

These remarks have all been made in the hope of establishing a sort of vantage point from which to view the question of what we mean by mission. They also bring us to broaden out that perspective still further, and to underwrite it with a theological rationale.

One reason why Christians must see, respect, and listen to other faith(s) traces to the nature of Christian understanding as such. Our reli-

gious *understanding* may no more exclude those whom Christ loved and
included in the grace of the Cross than may our religious *feelings*. We joyfully confess that God in Christ has spoken to *us,* has made himself known
to *us.* This can be known and confessed, however, only because God in
Christ has redeemed the *world.* The "us" to whom God has spoken includes us all. It is a universal grace we have been privileged to receive.
We are included in it *because it is given to all.*

This grace is confessed by faith as knowledge of God. It is right that
it be so confessed. Grace is essentially the gracious personal relation that
God establishes and maintains with our kind. It is a knowledge that has to
do, from our side, with what has happened to us in a quickened conscience, and been experienced by us as responding selves. At the same time
faith equally confesses grace as mystery. Our confession of faith in Christ
issues from experiences of grace in our own consciences, our own history.
But this faith also claims a certain kind of participation in Transcendence.
It speaks, to be sure, about our life, our time, our brothers and sisters, our
world; it speaks, as well, about God in Christ, about an *agapē* that alone
can account for creation and consummation, about perfection and destiny,
and about all those eternal energies of the Spirit that disclose the power of
the cross and the life of the soul as one. God's life and our experience flow
together in this faith. The knowledge is given and the mystery confessed
in a grace that is God's alone—but that is always confessed as truth and as
joy from within ourselves. If the *truth* of our confession is traceable wholly
to God (as I believe), the *special authenticity* of it includes our own responses and unique understandings. The truth of the confession is universally valid; the shape of our experience of that truth is not. Neither is the
experience transferable, as such, to others.

This latter fact reminds us that no helpful way is open by which we
may take *our* Bible, *our* creed, *our* Church, *our* experience, *our* style to a
Buddhist, Muslim, Hindu, or humanist, simply seeking his choice between *his* way and *our* way. We do not know the secrets that have been
disclosed in the reality of his own conscience, even as he has no way of
seeing our history and faith as we have experienced and shaped them from
within. Directly to seek his consent to our way is not only to eliminate the
mystery that remains even in our knowledge of God; it is to risk discred-
iting the reality and worth of his existence as an historical person—to deny
that God has been active in his history.

We confess a 'Way' in which there is truth and life. But if the way we walk is to reach to whomever we go, it must be cleared of misunderstandings and prejudices, be paved with mutuality, and remain open at both ends. Perhaps nothing is more insulting than to speak of Christ to one to whom we are unwilling to listen. No sacrifice of loyalty to one's faith is required by an attempt to be faithful to the world.

It is not really a question of loyalty to our faith, when we look at horizons wider than commonly recognized by Christianity. For "Christianity" is a historical and cultural phenomenon, and we "Christians" are notoriously parochial. The question, as I see it, is: In appreciating Gautama, Lao, or any other—or, in setting Christian understanding in contexts wider than Western—are we surrendering anything of the truth Jesus taught and showed, anything of the salvation he wrought, any of the ultimate meaning he has for us? To appreciate Buddhism must one reduce Christ?

Surely, to clarify or enlarge our doctrine of Christ is not a threat to Christ. To seek to relocate that doctrine in another language, culture, or religious context, is not to discredit Christ: this is how knowledge of Christ has come to ourselves. "We do not abolish the law (or gospel) but uphold it." We would not limit Christ to the West, but seek to show his significance against a universal horizon. We would interpret the gospel for all where the "all" are. This is more a moral and spiritual, linguistic and theological enterprise, than a geographic or programmatic one.

A reminder from the life of the early Church may lend support to such a point of view. The Church was born from the womb of Judaism, and grew up in the climate of Roman imperialism, Hellenistic thought and Mystery cults. It had both antecedents and context. What it had to confess, however, was wider than its context, and its most decisive affirmation— the human enfleshment of the creative and redemptive and eschatological Word of God—had no adequate antecedent, whether in the parent faith or in the cultural context. The Church had the incarnate reality on its hands, with no antecedent doctrine with which to account for it. How, then, was such a faith to be confessed?

The Church asserted an essential connection of the life and death of Jesus with both the tradition of Israel (see Acts 2, 4, 10) and the salvation of the whole world (Eph. 1:10; Acts 2:17). The early witnesses told of how Jesus had been faithful unto death, giving his very life on the cross. This death, they said, was of the righteous for the unrighteous, that he might bring us to God (1 Pet. 3:18). They interpreted this death as a revelation of God's love not less than of human sin. They said that God's love not only disclosed our death through sin, but, as well, the reality and possibility of eternal life through that love which was revealed in the grace of the cross (Rom. 5 and 8). The cross—as fact, as symbol, as power—defined a new center of health to which all persons could gather in faith and find healing. In Christ, the whole world was, and could know itself as being, God's redeemed family (Eph. 2). In this one, God himself is present.

Faith was confessed in this way—albeit more fully and more richly. But how was the confession to be given warrant? What rationale could make convincing so staggering an affirmation? Their answer was concise and unmistakable: In Christ, God was reconciling the world unto himself, not reckoning unto us our trepasses, and having committed unto us the word of reconciliation (2 Cor. 5:19). By such a confession, early Christian faith—which, I should suppose, is the only kind there is—was attributing to the work of Christ the qualities of both transcendence and universality. This means that faith was seen as corresponding to the reality and grace of God, on the one hand, and as being accessible always and everywhere to persons as persons, on the other. Such faith in God, by its very nature, includes the mission to all persons and to the world. Even in a local congregation, a universal gospel is preached, and what is not true for the whole cannot be true for the part. This is the human and theological reality that lies back of Emil Brunner's oft-quoted line that "the Church exists by mission as fire exists by burning."[40]

It was the early Church's actual and faithful interpretation of herself as mission that contributed so richly to the characteristic shape and accent of her theology. Perhaps a like serious involvement with the world in our time should not only serve to clarify for us the meaning of "faith," but, as well, to illumine the task of "mission." Possibly it would lend credibility, once more, to the Church's reason for being. For the true mission of the Church is not the establishment of herself as the world's religion; it is the extension to all the world, through her own fellowship and faith, of that love and light which God is, and saving knowledge of which he has disclosed to us all in the life and death of his Son. The calling of the Church in the world is simply and only to be who and what she is: (a) the extension of Christ's ministry as servant (Phil. 2:5-8); (b) the company of the com-

---

[40]*The Word and the World* (London: SCM Press, 1931) 108.

mitted (1 Pet. 1:3-8); (c) the historical embodiment of the divine righteousness (2 Cor. 5:21). These dimensions of the Church's life and calling have been rendered doctrinally as: the Church as the extension of the messianic ministry of her Lord, which sometimes is also phrased (I believe less helpfully) as the Church as the extension of the incarnation; the Church as God's pilgrim people, a committed company of disciples walking joyfully in the way, and carrying their load after Jesus; the Church as the paradigm of the Kingdom, that is, the Church in whose common life God's gracious activity is given concreteness in the world (according to the measure of faith) as it was manifest and exercised at absolute pitch by Jesus as Son and Christ.

Keeping in mind, now, what has earlier been said, and remembering something of the "spirit" of the approach by which we have come at the subject, let us try to say more exactly *what we mean by 'mission'*.

The word 'mission' refers to "sending forth," as with a commission to do the work of "ministry." In the everyday sense of the word "ministry" as "service" this anticipates that one shall be doing abroad what, in principle, he or she would have been doing if he/she had stayed at home. The missionary is not a "super-Christian" who somehow has interests and powers that transcend faith as such. He is "official" only in the sense that, ordinarily, the Church appoints and commissions him for this work.

What would he have been doing had he stayed at home? He would, as a Christian, have been living his life in faith, doing his job as best he knew how, and offering it to God, both as a form of human usefulness and as witness to Christ. In our society, he would have been doing this as a layman or as a "clergyman." As a layman, he might, at home, have been practicing law or medicine, teaching, or working at some level or another in labor or business. In whatever capacity, if he is a Christian witness, his vocation is to represent God in Christ to all whom he touches with his life. Medicine, teaching, business, and so forth, are media in and through which such a person does his primary work of "ministry." As a "clergyman," he may be teaching, "evangelizing" (that is, preaching the gospel) as pastor of a congregation, or serving through some other "office." In principle, his work and the layman's is the same. In role, they are different.

Such an understanding looks towards "mission" in ways less clerical and official than mission has traditionally been viewed. This understanding would also comport best with the needs and expectations of his fellow Christians who live in lands to which he would go. There the situation has greatly changed. Traditional mission might experience certain kinds of quantifiable successes today in, say, Latin America or Africa or China; but "truth in love," "truth in community," will be harder and harder to realize there through traditional missionary practice. Sensitivity to the *selfhood* of Latin American or Chinese or African Christian communities, involved concern for the fundamental social and political issues by which their lives and religion are so profoundly affected, readiness to help more than to control—such sensitivity must characterize the mission of the present and future.

A generation ago, the Church of England issued an important statement on evangelism, *Towards the Conversion of England.* In this document the evangelist's task is stated as being "so to present Jesus Christ in the power of the Holy Ghost that men shall come to put their trust in God through Him, to accept Him as their Saviour and follow Him as their King, in the fellowship of His Church."[41]

Such words, *mutatis mutandis,* could be applied, as well, to the missionary: (1) To "present Jesus Christ" requires serious reckoning with such issues as, What do we know of Jesus Christ, of his work, his teaching, the reality and meaning of his death? And are we prepared, in mind as well as heart, to interpret, for all persons and for the world's life, what this means—not simply to be able to say, "Here is what Christ means to me"? (2) To present Jesus Christ "in the power of the Holy Ghost" is never the same as urging a non-Christian to adopt the Christian religion through confession and baptism. It calls for the missionary's own penetration—in mind, heart, and will—into the undeserved mercy, into the cosmic meaning, into the ultimate purpose of God in Christ, so that hearers are exposed not so much to our words as to the Spirit who "searches the deep things of God," and who makes Jesus Christ contemporary with ourselves. (3) To "accept Jesus as Saviour and to follow him as King" is to see ourselves and all others as being involved in the judgment and promise of the Cross, its defeat and triumph, its shame and hope. It is to know oneself as infinitely obligated to the one Sovereign who conquers through suffering love and rules by giving what he demands. It is to know that God is not served

---

[41]*Towards the Conversion of England,* the report of a Commission on Evangelism appointed by the Archbishops of Canterbury and York (Philadelphia: Westminster, 1945). This is also quoted in John Mackay, *God's Order* (New York: Macmillan, 1956) 147.

by programs and principles that *agapē* has already rejected. (4) To serve as missionary through "the fellowship of the Church" is to be identified with both the world and the whole Church. Fellowship means the acceptance and full sharing of common life with our fellow human beings, not the giving of good advice from outside their circle. It also means that the missionary cannot be, *in any primary sense,* a representative of his denomination even though supported by it. He is a spokesman of the whole gospel of the whole Church of God. This Church takes its character not from its members but from its Head. The missionary is a representative of Jesus Christ, and though he uses his own understanding and experience to represent Jesus Christ, he is not a witness to them. His goals, and the means by which he seeks to realize them, are defined by the life and saving work of Jesus Christ—that is, by the sovereign and gracious will of God the King which is made known through the whole Church to the whole world.

All mission, conceived of as the life and work of the Church, derives from God's mission which is his own activity in the creation, reconciliation and consummation of the world. To be in mission is to be participating in faith in what God is "up to" in the world. To do this at home is to do what the Church of England report called "evangelism," to do it "abroad" is what is usually meant by "mission."

Being "God's fellow worker" is the essence of missionary service (1 Cor. 3:9). The Church serves God's mission; it does not seek its own vindication, and knows no means of advancing the cause of either truth or grace than by practicing them. The presence of truth and grace in the Church's life testifies to God's presence, through Jesus Christ, in the Church's faith. God in Christ by the Spirit is the ground and means of mission. God is also its goal or end. By his presence and power through the Church's faith, God certifies to all the world the realities of truth and grace which already are confessed in the Church and give identity to her.

Mission, then, is going on wherever Christian faith brings people to that mind of love which marked Christ's ministry as Servant. Such a company of faith understands its life, and orders its discipleship, by the model of Christ himself. It embodies (if imperfectly) the divine righteousness as God's vindication of right over wrong (as this is seen both in the forgiveness of sins and in the casting down of the strongholds of injustice). It works with singleness of heart. A missionary may be involved in tasks that appear diverse and maybe commonplace. He distributes food to the hungry and also seeks to improve understanding of food production or crop irrigation or to like. He may dig a well, build a windmill, and help provide safe drinking water. Missionaries may share "know-how" leading to improved farming or the care of animals. They may build schools or hospitals or Church buildings. They may lead worship, win converts (one might hope not too hastily), baptize, and teach. They may inoculate, deliver babies, and heal. But in all these diverse activities, "one thing" they do: they represent and set forward God's saving presence and purpose in Jesus Christ.

For this work, the individual missionary needs both freedom and discipline. The freedom for the doing of mission should be encouraged from the sending agency. His discipline and nurture should come from colleagues who work together as fellow missionaries. This order would discourage the growth of "benevolent authoritarianism" at home, and promote a more responsible involvement of each missionary within each mission.

The discussion immediately preceding has, I believe, disclosed that *what* the missionary is doing is never separable from *why* he is doing it. The discussion can be brought to a close by a consideration of *how* he should go about it. What follows attempts no "theology of mission," nor an examination of its motives. It deals only with attitudes and styles of approach.

6. Three approaches to other faith(s)

For this consideration, we need to recall all the argument of this book. Revelation is what God has done, is doing and shall do to make himself known unto salvation and eternal life, through Jesus Christ, unto all who have (do) faith. Faith is that faithful obedience or obedient trustfulness by which we respond in kind to the revelation, and begin to join in God's work of truth and love. Theology is the faithful and critical attempt to give intellective form to the meaning of this revelation and the nature of this faith. Mission is the work of faith in the world, aiming at truth, justice, and peace. It seeks to include all persons in the world in that community of love that is confessed as reality and possibility by the Church.

To focus upon the question of how all this is to be undertaken is to take up the subject of strategy (a somewhat nasty word)—or, better, the question of *right approach* to those who do not confess our gospel. Remember, we are talking here directly of neither motives nor goals, but of the spirit in which Christian faith is communicated, whether at home or abroad. The reader has surely been prepared already for much of what follows.

The possible missionary approaches available to us are, in principle, reducible to three. I shall suggest that one of them, more than the other two, appears appropriate to the claims of revelation, to the nature of faith, and to the actual condition of our humankind.

Granting some variety in the manner of formulating these three approaches, they may be listed as follows. First is the outlook that assumes the need for *the displacement by one religion of all of the others.* Sometimes called exclusivism, sometimes imperialism, this approach rides on the assumption that one religion is superior to all others (if not the only conveyor of truth), and that no alarming gap appears between the present institutional forms of that religion and the truth to which it bears witness. It is ready for wholesale adoption. Proponents of this approach have a visible anxiety towards the second approach, and suspect that the third is only another form of the second.

The second approach favors a policy of mutual agreement and adjustment, often called *syncretism.* This second approach assumes that the religions are alike in all essential respects, that none has a corner on truth; that since they represent the ''spiritual'' interests and convictions of our humankind, they are equally meritorious; that since absolute knowledge is beyond our historical and human capacity, all religions are equally relevant to the human condition. It might be observed, I hope with charity, that all this might make all religions equally irrelevant.

The third approach attempts a *dialogical exploration* of faith (both that of others and our own), and, therefore, a reconceiving of both doctrine and mission in broader and deeper terms. It refuses to see in the knowledge of God a basis for either self-justification or institutional self-aggrandizement; it recognizes the great gulf that lies between the knowledge of God as the truth of our existence, and the knowledge of God as doctrine—between God experienced as Life, and God found credible as idea. The ongoing reconception of faith through dialogue is a never-ending process, simply because God is too great to be taken in whether by reason or experience. This approach does not celebrate the correctness of our own understanding of faith: it encourages the awareness of the transcendent miracle—beyond all our computing and verification—that has come to faith as gift. Where this miracle is ignored or forgotten, ''reconception'' may easily become another form of syncretism.

My first acquaintance with ''reconception,'' as a missionary idea, came in student days through W. E. Hocking, from whom—along with

Hendrik Kraemer, Hugh V. White, and my own teacher, W. O. Carver—I learned much of the basics with which I have worked ever since.[42] I am, however, aware of using Hocking's term with a meaning that varies considerably from Hocking's own. Perhaps clarification would be helpful.

Hocking's use of the term "reconception" does not entirely avoid the charge of syncretism; nor, perhaps, does it fully escape an implied superiority of one sort of faith as compared with others.

The theological substance informing the idea of "reconception" as Hocking used it, assumed a common and basic core of truth, appearing in varying form, in all religion(s). This truth strikes the human intuition as self-evident, and the human conscience as a cosmic demand. Hocking was later to make explicit, in his *The Coming World Civilization,* that this core truth which unites all faiths is the sense of Being and Blessedness that appears in all the varieties of mystical experience. The reality and worth of this common truth outweigh the importance of such truths and values as appear in the diverseness. Avoiding both romantic syncretism and exclusivism, each faith (according to Hocking) should strive to reconceive *itself* in the light of the insights it discerned in other religions.[43]

---

[42]See W. E. Hocking, *Living Religions and a World Faith* (London: G. Allen & Unwin Ltd., 1940); Hugh Vernon White, *A Theology for Christian Missions* (Chicago: Willett, Clark, and Co., 1937), and *A Working Faith for the World;* H. Kraemer, *The Christian Message in a Non-Christian World* (Published for the International Missionary Council in London; New York: Harper & Brothers, 1938); W. O. Carver, *The Bible a Missionary Message* (New York: Fleming H. Revell Company, 1921); *Christian Missions In Today's World* (New York: Harper & Brothers, 1942); *The Glory of God in the Christian Calling* (Nashville: Broadman Press, 1954). This last book is a study of the *Epistle to the Ephesians* and contains the core of Carver's understanding of Church and of history. Along the way were added: Joachim Wach, *Types of Religious Experience: Christian and Non-Christian* (Chicago: University of Chicago Press, 1951); W. C. Smith, *The Meaning and End of Religion* (New York: The Macmillan Co., 1963); and *Towards a World Theology* (Philadelphia: Westminster, 1981); A. Kenneth Cragg, *The Christian and Other Religion* (London and Oxford: Mowbrays, 1977); Gerald H. Anderson, ed., *The Theology of the Christian Mission* (New York: McGraw-Hill Book Co., 1961); Donald G. Dawe and John B. Carman, eds., *Christian Faith in a Religiously Plural world* (Maryknoll NY: Orbis Books, 1978); E. Luther Copeland, *World Mission—World Survival, The Challenge and Urgency of Global Missions Today* (Nashville: Broadman Press, 1985).

[43]See also Cragg, *The Christian and Other Religion,* 76-77, and Paul Clasper, *Eastern Paths and the Christian Way* (Maryknoll NY: Orbis Books, 1980) 109.

Truth too important to ignore appears in this approach to interreligious understanding. It recognizes the distinction—noting which is necessary—between the truth of faith and even the good forms in which it might be historically carried. It respects persons (and their conscientious faith) as living before and unto God. It recognizes not only the value of learning as much as we can about others, it knows how knowledge of others teaches us much about ourselves. All of this should be remembered as valid in any faithful attempt at mission.

At the same time, matters of ultimate significance cry for attention. The tradition of faith that comes to us through the Jewish-Christian Bible, the faith we confess as Jews or Christians or Muslims, is not essentially mystical in character. It is historical and moral. It does, indeed, appeal to those deeps of meaning and existence that mystics everywhere acknowledge. Its entrance into those deeps, however, it is not unrelated to, nor is it continuous with, our human capacity for religious sentiment or vision. Biblical faith reckons with a *sovereign grace* which, at one and the same time, reveals both the divine love and the human condition-and-possibility. The deepest deeps are opened up by the recognition of guilt and reception of free forgiveness. Out of this moral redemption the reality-and-possibility of the "one new humanity" (Eph. 2:15) is disclosed. By this revelation, which is also an experience of faith, our separation from God, as well as our relationship to God, has been given both accent and clarity. Our identity as Christians is not the same as acknowledgment of membership in the one human race. We do not lose our Christian identity through our membership in the one human family. That is, we do not cease to be Christian witnesses, for that is who we are. But we do not say, "Our form of religious understanding and practice is better for you than what you presently observe." We do say, "Hitherto, in Christ, has the Lord led us"; "we will seek and serve your good as humbly and usefully as we know how"; "we would like the opportunity of dialogue and fellowship, and will seek to be as ready to learn as to teach"; "meanwhile, we hope and expect for you the same mercies and blessings which we, as Christians, have come to know in Christ, and we cannot help but wish that you might come to associate your own truth and grace with his name."

Missionary approaches are means to an end in view. They are not forms of "doctrine" that we are seeking to establish. Neither are they "values" in themselves for which one is morally obliged to contend. In the Bible one does not read of "continuity" and "discontinuity," of "dialogue" or "reconception." There, one reads of God, of grace, of faith, of duty, of the possible. These are the "values," and all three of the above missionary approaches have been proposed as means to their realization on a divinely intended scale. They are not, as I see, it, equally valid or equally helpful ways of realizing the ends, but each, surely, was originally developed with the protection of some authentic value in view.

When some Christian thinkers have proposed "radical displacement" of other religions by our own, they would appear to be saying, "Christ is the decisive disclosure of God's purpose and activity"; "in no other name is there salvation"; "Christ is the Way, the Truth, and the Life, no one comes to the Father but by him"; "it has pleased God to sum up all things in the Son." This approach, certainly, has caught the note of the *uniqueness* of the revelation in Christ of which one hears so much in the New Testament. If some other approach to mission must discard all this, in order to be consistent with itself, it would appear—to Christian faith— to be disastrously flawed. At the same time, note well, *some interpretations* of these texts conflict with—if they do not outrightly set at naught— affirmations of faith that find equal accent in the New Testament.

For the New Testament considers the revelation in Christ to be as *universal* as it is unique.

When, as a missionary approach, some Christians propose dialogical exploration and "reconception," both of their own faith and that of others, they have (or should have) in mind that "God so loved the *world*"; that "he has not absented himself from any place or people and that evidences of his presence, therefore, are to be sought and found"; that "the heavens declare God's glory and the firmament his handiwork"; that the Word which became human person in Jesus is "the light coming into the world which lightens every person"; that "it is not God's will that any should perish but all come to eternal life"; that all our best thoughts of God are still human thoughts of One "whose ways are not our ways"; and that "to condemn other peoples or cultures is either to set God at naught or to affirm his absence from those whom he is said to love and will to save."

Syncretism is unlike either of these. It seeks, in what appears to be a simplistic way, to build a new religious whole out of already existing parts. It manufactures a construct; it does not engender an organism. It rightly feels that religions, since they claim truth, should not be alien to each other, but finds small, or no, place in faith for variety in the understanding of faith: faith is only a conceptual approximation of truth; it must have no decisive content. Syncretism does have about it, in the absence of positive theologial conviction, a strong sense of fair play. If the perspectives suggested in what has already been discussed in this book are generally valid, we may safely drop the approach of "syncretism" as a viable option. In syncretism, the universal is dehistoricized, and the unique seems to be lost. But what are we to do with "displacement" and "dialogical reconception"?

Reflect. In regard to mission, two considerations seem implicit in Christian faith as such. It would appear that that would be the best approach to mission that most fully confesses and makes sense of both. One, is the conviction of *uniqueness:* the conviction of the total adequacy of Jesus Christ, and the absence of flaw both in him as person and in the revelation from God that comes through him. Christian thought has never sought to improve on Jesus. He is seen, by Christian faith, as the fruition of the revelation to Israel and as its partial transformation. As we insisted earlier, the Christ emerges out of that tradition as its end point, its *telos*—the goal towards which the whole process of creation and history had aimed. But Christian faith also sees the event of Christ as carrying beyond the earlier revelation as its "ideal" fulfillment. This is why Christ was described earlier as the *teleiōsis* of the earlier revelation (as well as its *telos*)—the quality of reality beyond which another *telos* is unimaginable. Furthermore, this seemed a "natural" conclusion for people who had begun to associate the name of Jesus with their very worship of God.

The second consideration, equally implicit in Christian faith as such, is the conviction of *universality:* the conviction of God's gracious and sovereign presence amongst people who have never heard of Jesus Christ; the confidence that God has not failed to give effective witness of himself amongst any people, and that authentic responses to that Presence are discoverable to eyes of love. Right perceptions of the nature of either faith or truth never produce narrowed perceptions of community or of love. In the Cross of Christ, God has forever broken down the wall of separation that divides humanity into fragments, and offers human unity, human community, to us as both fact and possibility (Eph. 2:11-16). All persons are to be accepted because all *have been accepted.*

"Radical displacement" affirms the full and final adequacy of Jesus Christ, but tends to run afoul of the saving presence of God among all peoples. "Dialogical exploration" is capable of affirming both, but perhaps is stronger on the universal than the unique. Still, perhaps, as a missionary approach, it can come closest to being both loyal to itself and faithful to the world of this present time.

No hostility between Christianity and another religion is finally defensible where the Church's primary aim is the doing of truth in love. The real (and most painful) hiatus is not between religions; it always appears as a yawning gulf between the Church's own profession of faith and our actual performance in the world.

The Church must work to close this gap. She must not only *have missionaries;* the Church must *be mission*—the extension of God's mission in the world. We Christians may not simply devise strategies by which to set forward the cause of "Christianity" in the world; we must discover depth and range in our own faith, knowing all the while that unique and universal truth transcends us and is inexhaustible. Because we can do this, we must do it.

The last word, however, is never "obligation." Realities such as grace, salvation, eternity, reach beyond even so sublime a word as duty. For faith, confessed in gratitude, in joy and freedom, is always as well a form of certain hope—a hope that desires, but, even more, expects and realizes those great realities that have laid us under obligation. This Christian hope is one form of faith's present reality; it also is identical with faith's final destiny under God.

Even decimation by world anarchy or obliteration by nuclear holocaust cannot thwart this destiny. This destiny of faith is to realize, whether in history or beyond it, the dream of Teilhard de Chardin: "Someday, after we have mastered the winds, the waves, the tides and gravity, we shall harness for God the energies of love. Then, for the *second* time in the history of the world, man will have discovered fire."

On that someday, too, we shall know adequately, as if for the *first* time, what is meant by revelation and faith, and shall then, perhaps, have less need for theology.

Dominus regnavit, regnat, regnabit; Sursum corda.

INDEXES

INDEX OF NAMES

INDEX OF SUBJECTS